Unpicking Gender

Unpicking Gender
The Social Construction of Gender in the Lancashire
Cotton Weaving Industry, 1880–1914

JUTTA SCHWARZKOPF

ASHGATE

© Jutta Schwarzkopf 2004

All rights reserved. No part of this publication may be reproduced, stored in a retrieval system, or transmitted in any form or by any means electronic, mechanical, photocopying, recording or otherwise without the prior permission of the publisher.

Jutta Schwarzkopf has asserted her moral right under the Copyright, Designs and Patents Act, 1988, to be identified as the author of this work.

Published by
Ashgate Publishing Limited
Gower House
Croft Road
Aldershot
Hants GU11 3HR
England

Ashgate Publishing Company
Suite 420
101 Cherry Street
Burlington, VT 05401-4405
USA

Ashgate website: http://www.ashgate.com

British Library Cataloguing in Publication Data
Schwarzkopf, Jutta
  Unpicking gender : the social construction of gender in the Lancasthire cotton weaving industry, 1880–1914. – (Studies in labour history)
  1. Women textile workers – England – Lancashire 2. Cotton manufacture – England – Lancashire – History – 19th century 3. Cotton manufacture – England – Lancashire – History – 20th century
  I. Title
  331.4'87721'094276'09034

Library of Congress Cataloging-in-Publication Data
Schwarzkopf, Jutta.
   Unpicking gender : the social construction of gender in the Lancashire cotton weaving industry, 1880–1914 / Jutta Schwarzkopf.
       p. cm. – (Studies in labour history)
    Includes bibliographical references.
    ISBN 0-7546-0980-4 (alk. paper)
       1. Women textile workers–England–Lancashire–History. 2. Sexual division of labor–England–Lancashire–History. 3. Sex discrimination in employment–England–Lancashire–History. 4. Women–Employment–England–Lancashire–History. 5. Cotton weaving–England–Lancashire–History. 6. Industrial relations–England–Lancashire–History. I. Title. II. Studies in labour history (Ashgate (Firm))

HD6073.T42 G697 2003
331.4'877'00942609034–dc21   2002190876

ISBN 0 7546 0980 4

Typeset by Bournemouth Colour Press, Parkstone, Poole
Printed and bound in Great Britain by MPG Books Ltd, Bodmin, Cornwall

Contents

General Editor's Preface		vii
Acknowledgments		ix
List of Abbreviations		xi
1	Unpicking Gender: Introduction	1
2	Setting the Scene: the Indian Summer of the Cotton Industry	15
3	The Trouble with Weaving: Deriving Satisfaction from Work	53
4	The Weaver's Rest: the Ultimate Escape from Weaving	83
5	Making a Bid for a Family Wage: the Struggle around the Automatic Loom	103
6	Weaving Fair and Weaving Free: England's Web of Destiny – Interweaving Shopfloor, Home and Street	137
7	Gender Unpicked: Conclusion	183
Glossary of Technical Terms		193
Bibliography		197
Index		223

Studies in Labour History
General Editor's Preface

Labour history has often been a fertile area of history. Since the Second World War its best practitioners – such as E.P. Thompson and E.J. Hobsbawm, both Presidents of the British Society for the Study of Labour History – have written works which have provoked fruitful and wide-ranging debates and further research, and which have influenced not only social history but history generally. These historians, and many others, have helped to widen labour history beyond the study of organized labour to labour generally, sometimes to industrial relations in particular, and most frequently to society and culture in national and comparative dimensions.

The assumptions and ideologies underpinning much of the older labour history have been challenged by feminist and later by postmodernist and anti-Marxist thinking. These challenges have often led to thoughtful reappraisals, perhaps intellectual equivalents of coming to terms with a new post-Cold War political landscape.

By the end of the twentieth century, labour history had emerged reinvigorated and positive from much introspection and external criticism. Very few would wish to confine its scope to the study of organized labour. Yet, equally, few would wish now to write the existence and influence of organized labour out of nations' histories, any more than they would wish to ignore working-class lives and focus only on the upper echelons.

This series of books provides reassessments of broad themes of labour history as well as some more detailed studies arising from recent research. Most books are single-authored but there are also volumes of essays centred on important themes or periods, arising from major conferences organized by the Society for the Study of Labour History. The series also includes studies of labour organizations, including international ones, as many of these are much in need of a modern reassessment.

Chris Wrigley
British Society for the Study of Labour History
University of Nottingham

Acknowledgments

This book has been a long time in the making. During the period of its gestation my colleagues in the History Department at the University of Hanover provided a congenial setting for the development of my ideas, and to Adelheid von Saldern I owe a particular debt of gratitude. Her unwavering support of my line of research, despite occasional reservations, bears ample testimony to her personal and intellectual generosity.

A number of people have read parts or all of the manuscript at some stage of its production, and I would like to thank Harriet Bradley, Claus Füllberg-Stolberg, Janet Greenlees, Karen Hunt, John Walton, Volker Wünderich and the two anonymous referees for their helpful comments and constructive criticism.

The research for this book was largely based on material stored in the various local archives in the Greater Manchester area and the Lancashire Record Office at Preston. I would like to thank the staff of all these archives for tirelessly delving into their treasures and producing the documents that have made this book possible. Winnie Clarke, Keeper of Special Collections at Lancaster University Library, is particularly memorable for instantly recalling the exact whereabouts of a particular set of oral history material – the Lancashire Textile Project – as well as the fact that the embargo the depositor had placed on the material had expired by the time I wished to look at it.

I would like to acknowledge that an earlier version of part of Chapter 3 was published as 'Die soziale Konstruktion von Qualifikation. Eine historische Untersuchung der Weberei von Lancashire zwischen 1885 und dem Ersten Weltkrieg', *PROKLA, Zeitschrift für kritische Sozialwissenschaft*, **23**, 1993 (Westfälisches Dampfboot); part of Chapter 4 as 'Gendering Exploitation: the use of gender in the campaign against driving in Lancashire weaving sheds, 1886–1903', *Women's History Review*, **7**, 1998 (Triangle Journals); and part of Chapter 5 as 'Gender and Technology: Inverting Established Patterns. The Lancashire Cotton Weaving Industry at the Start of the Twentieth Century', in Margaret Walsh (ed.) (1999), *Working Out Gender: Perspectives from labour history*, Aldershot: Ashgate.

Last, but by no means least, I thank Albert Grützmann for sharing with me the joys and sorrows of a historical researcher and much else besides.

List of Abbreviations

CFT	*Cotton Factory Times*
GTC	Gertrude Tuckwell collection
M&SWTC	Manchester & Salford Women's Trades Council
MSU TLSL	Manchester Studies Unit, Oral History Tapes
TUC	Trades Union Congress
WTUL	Women's Trade Union League

Chapter 1

Unpicking Gender: Introduction

This study is concerned with unravelling gender in a way not dissimilar to the weaver who, unpicking a fault in the cloth, neatly has to disentangle warp from weft. The legitimacy of, if not the need for, placing gender at the centre of this investigation derives from the fact that, along with class and ethnicity, gender is one of the chief axes along which inequalities of power are organized. Despite the wide variety of forms which it has assumed over time and across cultures, gender as a principle of classifying human beings is a universal, all-pervasive characteristic of society, in fact so much so that referring to human beings obscures the fact that they are always perceived as gendered. Consequently, history is understood as a series of events shaped by groups of gendered beings over time.

A significant advance in both the theory and practice of gender history is marked by Joan Scott's 1986 article on gender as a category of historical analysis,[1] in which she proposed a concept of gender that is divested of the last vestiges of essentialism and has the potential of revolutionizing the writing of history. Influenced by French post-structuralism, she has put forward a definition of gender as a volatile system of classification which results from a continuous struggle for the power to determine meanings. Following Michel Foucault, she conceives of knowledge as the socially produced understanding of human relationships, including those between women and men. According to this view the uses and meanings of knowledge are contested as well as being constitutive of power relations. Thus gender denotes both the knowledge of sexual difference and the social organization of that difference. By producing knowledge of the changes in that system of classification over time, historiography itself becomes embroiled in the contest for power.

Thus a concept of gender as a discursively produced construct has emerged. Following Jacques Derrida, methods of textual analysis, mostly borrowed from literary criticism, are employed to unravel – deconstruct – a multiplicity of meanings of masculinity and femininity, meanings that derive from both terms being oppositional rather than from signifying actual men and women.

Previous understandings of gender are marred by their grounding in an ahistorically conceived 'nature'. In this view gender denotes a social status acquired in the process of socialization and attaching to sex as the biologically given and hence immutable physical essence or core. As a result an unproblematized parallel is assumed between male and masculine as well as female and feminine. Yet sex, as a biological or physiological category, does not exist outside the social. Like gender it is similarly constructed socially,[2] their relation being one of contingency.

Once recognized as a construct, gender can and must be historicized. As a binary opposition, gender evolved comparatively recently. As Laqueur, among others, has shown, in the early modern period, for instance, masculinity and femininity were thought of as being on a continuum. This notion of gender was buttressed by contemporary physiology, which saw no stable or uniform opposition between male and female bodies. In accordance with humoral understandings of the body, maleness and femaleness, in the bodily sense, were seen as being at least in part the result of regimen, diet and exercise.[3]

In the modern period, by contrast, an understanding has come to predominate according to which gender as a binary opposition is grounded in a 'natural' difference that inheres in the body. According to this naturalization, which the sciences have played an important part in legitimizing, human bodies bear unambiguous markers of either sex. Yet differences that are constructed as binary opposites introduce oppression and are a device for exercising power in a multiplicity of ways. The suffering inflicted on intersexuals, who are made to fit either category by a variety of interventionist methods, including physical mutilation, is but a particularly glaring example of the way in which conformity with binary opposition is enforced by arbitrarily defining the point of transition between sameness and difference.[4]

Despite its adherence to a concept of gender as a relational category which is socially produced, it is in its rejection of the emphasis placed on language and textuality and the concurrent recourse to methods of literary analysis that this study parts company with those historians whose work has been inspired by the linguistic turn. For them experience and agency have become questionable as concepts of a historical analysis which is concerned with representation rather than with the pursuit of a discernible and retrievable historical reality.[5] Though steering rigorously clear of any psychological and sociological reductionism, these historians, as Toews has argued, stand guilty of a new kind of reductionism, which dissolves experience into the meanings shaping it. For Toews this approach signals the emergence of a new form of intellectual hubris, 'the hubris of wordmakers who claim to be makers of reality'.[6] This study, by contrast, emphatically maintains that is is people rather than discourses that make history.

Agency is therefore crucial to the concept of gender informing this study. Gender is understood here as denoting both inter- and intra-relations of men and women, thus facilitating exploration of the ways in which gender, class and ethnicity are interlinked with, and fractured by, each other. These relations are evolved in an interactive process in which people relate to each other as masculine or feminine, thereby producing masculinity and femininity in their specific forms. This process has come to be known as 'doing gender',[7] which involves men doing dominance and women doing deference. Everyone's active involvement in this process is emphasized here in contrast to the belief according to which women passively let themselves be acted upon by men intent on rendering them subservient to their interests, thereby making women the helpless victims of a greed for power believed to inhere in all men.

The emphasis on doing gender as an interactive process draws attention to the multiplicity of masculinities and femininities thus created – or constructed – in the various spheres inhabited by the individual. This entails the possibility that the way gender is being done – the specific masculinity or femininity enacted – may vary with social sphere. Differing versions of masculinity or femininity may interact in a variety of ways, reinforcing, coexisting, but also clashing with each other. The potential conflict arising between different versions of gender introduces an element of dynamism into what might otherwise appear as a closed system reproduced indefinitely.[8] By highlighting the multifaceted, not of necessity exclusively linguistic, process of social construction, gender is focused as an arena of struggle in which the meanings of femininity and masculinity are contested and negotiated. Despite the varieties of masculinity and femininity produced in this manner, the line of demarcation may shift, yet does not dissolve. This is because difference is inextricably linked to hierarchy.[9] Consequently, deconstructing difference, breaching the 'sameness taboo',[10] always implies deconstructing hierarchy as a prerequisite of a more egalitarian society.

In this study the social construction of gender is explored in the context of the Lancashire cotton weaving industry, which is particularly suited to an investigation of this kind, affording as it does the opportunity of catching the constructors of gender in the act, as it were.[11] Lancashire cotton weaving, it should be stressed, has not been selected for study on grounds of representativeness. On the contrary, both the notions of masculinity and femininity current in the working-class communities of the cotton district and the conditions in which they had been fashioned were quite exceptional in the context of the late nineteenth-century British working class. Equally singular is the clarity with which processes of the contruction of difference become apparent.

Given its working-class setting, this investigation, apart from historicizing gender, also contributes to the writing of a labour history that is informed by gender.[12] Unlike women's labour history, which has yielded important insights into the significance as well as the diversity of women's participation in economic life and collective protest,[13] this study aims to contribute to a labour history which uses gender as a core analytical concept. It moves beyond the concerns that have been central to women's labour history by considering those social groups that form the subject matter of labour history – workers and employers and their respective organizations – as made up of gendered beings in whose actions mesh concerns shaped by both their class and their gender positions. In particular this study explores the ramifications of the extent and conditions of their employment for women weavers' identities and for the understandings of femininity and masculinity current in the cotton communities. Ultimately, it reveals women weavers taking collective action for a gender-specific demand (women's suffrage), thus claiming for themselves a subjectivity that encompassed the allegiance to both class and gender. Their self-conception as being socially positioned in terms of both class and gender is traced back to the way the labour process in cotton weaving was organized.

This allows the investigator to observe the various social practices resorted to in constructing difference. In the heartland of the cotton-weaving district of Lancashire, men and women were working side by side, producing the same types of cloth on the same kind of machines. Moreover, these identical tasks were remunerated on the basis of identical piece rates, which varied, not with the gender of the worker, but with the type and quality of the cloth produced. The specific organization of the labour process thus failed to offer any of the opportunities present elsewhere of anchoring differentiations by gender as a way of bestowing on them a seemingly objective quality.

Firstly, there was no division of labour by gender, which is one of the powerful mechanisms by which relations between men and women are structured. As a result of the large body of work produced over the years it has become clear that the allocation of tasks by gender, far from being a 'natural' given, has been in constant flux.[14] The changes that have occurred in the distribution of paid work range from inversion – as in cotton spinning in the course of industrialization[15] – through the tenaciousness of male domains in the face of technological innovation, as in typesetting until the comparatively recent introduction of computers,[16] to the opening up of new fields of female labour, as in office work.[17]

Furthermore, it has been demonstrated that definitions of what constitutes the gender-specificity of a given job are quite unstable, and that not only historically, but also concurrently. Characteristics allegedly making a given job particularly suitable for women may serve at the same time to claim some other task to be cut out for men.[18] The division of labour by gender is enforced by social practices that aim at giving the arbitrary allocation of tasks some seemingly objective grounding. The effectiveness of these practices is demonstrated by workers' own belief in their tasks being an expression of their inherent natures, a belief adhered to in even the most unlikely circumstances.[19]

Secondly, the gendering of machinery, equally absent in Lancashire cotton weaving, has been a potent mechanism of allocating work by gender. Male workers, in collusion with employers, may give preference to a machine design that can be accorded masculine connotations. One example from the cotton industry is the spinning mule, operating which, male spinners claimed, required strength and skill beyond the scope of women.[20] This claim was buttressed by machine designers expanding the length of the mule as a way of increasing the number of spindles mounted on the frame. The throstle-spinner, by contrast, was operated exclusively by women. When the ring-spinning machine was introduced, which represented an advance on the throstle-spinner's design, the new machine appears to have inherited its feminine connotation from its predecessor and was thus operated by women alone.

Cynthia Cockburn has analysed what she has termed the 'technological sexual division of labour' with particular regard to typesetting. In this trade men eager to obliterate the similarity between their machines and 'feminine' typewriters opted for a machine design underscoring the desired difference. Cynthia Cockburn's findings show how the gendering of technological competence, whereby competence correlates strongly with masculinity and incompetence with femininity, shapes technical artefacts.[21]

Finally, piece rates failed to vary by gender in the Lancashire cotton industry. In her exploration of the various meanings 'a woman's wage' has assumed in the United States in the course of the twentieth century, Alice Kessler-Harris has emphasized the ways in which gender is inscribed into the wage and how the wage helps to construct gendered expectations for both men and women.[22] Her findings render the absence of gendered piece rates in cotton weaving even more salient. Payment by the piece, generating as it does the illusion that each worker can determine his or her earnings by the amount of effort dispensed, is a potent mechanism of increasing productivity and undermining solidarity by pitting worker against worker. In cotton weaving the outcome of setting the male weaver against his female counterpart was no foregone conclusion and had important repercussions on the versions of masculinity and femininity created by the cotton workforce.

In the absence of any of these possibilities for objectifying gender difference, male weavers, and the equally male trade union officials in particular, could be seen constantly striving to distinguish themselves from their female co-workers in a variety of ways. Women weavers, by contrast, could derive a great deal of satisfaction and self-confidence from performing a job that was not unequivocally gendered. They formed a group of women some of whom, at least, fashioned for themselves an identity as waged workers rather than as mothers of families.[23]

Women's desire, over and above the economic necessity, to combine family responsibilities with paid employment away from home has been theorized sociologically as their 'double socialization',[24] leaving women with the need to reconcile the contradictory pulls exerted by their involvement in both social spheres. This conceptualization of the ways in which they are integrated into society is particularly helpful when dealing with women in employment, alerting researchers, whether sociologists or historians, to the potential sources of personal satisfaction to be derived from performing paid work.

The example of the female weavers of Lancashire underscores the impossibility of generalizing about which are the key experiences in which female subjectivity is grounded.[25] Instead, the relative importance of paid employment and family care needs to be established for each specific group of women anew.

The construction of difference was cast in particularly sharp relief when conflicts erupted on the shopfloor. Whether the issue was one of demarcation between weavers and supervisory staff, the impact of pressure to increase output or the introduction of new machinery, each was saturated with gender, and in the ensuing struggles the meanings of femininity and masculinity were contested and renegotiated.

The approach adopted to unravel the different layers of these conflicts has been that of the case study, for this permits close attention to be paid to detail and nuance as a prerequisite for teasing out what implications for gender the words and acts of the parties involved had. Chapters 3 to 5 represent a case study each, organized around a specific conflict and highlighting the part played by different groups of actors in the process of construction. Read in conjunction, they add up to the case study which forms the subject of this investigation.

The survey of the state of the cotton industry in the period 1880 to 1914, given in Chapter 2, provides the backdrop against which the conflicts around gender were being played out. That period was chosen because it marks the heyday of the industry before the onset of terminal decline after 1918. In the decades prior to the First World War the industry achieved its highest growth rates in the face of increasing international competition. The means adopted to meet the challenge to its position of erstwhile global leader had repercussions on conditions on the shopfloor.

Chapter 3 takes a close look at the labour process, dissecting it with regard to the requirements of skill and the potential job satisfaction to be derived from it. By training the spotlight on the interactions of three groups of workers on the shopfloor – male and female weavers as well as supervisory staff – the chapter explores issues of demarcation in terms of both skill and gender, thus highlighting the degree to which the notion of skill is saturated with gender.

In Chapter 4, trade union officials step onto the scene, on which male and female weavers are seen battling to fend off the effects had by the intensification of labour on both their earnings and their work identities. The way of acting adopted by a disconcertingly large number of young female weavers – committing suicide, preferably by drowning themselves in the mill-pond – has been made sense of by means of 'thick description'.[26] By being placed within the context of the culture produced by the weaving communities, these seemingly senseless acts become intelligible as symbolizing the relevance of achieving the status of skilled weaver to the female members of these communities.

Chapter 5, finally, introduces employers as protagonists, highlighting their attempt to collude with male weavers over the introduction of new technology at the expense of women. Employers are presented as acting in their dual persona of capitalists seeking profit and as men[27] deviating from the path of strict economic rationality by offering to pay their male weavers a family wage in exchange for the latter's consent to operate new machines.

In Chapter 6, women weavers take centre stage successively as mothers of families, unionists and suffragists. This chapter pursues the ways in which women translated their self-perception as men's equals in the labour process into rather more equitable family relationships and in which it both motivated and empowered them to engage in political activity for their own benefit. The women weavers of Lancashire formed the largest contingent of working-class women in the movement for female suffrage.

The Lancashire cotton industry doubtless counts among the most thoroughly researched industries in Britain. Cotton processing has attracted attention both as the pioneer of industrialization and as the harbinger of industrial decline, in many ways typifying the development of the British economy from unchallenged global leader to the demise of large sectors of its manufacturing industry.

Yet among the spate of books and articles published about the industry there is a conspicuous lacuna. Gender, though rarely addressed explicitly, permeates the industry's historiography nonetheless. The spinning department has been privileged as an object of investigation beyond all proportion. Mule-spinners have been accorded prominence, displaying as they did all the paraphernalia of working-class masculinity.[28] By contrast, the weaving department has been construed as spinning's 'other'. Blinded by the large contingent of women among the workforce, historians of the industry have given weaving short shrift as a feminine occupation, which is by implication unskilled and ill-paid. The high degree of unionization among weavers is portrayed as having been achieved against all odds and being constantly threatened by women's assumed volatility in matters of employment. It is also to redress the balance that this study with its focus on weaving has been undertaken.

What attention weavers have received has been confined to historians not primarily concerned with the cotton industry, such as Michael Savage, whose work is both drawn upon and critically assessed below. Of particular importance has been the writing of Jill Liddington and Jill Norris, who have brought to light the involvement of female cotton workers in the campaign for women's suffrage.[29] They see women's large-scale employment in the cotton industry, coupled with a long tradition of trade-union involvement, as lying at the heart of their political activism. Heavily indebted to the work of these two historians though it is, this study differs from it in its major concern – the construction of gender – and the pride of place accorded to the labour process in pursuing this concern.

Carol Morgan has confined her investigation of the gender identity of women cotton workers to the period up to the 1840s,[30] focusing in particular on their involvement in the Ten Hour Movement. Her study pays little attention to the specific organization of the labour process in the different branches of the industry and plays down the extent to which class was fractured by gender.

Finally, Sonya Rose has dealt with Lancashire cotton weavers. In the introduction to *Limited Livelihoods* she makes the claim that, although the industry was sexually integrated and women and men received roughly the same wages, male and female weavers had different experiences at work and in the labour organizations. In the chapter of her book given over to Lancashire cotton weavers she elaborates upon this claim by arguing that, given the emphasis on female domesticity and male performance of the bread-winner role in the discourse on gender prevalent in nineteenth-century England, women weavers were both made to feel an anomaly in the workplace and sidelined in trade union struggles.[31]

Her conclusions are marred by the way in which she stresses the normative power of the discourse on gender in shaping conceptions of the masculine and the feminine at the expense of a notion of gender that emphasizes contestation and conflict, that conceives of gender as a terrain on which ideas of what constitutes masculinity and femininity are battled out. This undue privileging of the normative and static over the fluid and dynamic, to the extent of actually blinding her to contrary evidence, derives largely from Sonya Rose's view from above. While paying a great deal of attention to the ways in which gender was deployed by the state, employers and trade union officials alike, she has failed to consider gender from below, as it were. As a result the actors and actresses in the story she recounts act out a gender script involving a restricted repertoire of male and female roles, rather than creating specific masculinities and femininities in the process of mediating between the gender roles made available by the repertoire and the social conditions in which weavers lived.

Without losing sight of the constraints imposed by gender, which positions masculine and feminine differently with regard to wielding power, this study discards an approach in which men and women are placed in a position of passivity where they are acted upon by forces beyond their control. On the contrary, the approach adopted here draws attention to the various ways in which men and women appropriate historically specific precepts of masculinity and femininity, adopting some elements while rejecting or refashioning others. Through this focus on agency, men and women emerge as actively pushing against, and expanding, the boundaries circumscribing their gendered scope of action. Through the highlighting of the dynamics of gender, which feed upon the tensions generated by the disjuncture of gender and power in different social spheres,[32] change becomes both apparent and explicable.

An important precondition for this study was the rich documentation available on the Lancashire cotton industry. The investigations carried out by numerous Royal Commissions and Parliamentary Committees, which often touched upon, or were specifically devoted to, aspects of the industry, have been useful for the evidence collected by interviewing witnesses, that is people directly involved in the industry in a variety of capacities. Those selected to make a statement before the members of such bodies were acutely aware of operating within a politically significant context, using this opportunity of voicing what they perceived as their grievances and urging upon their audience what they considered the most desirable course of action.

In addition much information has been culled from the pages of the *Cotton Factory Times*. Founded in 1885 by a newspaper proprietor wishing to give cotton unions a means of publicizing their concern with improving the position of the cotton operatives, the weekly remained in existence until 1937. Both the detail and the breadth of its coverage render it indispensable as a source of information for anyone interested in the history of the cotton industry, and this despite the rather haphazard way this information was obtained. Operating with a minimum number of permanent staff, the paper relied largely upon its readers sending in reports about events in their localities. It is impossible to ascertain to what extent and on the basis of which criteria a selection was made from the material submitted. Though set up to serve the purposes of the cotton unions, from its inception the paper catered to what it perceived as the needs and interests of all members of a cotton operative's family, not least in order to secure the regular custom of what was a large and relatively prosperous occupational group of men and women,[33] of juveniles and adults. Nevertheless, the dominant voice making itself heard in the columns of the *Cotton Factory Times* was that of the exclusively male trade union officialdom.

The paper's particular importance lay in transcending the pronounced localism[34] characteristic of the places in which cotton processing went on. The *Cotton Factory Times* played a crucial role in constructing a community to which belonged all those involved in the industry, whether directly or indirectly, as workers or employers, no matter how fraught the relationship between the two groups could at times become. The individual fortunes of the members of this community were without exception, though in different ways, subject to the vicissitudes of the global market on which raw cotton and cotton goods were traded. Guided by its overriding concern with cotton, the paper achieved international coverage, regularly reporting about the state of the cotton crop as far afield as India or Brazil. Closer to home, the weekly formed an important weapon in the arsenal of the cotton unions intent on establishing uniform conditions of work and pay throughout the entire district by helping to raise cotton workers' awareness of conditions elsewhere.

Statements made in the columns of the *Cotton Factory Times* or before government commissions, like any other type of source, need to be contextualized for their import to become intelligible. These utterances can then be read as the self-representations of specific, often influential, groups within the cotton community, chiefly trade union officials, in the public, even explicitly political, domain. Gender was an important component of their self-representation.

Government investigations, trade union records and, to a lesser extent, the *Cotton Factory Times*[35] were not conceived, nor did they function, as the mouthpieces of female cotton workers. Who wants to hear women's voices needs to turn elsewhere. Fortunately, breaking women weavers' silence does not pose much of a difficulty. There is an abundance of interviews that were conducted with cotton operatives at a time when awareness began to grow in Lancashire that the county's staple industry was nearly extinct, and with it the know-how, traditions and way of life of those who had worked in it threatened to die out, too. Fortunately coinciding with the general upsurge of interest in oral history, both people willing and able to conduct the interviews and the requisite funding were available to rescue an industry and its workforce from sinking into oblivion. It has been one of the greatest pleasures involved in the research on which this study is based to read, or listen to, women weavers talking about their lives both inside and outside the mill.

This oral history material has been used to elucidate women weavers' subjectivity moulded by their experience. In the analysis of their accounts experience has not been understood as leaving an immediate imprint on individuals' minds. Rather it has been conceived of as having been crucially mediated by consciousness.[36] By virtue of being used to accord meaning to events by those living through them experience has a narrative structure, within which reality supplies the material from which the subject fashions an understanding of self. Experience thus grounds subjectivity.

Obviously, in making sense of their experience, people draw upon contemporary discourses. Yet self-perception is not fully determined by discourse. Human agency can be discerned in the way people select from, and adapt to their own purposes, the range of discourses available to them. As Ava Baron has observed, 'Discourses, located in social institutions, mediate and shape our experiences. But ... the agency of individuals is required before the social and political implications of a discourse can be realized.'[37] Particular attention has been paid to the ways in which women weavers mediated or transformed contemporary discourses to make sense of their lives,[38] an issue explored more fully in Chapter 3.

What becomes apparent from their accounts is the degree to which their self-representation as skilled workers whose lives revolved around the factory was embedded in, and derived its acceptability from, the cultural values shared by the weaving communities of which the interviewees formed part.[39] Community, both understood narrowly as that of the workplace and more widely as that of the locality, looms large in the women's memories. They constructed a workplace community, chiefly composed of women, who shared the joys and sorrows of life at work and in the home. In their representations of the weaving community, co-workers, friends and kin merge into each other.

A great deal of this oral history material was collected at a time when the memories of quite a few among the interviewees stretched back into the period under consideration. The only exception, the Lancashire Textile Project, was not only carried out in, but also specifically referred to, the late 1970s. Prior to the imminent closure and demolition of one spinning mill and one weaving shed, both the processes and the environment in which they were performed were recorded, with particular attention being paid to the technology in use and the ways of operating it. The method adopted involved taking detailed photographs of the various stages of the work process. These were then used as stimuli inducing workers to explain as fully and exactly as possible what they could be seen doing in a given photograph.[40] In this way it has been possible to build a detailed picture of the complexities and intricacies of weaving. This is the first study making use of this rich source, which has long lain untapped.

Though relying on material relating to technology in use in the 1970s may appear anachronistic in a study concerned with the period 1880 to 1914, in fact it is not. Not only has the Lancashire cotton industry frequently been castigated for its tardiness in adopting technological innovation (an issue that will be addressed further in Chapter 5) but this particular shed, built in 1922, had been equipped with looms bought second-hand from firms that had closed down after the end of the post-war boom. At the time of the interviews, in 1978–9, the looms at this shed were probably more than 100 years old.[41] Though minor changes, such as the hiring of ancillary labour to relieve weavers of the need to sweep their looms at regular intervals, had occurred in the organization of the labour process, the technology in use was the Lancashire loom in exactly the same shape that would have been familiar to weavers around 1900.

Furthermore, this material has occasionally been drawn upon to elucidate the way in which female weavers shaped their home and family life. Again, rather than being anachronistic, these references serve to underline the tenacity, well into the 1970s, of beliefs and practices that had changed very little since the turn of the century, precisely because they were embedded in a culturally specific way of life that had been evolved by weaving communities as part of their response to the industrialization of cotton processing.

Scrutinizing this wealth of material for clues to the construction of gender has produced the central argument of this study: It was the organization of the labour process in the cotton weaving industry, making possible women weavers' self-perception as men weavers' equals, and the varying degrees of gender inequality in the other spheres their lives encompassed, that caused many of them to organize themselves around the demand for the franchise. Their experience of equality in the labour process both sensitized them to inequality elsewhere and empowered them to fight against it by showing it to be humanly produced rather than naturally or divinely ordained. Drawing on the discourses deployed by disenfranchised working-class men and middle-class women alike, they accounted for their inequality in terms of their exclusion from the polity. In the process of holding their own against male co-workers, supervisory staff, employers, labour activists, politicians and, last but not least, middle-class women, they evolved their own version of working-class femininity, which differed in important ways from the female domesticity that had a vibrant existence in labour rhetoric, but rarely beyond.

Notes

1   See Scott (1986), reprinted in Scott (1988, 1996).
2   See also the distinctions between 'gender', 'sex' and 'sexuality' made by Lorber (1994, pp.ix–x).
3   See Laqueur (1990, pp.125ff).

4   For a survey of the vast array of literature exploring the operation of gender as a binary opposition in homogenizing variations, see Lorber (1994).
5   For an unequivocal rejection of 'experience', a subject's own account of what they have lived through, as uncontestable evidence and an originary point of explanation, see Scott (1991). As against such an allegedly naive conception of experience as reflecting the real, Scott posits experience as the object of investigation. For the epistemological issues raised by the linguistic turn, see also the somewhat acrimonious interchange between Laura Lee Downs and Joan Scott in volume 35 of *Comparative Study of History and Society*.
6   See Toews (1987, p.906), whose article is criticized by Scott (1991, pp.787–90); see also the rather more tempered critique of the negation of experience and agency in Canning (1994).
7   This concept owes a great deal to the research by Kessler and McKenna (1978), which has been informed by ethnomethodology.
8   For the potential stasis inherent in a social constructionist approach to gender, see Lorber (1994, p.49).
9   See Gildemeister and Wetterer (1992, p.229).
10 Rubin (1975, p.178).
11 This expression plays upon the title of an article by Carol Hagemann-White (1993), 'Die Konstrukteure des Geschlechts auf frischer Tat ertappen?' (Catching the contructors of gender in the act?).
12 See Rose (1993) for the need to write such labour history.
13 For an overview of the issues investigated by women's labour history, see, for example, Frader and Rose (1996b, pp.16ff).
14 See, for example, John (1980; 1988), Cockburn (1981); Collinson and Knights (1986), Bradley (1987), Milkman (1987), Valverde (1987), Jordan (1989), Williams (1989), Valenze (1991), Hausen (1993); for the professions in particular, see Wetterer (1995); for an overview of the broadening out of current investigations of the gender division of work into the cultural and representational, see the special issue on 'Gendering Work', *Labour History Review*, 1998.
15 See Hall (1982).
16 See Cockburn (1991).
17 See, for example, Anderson (1988).
18 See Leidner (1991, p.158); for geographical variation in the gender division of labour, see Lewis (1984, p.162).
19 See Leidner (1991).
20 See Freifeld (1986).
21 See Cockburn (1981; 1986).
22 See Kessler-Harris (1990).
23 This is corroborated by the differences found between female 'casual' workers and Lancashire cotton weavers in Glucksmann (1995 and 2000) or the Scottish textile workers investigated in Gordon (1991).
24 See Knapp (1990).
25 For the tendency to accord primacy to their familial duties for the formation of women's self-perception, see, for example, Barrett and MacIntosh (1980), Davidoff and Westover (1986b), Roberts (1986). By contrast, Glucksmann has concluded from her study of women workers in the new industries that sprang up in inter-war Britain that women's position at work actively produced gender inequality rather than simply

reflecting it. Women's position in the work process was not just carried over from other social institutions and did not simply reflect or reinforce an already fully formed subordination created outside of paid employment and prior to it. She has therefore underlined the legitimacy of viewing the work process as a distinctive site for the construction of gender; see Glucksmann (1990, pp.208–9). For surveys of sociological approaches to the gender division of labour which distinguish between those arguing that women's subordination in the family carries over into employment and those which maintain that gender relations in employment have to be analysed separately, see Beechey (1987) and Beer (1990).

26 See Geertz (1973, esp. ch.1).
27 Judy Lown, too, has demonstrated that employers' identities are shaped by considerations of both class and gender, see Lown (1990, p.212).
28 For aspects of working-class masculinity, see, for example, Alexander (1984), Rose (1986b; 1988; 1992), Thompson (1988), McClelland (1989), Clark (1997).
29 See Liddington and Norris (1985) and Liddington (1984).
30 See Morgan (2001).
31 See Rose (1992).
32 For the subversive potential of such fractures within the system, see Downs (1993a, pp.430–31).
33 For the history of the *Cotton Factory Times*, see Cass (1994) and Cass et al. (1998).
34 This has also been stressed by Miriam Glucksmann as one result of her contrastive study of patterns of living in Lancashire; see Glucksmann (2000, p.153).
35 The few identifiable female contributors to the paper include Ethel Carnie, cotton winder and writer of socialist leanings, whose stories were published and whose novels were reviewed, and Alice Smith, a cotton worker from Oldham, who sent in dialect sketches and articles on cardroom union affairs; see Cass et al. (1998, p.158).
36 This understanding of 'experience' is influenced by Raymond Williams who used the term 'experience past' to denote 'knowledge gathered from past events, whether by conscious observation or by consideration and reflection' (Williams 1976, p.126). This is different from 'experience present', which he defined as 'the fullest, most open, most active kind of consciousness, ... [which] includes feeling as well as thoughout' (ibid., p.127).

For a charting of the course that 'experience' has taken from being a central category of analysis in social history to being virtually discarded, as discourses's other, in the wake of the 'linguistic turn' and its recent re-emergence as a much refined and hence revalidated category, particularly in historical writing on memory, the body and subjectivity, see Canning 2002.
37 Baron (1991b, p.31).
38 For such use of personal testimony, see, for example, Summerfield (1998).
39 In her study of women's reminiscences of the Second World War, Penny Summerfield has emphasized the determining influence upon the way a narrative is told of the cultural values shared by the public to which it is addressed; see Summerfield (1998, p.20). This influence has not been discernible in the material produced by women cotton workers, which is far more expressive of the embeddedness of these women's subjectivity in a particular working-class culture.
40 See Graham (1980).
41 See Lancashire Textile Project, respondent AI2, p.7.

Chapter 2

Setting the Scene: the Indian Summer of the Cotton Industry

The relevance of the cotton industry to the British economy in the period from the 1770s to the beginning of the First World War can hardly be overrated. Not only was it the first industry to make the transition to factory-based mass production, but from that time until the First World War it also was consistently one of the major contributors to national wealth.

Domestic textile production had been expanding rapidly on the basis of the putting-out system when in the 1770s spinning was mechanized and transferred to factories, where it was followed by weaving some decades later. Thus began the industry's era of expansion, which comprised three distinct periods, each of which was characterized by successively slower rates of increase in production and which ended in 1840, 1872 and 1913, respectively.[1] The industrialization of spinning and weaving along with the preparatory processes spanned the period from the 1780s to the 1840s. The industry's growth rate reached its height because the power-driven carding and spinning machines rendered English cotton cloth cheap without detracting from its quality.[2] During the subsequent phase, from the 1840s to the 1870s, the industry took on its typically 'modern' form in terms of organization and technology. Both were to survive fundamentally unchanged until the Second World War. This phase was characterized by unparalleled prosperity, based on supremacy in overseas markets.

The Economic Development of the Cotton Industry, 1873 to 1914

The commercial crisis of 1873 ushered in the next phase, dubbed the 'Indian summer' by historians of the cotton industry.[3] It was to last until the beginning of the First World War, which saw government regulation of the economy on an unprecedented scale.

By the 1870s, the industry's global supremacy began to be challenged. In overseas markets the industry began to feel the pinch of competition by the USA and the Continent. Yet the greatest threat was posed, not so much by competition from other industrial states, but from the nascent industrialization of former importers of British cotton goods. As a result exports went increasingly to less developed economies with lower income and greater demand for coarser yarn and cloth, such as India. In this market Britain retained her competitiveness by reducing the quality of the cotton input at each stage of the production process. The technology in use, the self-acting spinning mule and the powerloom, were particularly suited to producing this type of goods.[4]

At the same time that Britain managed to hold her own by satisfying the demand for coarse and heavily sized cloth in poor economies overseas, she also concentrated on producing higher-quality yarn and cloth directed at the domestic and European markets.[5] This bifurcation of production enabled the industry to retain its export markets as a prerequisite of expansion. Between 1882 and 1913, the industry's export volume reached its highest point, consistently oscillating around 80 per cent.[6] In the decade immediately prior to the First World War, capacity and output increased more rapidly than in either of the two previous decades.[7] Jones gives the following figures for Lancashire alone:[8]

Date	Spindles	Looms
1884	40 533 882	534 403
1893–4	42 970 528	606 627
1904	45 195 641	653 120
1914	59 317 187	805 452

These figures yield the following rates of increase per decade:

Period	Spindleage	Loomage
1884–1893	app. 6.0%	app. 7.4%
1894–1903	app. 19.3%	app. 13.1%
1904–1914	app. 28.6%	app. 23.3%

Despite this absolute increase in capacity, the relative importance of textile yarns and fabrics to the country's export trade had been declining steadily, from 60 per cent of UK export values in 1850, to 46 per cent by the period 1880 to 1884, to 34 per cent by the period 1909 to 1913. In spite of this decline in proportion, absolute quantities of textiles exported remained unchanged, with those of some important types of goods even exceeding previous levels. Thus the yardage of cotton piece goods shipped annually between 1909 and 1913 was 40 per cent greater than in the period 1880 to 1884.[9] This rise in volume at the same time that value declined reflected the increase in exports of cheap varieties of cloth.

The industry's capacity grew steadily in terms of output, consumption of raw cotton and labour force. Output of yarn and cloth more than doubled between 1870 and 1913, the latter year marking the highest point ever achieved. In 1870, 1075 million lbs. of raw cotton were consumed, while the corresponding figure for 1913 stood at 2178 million lbs.[10] In 1901, the industry employed 544 000 people, or 3.26 per cent of the UK labour force.[11] Just prior to the First World War, with a workforce numbering more than 600 000 people, the cotton industry was still Britain's largest manufacturing employer.[12]

The skill and efficiency of these workers became increasingly important in a more and more competitive environment. Thus the number of spinners per 1000 spindles was lower in England than on the Continent, though the English spinning mules were running faster and had a longer traverse than their Continental counterparts. In weaving, too, machines ran faster, while time lost through breakages was lower than on the Continent.[13] As a result of increasing size and speed of machinery and despite shorter-staple cotton making up an ever larger proportion of the raw material used, spinning output per worker rose from 5520lbs. in 1880–82 to 8737lbs. in 1913. In weaving, though the amount of cloth produced per worker appears to have fallen – from 4039lbs. in 1880–82 to 3868 lbs. in 1913 – the value of the cloth produced rose from £222.25 per worker in 1891–3 to £280.76 in 1913.[14] These figures reflect not only the general rise in prices, but also the tendency towards the production of finer cloth of higher value.

Yet hidden beneath the growth in volume attained by the industry between 1870 and 1914 lay relative decline. The rate of growth increased but little, and the proportion of people employed in cotton processing declined, as did Britain's share of the world's output. In 1875, the industry possessed 56 per cent of the world's spinning spindles. By 1893 that proportion had fallen to 50 per cent and continued to decline thereafter. A similar trend was shown by cloth exports, which had made up 81.9 per cent of the world's exports in 1882–4, but had fallen to 69.9 per cent by 1909–13.[15]

Despite the continuing expansion of the industry, the period 1885 to 1914 did not see an unchecked boom. In the years 1883, 1898 to 1901 and 1905 to 1907, the industry boomed, while the years 1878 to 1880, 1885 to 1888 and 1903 to 1905 were periods of depression.[16] The years 1891 to 1893, moreover, saw a cyclical depression, while in 1904 the previous peak in the gross volume of production, reached in 1872, was surpassed. The 12-year span from 1895 to 1907 was relatively stable, but followed by a deep recession lasting from 1908 to 1910. The period from autumn 1910 to the early summer of 1914, finally, witnessed a boom in productivity, though not in profits.[17]

During the four decades prior to the First World War the expansion of the British cotton industry relied solely on its high export rate. In the face of growing competition both from more recently developed industrial countries on the Continent and from newly industrializing economies overseas, the British industry remained competitive thanks to its highly skilled workforce. Operating well-tried technology, British cotton workers were able to produce yarn and cloth more cheaply than its newly arisen rivals and goods of higher quality than its Continental and US competitors, despite increasing resort to inferior raw materials.

Relying on export as heavily as it did, on the eve of the First World War the cotton industry had attained a position it could not realistically be expected to maintain.[18] The war economy brought the industry an artificial boom, which crashed in 1920, whence the industry embarked on its way towards terminal decline.[19]

Regional Concentration and Local Specialization

By the closing decades of the nineteenth century, the British cotton industry had come to be characterized by a high degree of regional concentration, coupled with a marked diversity of local specialization. Linked to this was a specific internal structure.

In the late 1830s, cotton was being processed in at least 15 counties of England and Wales as well as in Scotland and Ireland. By the last third of the century, by contrast, the industry had come to be concentrated in Lancashire and the adjoining fringes of Cheshire and Derbyshire. By 1911, Lancashire employed nearly 90 per cent of the industry's workforce.[20] Scotland sank into insignificance as a producer of cloth, and only Yorkshire retained a sizeable proportion of the industry, boasting one in every 10 cotton mills in Britain and employing 5 to 6 per cent of the cotton workforce.[21] Yet on average mills were considerably smaller than their counterparts in Lancashire, employing only half as many workers and using only half as much power and machinery.[22] The concentration of the industry in Lancashire's south-eastern corner was largely the result of the Cotton Famine caused by the American Civil War. The peripheral country districts proved unable to sustain the impact of rising raw material prices.[23]

Within Lancashire the industry was geographically segregated, with spinning being concentrated in a semi-circle around Manchester and weaving predominating in the north and north-east of the county. This had not always been the case. When weaving had eventually been mechanized, spinning factories already in existence had added on a weaving department to their plant, partly in order better to survive a concurrent depression in the spinning trade, partly in order to make use of spinners' knowledge of handling machinery. Though spinning firms predominated at that stage, integrated firms were larger in terms of their workforce both in the aggregate and per firm.

Between 1840 and 1880, a large number of firms specializing in weaving set up in the north of the county, where they were able to tap a pool of cheap labour with the requisite skills acquired from a long tradition of handloom weaving.[24] The self-reinforcing influence of localization,[25] coupled with the decline of the small spinning firms in the north unable to compete with their much larger counterparts in the south, deepened the geographical divide.[26] In addition, Farnie has pointed to the low price of land in the north as particularly conducive to the erection of weaving mills.[27] The greater weight of the machinery and the warp beams militated against the use of multi-storey buildings, the typical locale of spinning. Hence the emergence of the single-storey 'shed' with its typical 'saw-tooth' profile, formed by north-facing windows. These allowed reasonable natural lighting, while enabling an optimum balance of temperature and humidity for weaving to be maintained.[28]

Despite the comparative advantages of the north, a clear-cut north–south division between weaving and spinning did not emerge until the 1880s. By 1884, the largest manufacturing towns usually combined both sectors. In the newer, rapidly expanding manufacturing centres, by contrast, mills specializing in either process were being built. The old, combined firms survived in the peripheral areas, such as the Pennine valleys, and on the western edge of the cotton-producing region, in Preston, Chorley and Wigan.

In the period from 1884 to 1914, each regionally dominant sector came to monopolize resources, labour, sites, capital and buildings. Process specialization was encouraged as the range of products increased. Each type of cloth required a particular count of yarn, which was available at lower cost in the competitive open market than from the spinning department of a combined mill.[29]

At the beginning of the twentieth century, when the industry was experiencing its most rapid growth, the divide deepened further. The spindleage of spinning-only mills approximately doubled and the loomage of weaving-only firms grew by nearly 150 per cent, while the number of spindles and looms in combined firms decreased both relatively and absolutely. The spinning sector expanded most rapidly in Oldham, Bolton, Rochdale and Ashton, thereby reinforcing the position of these towns as the foremost producers of yarn, with the growth in Oldham exceeding that attained elsewhere. Weaving, though expanding throughout the region, grew fastest in the north, concentrating especially in the Burnley–Nelson–Colne and Blackburn–Darwen–Accrington areas.[30]

Burnley provides a particularly good example of the regional specialization experienced by the Lancashire cotton industry. In 1850, the town boasted 400 000 spindles along with 9000 looms. By 1910, the corresponding figures were 581 000 spindles and 99 000 looms, that is an increase in spindleage of only about 45.25 per cent, as compared to 1000 per cent in loomage. Moreover, 30 firms closed down their spinning departments between 1866 and 1886. Weaving increased so rapidly that, by the latter year, Burnley boasted of being the greatest producer of cloth in the world.[31] Blackburn underwent a similar development, with the number of looms increasing from 48 000 to 88 770 between 1870 and 1914, an expansion matched by a corresponding decline in spindleage.[32]

Towards the close of the nineteenth century, the British cotton industry thus emerged as highly concentrated in Lancashire, where weaving and spinning were to a large part carried out in different parts of the county by mills specializing in either process. The expansion of spinning in south Lancashire, where it was closely linked to the perfection of steam power and the growth of textile engineering, contributed to this geographical separation of spinning and weaving.[33] Vertical specialization was accompanied by marked differences in the internal make-up of spinning and weaving firms, respectively.

In spinning, there occurred a movement towards the limited liability company from the 1870s onwards, with Oldham emerging as the epitome of the joint-stock company town. Weaving, by contrast, continued to be dominated by the private company. This was largely due to differences in capital formation between the two sectors. Labour accounted for 77 per cent of the cost of production in weaving, but for only 47 per cent in spinning.[34] By enabling reasonably well-off individuals to take out shares,[35] joint-stock spinning companies gained access to the capital needed for investment in machinery. Yet, as Toms has demonstrated,[36] in the Lancashire cotton industry private companies were more profitable and grew faster than public companies. Moreover, the collapse of share values on the Oldham stock exchange in the early 1890s, forcing investors to sell at a loss, ushered in a new type of entrepreneur able to accumulate enough private capital to engage in the building of business empires.

In weaving, by contrast, it continued to be possible for private individuals, including self-made men, to set up in business, not least through the room-and-power system, which further reduced the necessary outlay of capital for plant. Under this system an enterprising individual would hire mill space, and sometimes even looms, pay for the proportion of energy used by his machines, and acquire his raw materials on extended credit. This form of ownership made for cut-throat competition, which had repercussions on working conditions as well as leading to a high turnover of firms. Though different types and sizes of weaving enterprises were to some extent localized, variations from place to place were not as pronounced as in spinning. In Colne, Nelson and Manchester, where the proportion of private mills was highest, the average size of weaving sheds was smallest.[37] The small firm also remained the typical unit of production in Blackburn, Darwen, Burnley and Rossendale. The only large firms to be built in the weaving district were to be found in Preston and Chorley.[38]

Burnley stood out as having a number of weaving firms run along cooperative lines. The first of these, set up by local operatives, lasted from 1863 to 1870. In March 1886, the Burnley Self-Help Manufacturing Society was founded to obtain for workers a greater interest in the results of their labour.[39] The society leased Healey Royd Mill, equipping it with 400 looms[40] and some spinning frames. The necessary capital was subscribed by operative members and others in £5 shares. No interest or bonus was paid in cash to any working shareholder but was added to his credit until his holding amounted to £20. Thereafter 5 per cent interest was paid in cash on each £20. Non-working shareholders received cash interest on each share. If interest could not be paid out of profits, it was paid out of wages. Of the £3700 share capital owned during the first year, £1400 had been subscribed by workers.[41] Eventually the company owned 1032 looms and had 400 operative shareholders. It failed after only four years owing to bad trade. Several other cooperative ventures were equally short-lived.[42]

Nelson, which evolved only in the 1870s from a place called Marsden, was the final Lancashire town to owe its existence to the cotton industry, and to weaving in particular. It was the fastest growing town in Victorian Lancashire,[43] its population of 5589 in 1871 rising to 39 479 by 1911.[44] The number of inhabitants had increased more than sevenfold in a period of only 40 years. Owing to the predominance of the room-and-power system, Nelson's unit of production was smaller than the industry's average. In Edwardian Nelson the average number of looms per firm stood at 437, as compared to 715 in Burnley and 822 in Blackburn.[45]

Apart from being largely distinct geographically, cotton spinning and weaving were internally subdivided in that virtually each district specialized in a class of goods of its own. In spinning, the fine trade was centred in and around Manchester; the medium fine trade was carried on mainly in Bolton, but also in Chorley and Preston; the medium trade, forming the bulk of the industry, was located in south-east Lancashire; the coarse trade was the domain of Oldham, Rochdale, Todmorden and the Rossendale Valley. The waste trade, finally, spinning up the refuse material of the preceding branches, was located in Oldham.[46]

In weaving, the western towns – Bolton, Chorley and Preston – specialized in fine, high-quality cloth, as did parts of south-east Lancashire, such as Ashton. Trade in the easterly towns – Oldham, Blackburn and Burnley – was geared to coarse cloth. While Blackburn specialized in plain dhooties, Burnley did so in medium weight grey cloths.[47] Local specialization had evolved from existing pockets of skill, which in turn re-enforced the development of distinctive capabilities in particular communities.[48]

Around 1900, cotton had become synonymous with Lancashire. The bulk of cotton processing in the heartland of the county's cotton district was divided geographically between weaving in the north-east and spinning in a semi-circle around Manchester in the south-east. Accordingly, vertically integrated firms were fairly exceptional. Furthermore, the greater capital outlay required in spinning caused limited liability companies to be set up, while weaving continued to be dominated by privately owned small units of production.

Industrial Relations

The vertical segregation typical of the Lancashire cotton industry was reflected in the organizations of both workers and employers. Spinners and weavers of each locality formed separate associations of their own, while employers, too, organized along departmental lines.

The cotton industry had not only pioneered the mechanization of textile production, but it also saw the unionization of the world's first-ever factory workforce. An early, rather short-lived, spinning union combining mule spinners from Manchester and Stockport was formed in 1792, while the first powerloom weavers' unions were set up in Glasgow, Oldham and Preston between 1834 and 1837.[49]

Spinners' and weavers' associations differed in significant ways. The former were closed, exclusivist organizations conferring upon their members bargaining strength, high wages and status through control of the labour supply into spinning. The unions marked their exclusiveness by relatively high dues and pronounced lack of interest in organizing other grades of cotton operatives. This reluctance came to the fore in spinning unions' consistent refusal to organize the exclusively female ring spinners, who were eventually accepted as members by the Cardroom Amalgamation.

Weaving unions, by contrast, were open, never attempting to restrict entry into the occupation. This was partly because, in handloom weaving, apprenticeship had been eroded a long time previously, and partly because of the specific way in which the weaving factory workforce evolved. Initially, weaving sheds had been staffed overwhelmingly by women and children, while men clung to the increasingly elusive independence of domestic handloom weaving. Only when their resistance to working in the mill finally collapsed in the mid-1840s, under the impact of increasing competition from factory production, did they follow women and children into the weaving sheds. Their only chance of gaining a foothold in the industry consisted in pressing for non-gender-specific rates of pay in order to prevent women from being preferentially employed for lower wages than men.[50] When subsequently becoming accustomed to operating a larger number of looms with the help of a juvenile assistant, or tenter, paid out of their wages, weavers made no attempt to convert their form of subcontracting into an entry restriction. In spinning, by contrast, promotion from piecer, or learner, to spinner had been made dependent upon seniority and the availability of a pair of mules.[51]

Enforcement of the standard rate for the job was by means of price lists agreed between employers and unions. The first of these, the Blackburn List of 1853, as Kirk has noted, was crucially important in setting the precedent of a standard list to be used as a reference point in subsequent negotiations.[52] By 1887, there were 22 lists in existence, each setting the rate due for the type of cloth in the production of which a particular district specialized. Price lists were highly intricate, specifying in minute detail the cloth to which a particular rate applied. They allowed adjusting the wages of operatives engaged in weaving different kinds of cloth by reference to the fineness of the yarn supplied, the width, length, the number of picks, healds and reeds of each class of cloth, the kind of weave and whether the cloth was patterned or plain. All these variables had a bearing on the kind and amount of labour required.[53] As Biernacki has demonstrated in his comparative study of the textile industries in Germany and Britain, the employment relation was understood by British employers and workers alike as the appropriation of workers' labour, which had been given physical expression in their products. Textile workers in Britain saw themselves as being allowed the use of machines for the making of a product that on completion was sold to the employer. Hence the appellation 'price list' for the list of piece rates. In Germany, by contrast, the employment relation was understood as comprising the purchase of labour effort and the disposition over workers' labour activity.[54]

It was not until 1892 that piece rates in the different districts were brought into line through the adoption of the Uniform Standard List. The list, which was a compromise between those of Blackburn, Preston and Burnley, was recognized throughout the entire weaving district of Lancashire except for part of Ashton-under-Lyne, which continued to adhere to the 1853 Blackburn List.[55] Standardization was resisted most by those manufacturers specializing in low-quality goods. Subscribing to the list here involved increasing the wage bill. Conversely, on the operatives' part, pressure for a uniform list was strongest in areas specializing in less skilled production. Though attempting to allow for variations in quality, the Uniform List, as Savage has observed,[56] tended to benefit workers employed on less skilled weaving, because it increased earnings in proportion to the number of looms worked and the speed of production.

Attainment of the standard rate presupposed collective bargaining and union recognition. Negotiating pay rates on the basis of locally agreed lists became the prerogative of a permanent and salaried officialdom, who stood out from the rank and file for their amount of expertise as regards the intricacies of the lists. As a result, in the 1850s and 1860s, weavers' unions became increasingly centralized and bureaucratized.

Furthermore, attainment of the standard rate acted as an incentive for amalgamation so as to prevent districts from undercutting each other. In 1858, the North Lancashire Power Loom Weavers' Association, which is often also referred to as the 'First Amalgamation', was formed.[57] It comprised all the weaving towns and villages between Colne and Chorley with the exception of Preston, Blackburn and Darwen, and had 28 000 members.[58] It was relatively short-lived and in 1884 was succeeded by the Northern Counties' Amalgamated Association of Weavers, or Second Amalgamation, which was to survive into the 1960s. At its inception it had 37 539 members[59] in 28 districts in Lancashire, Cheshire, Yorkshire and Derbyshire.[60] Weavers' unions were further pushed towards amalgamation, as Kirk has maintained,[61] by their reliance on financial assistance from external sources in the event of strikes. Keeping subscriptions low to preserve their openness, unions were forced to solicit the financial aid of weavers unaffected by any current strike action, of the labour movement in general and often even of the public. This necessitated close cooperation between unions throughout the cotton district.

Despite their amalgamation, weaving unions retained a high degree of local independence. As Cole has noted,[62] they were more disposed to take common action for political purposes than for collective bargaining with employers, channelling their energies into securing the passage of factory legislation. Only to this end was the United Textile Factory Workers' Association set up, though cotton workers from the industry's different departments refused to federate otherwise.[63] Along with the miners, the cotton unions were pre-eminent in the labour movement in making use of parliamentary action, recognizing that in certain areas, such as working hours or safety at work, legislation was the best way of ensuring control. With their large forces concentrated into a relatively small number of constituencies, they disposed of an electoral strength unmatched by any other body of workers.[64]

Increasing unionization of workers in conjunction with the setting up of elaborate organizational structures was mirrored on the employers' side by the establishment of masters' associations,[65] with manufacturers in the three largest weaving towns, Blackburn, Preston and Burnley, taking the lead in 1866. These associations were partly motivated by trade union growth and militancy, but were also, and perhaps chiefly, a response to declining profitability as a result of increasing competition. Employers' associations helped to maintain roughly equal standards of work and pay among members. Furthermore, as McIvor has noted,[66] the structure of British industry facilitated the externalization of industrial relations through delegation to an organization. This was particularly true of the cotton weaving industry with its prevalence of small, family-owned firms lacking any sophisticated management bureaucracy that could have effectively met the challenge posed by trade union activity.

Nevertheless, in the early 1890s, only 25 to 30 per cent of the loomage of all Lancashire cotton employers were registered as being within the manufacturers' association, which was confined on the whole to the larger urban areas as opposed to the outlying country districts. Between 1900 and 1914, the proportion of looms registered rose from 40 to 61 per cent, mainly as a result of expansion of members already federated rather than addition of new ones,[67] but possibly also, as Toms has argued,[68] as a result of a shift away from the localism that had previously prevailed. Mirroring the United Textile Factory Workers' Association, the Cotton Employers' Parliamentary Association was set up in 1899, concerning itself with parliamentary and trade action rather than with wages.[69]

By the 1880s, mill owners predominantly opted for the institutionalization and incorporation of unions into forms of bureaucratic and procedural control, epitomized by the Brooklands Agreement of 1893. This had been reached following a protracted strike called by spinners and cardroom operatives against an announced 5 per cent cut in wages. The Agreement not only terminated this particular strike, but also laid down procedures to be followed in settling disputes at individual mills and in industry-wide negotiations of changes in wage rates. It remained in place for 20 years and has been described by Joyce as the most thoroughgoing institutionalization of labour relations in nineteenth-century Britain.[70] Yet, as Porter has argued,[71] it effectively limited spinners' ability to use their bargaining power to secure any increase in wage rates.

In weaving, the Joint Standing Committee of Employers and Operatives was created in 1881 to consider in their preliminary stages all weaving disputes in north and north-east Lancashire, thereby endeavouring to preserve good feeling between both parties. The committee consisted of six representatives of each side, who had equal voting rights. Though confined to making recommendations, the committee had the satisfaction of seeing its decisions being by and large adopted.

In negotiating pay rates, the selling price of the employers' finished product and the state of the trade were accepted as wage regulators by both parties.

Although, as McIvor has noted,[72] a system of procedural control had come to replace coercion and the strategic use of mill paternalism as the dominant mechanism of labour control, the period from 1875 to 1914 was far from being quiescent. He has shown that, in the 1890s and 1900s, master weavers were highly committed to conciliation and incorporation. They displayed a relatively low level of sensibility to short-term fluctuations of the trade cycle, calling neither for wage reduction nor for lock-out.[73] Yet employers' conciliatory attitude was not always reciprocated by operatives. White has distinguished three phases which industrial disputes in that period went through. From 1875 to 1893–4, strikes were called in order to fend off wage cuts and press for union recognition. The subsequent phase, lasting until 1906, was one of consolidation and relative industrial peace. By contrast, the years up to 1914 were marked by a wave of conflict spreading throughout the industry, reaching its height in 1913.[74] In 1911, the weaving industry witnessed the first general lock-out since 1878. This occurred in response to the demand – unprecedented in any branch of the industry – for an industry-wide closed shop.[75] The Amalgamation had been emboldened to take this audacious step by constantly mounting membership figures, which had risen from 112 462 in 1911 to 137 196 in 1912, to 179 391 in 1913, and reaching their pre-war peak of 197 957 in 1914.[76]

Until 1914, both cotton workers and employers' organizations were characterized by a high degree of localism and sectionalism. While amalgamation did occur, no attempt at federation was made at any stage. At the same time the workforce was highly unionized and being led by carefully selected professional bargainers, who concurred with employers in the most elaborate institutionalization of labour relations.

Factory Legislation and Working Conditions

Once having been transferred from workers' homes to factories, cotton processing became the object of government regulation, setting a precedent for state intervention in the economy. This open breach of laissez-faire principles, which dominated economic thinking at the time, had been facilitated by the large number of women and children employed in the cotton industry. Initially, factory legislation was primarily concerned with the working conditions of infant labour. Beginning in 1802, a number of Acts were passed restricting the employment of children. Not until 1833 were provisions made for the appointment of factory inspectors by government to enforce the law. As long as their number remained small, enforcement was lax.

The Factory Act of 1844 was the first explicitly to include women in its purview by limiting their hours of work.[77] Following the successive shortening of hours, in 1878 factory law was consolidated into a single great Factories and Workshops Act. This fixed the standard working day at 10 hours (at six-and-a-half hours on Saturdays) and ruled for it to fall either between six o'clock in the morning and six o'clock in the evening, or between seven and seven. The Act defined a child as anyone under the age of 14 and a young person as anyone under the age of 18. This Act also excluded women and children from certain occupations as well as from nightwork.[78] The latter two regulations, however, were irrelevant to the cotton industry.

By the twentieth century, regulation had been extended to the internal make-up of the working day, two hours of which had to be given to meals. One meal hour had to be granted before three o'clock in the afternoon, and no-one was to work for more than four and a half hours without a meal break. In addition, six holidays were fixed beside Sundays. These were Christmas Day, Good Friday and the four bank holidays.[79]

Although the bulk of nineteenth-century factory legislation concerned hours of work and the age of entry into factory work of juvenile labour, other aspects of the labour process were regulated as well. The Truck Acts of 1831, 1887 and 1896, for example, aimed at securing for workers of either sex payment of all their wages in cash rather than in goods and without stoppages. These Acts were invoked whenever an employer fined an operative for alleged faulty weaving and damaged cloth. The 1896 Truck Act restricted employers' right to make deductions from wages as fines (considered in more detail in Chapter 4) or to receive payment in recompense for bad work. The Act ruled that a fine could only be imposed for an act, omission or fault likely to cause damage to the employer. The amount of the fine had to be reasonable, as had the payment or deduction for damaged goods.[80] The Weavers' Amalgamation, objecting as it did to the framing of the Act, successfully applied to the Home Secretary for exemption.

Cotton unions' parliamentary action caused a number of Factory Acts to be passed,[81] such as that of 1891. This contained a Particulars Clause stipulating that all factory owners furnish their piece workers with the particulars of the rate of wages for the work on hand and of the work to which the rate applied. The Cotton Cloth Factories Acts of 1889 and 1897, which laid down maximum levels of humidity for weaving sheds, had equally been passed as a result of pressure applied by unions. Steam was injected into weaving mills in order to prevent the yarn from breaking. The practice became increasingly widespread as manufacturers resorted to progressively inferior yarn in order to cut costs. Frequently, steam jets were situated within a few inches of weavers' heads, causing severe headache. Moreover, especially in the summer, shed floors were flooded with water, sometimes above weavers' clogs.[82] By 1909, about 45.5 per cent of all females employed in weaving and incidental processes worked in mills where steaming was used.[83]

According to the typology proposed by Alice Kessler-Harris, Jane Lewis and Ulla Wikander, those nineteenth-century Factory Acts that had a bearing on the cotton industry, though concerned with regulating the hours worked by women and children, tended towards the gender-neutral,[84] at least with regard to the effects they actually produced. Yet factory legislation was also always informed by the wish to buttress gender hierarchy at work. Many of those pressing for government measures hoped that the reduction in the hours women could work would encourage manufacturers to give men preference in employment over women.[85] Yet, given the interconnectedness of the labour process in cotton factories, any reduction in the hours of specific groups of workers had to be extended to all operatives.

The Ten Hour Movement had focused on a reduction in the hours worked by women only. This may be seen as a necessary subterfuge to make the demand for shorter hours palatable to legislators imbued with laissez-faire economics, which ruled out any government interference in the economy, in which free agents were believed to act subject to the market laws of supply and demand. The perception of agency as a corollary of masculinity, but an opposite of femininity,[86] paved the way for state interference on behalf of women and children, who were construed as being in need of protection and therefore being positioned differently from men in relation to the state.

The 1901 Factory Act signalled the shift of legislators' concern in the 1890s from the 'working woman' to the 'working mother', as Jane Lewis and Sonya Rose have argued.[87] This act was explicitly gendered in making it punishable for an employer knowingly to employ a woman within four weeks of the birth of her child.[88] Yet, in the absence of any maternity benefit, women workers were only too keen to collude with employers evading the law.[89]

Despite the spate of Factory Acts regulating the conditions of factory labour, these were far from satisfactory. The threat posed generally by machinery in motion was exacerbated in weaving sheds by the closeness with which looms were arranged in straight rows, or alleys. Only experienced workers were able to manoeuvre through them in relative safety and without being knocked about by moving parts.[90] Of the machine parts in motion, the shuttle was by far the most dangerous. Shuttles were prone to 'fly out', that is to leave their prescribed trajectory across the warps. Flying out was caused by ends broken and sticking fast in the shed so that, instead of opening when the shuttle arrived, the shed stayed close.[91] Shuttles flew so fast that they could not be seen coming and sometimes even landed in another weaver's alley. Although factory legislation stipulated that all looms be fenced in, in some districts guards were completely unknown, and in only a few mills were guards found to have been attached to all looms.[92] As a result, many a weaver had lost an eye through a shuttle flying out.

Even when running smoothly, the shuttle posed a health hazard by continually having to be replenished. In response to persistent trade union demand, an inquiry into the risks involved in the prevailing practice of shuttle changing was conducted by a panel of experts, who submitted a report to the Home Office and the Local Government Board. In this report shuttle changing was described thus: in order to thread a shuttle, a cop is placed on a skewer fixed by one end inside the shuttle on an axis which allows the free end to be raised vertically so that the cop may be placed on the skewer. The skewer is then depressed so as to lie lengthwise inside the shuttle. A little of the thread is drawn off the end of the skewer, loosely rolled into a little bunch, and pushed by a finger towards the inner opening of the eye. The opening on the outside of the shuttle, which may be clean or dirty, is then placed to the mouth. By means of a sudden and forcible inspiration, a strong draught of air is induced through the eye and carries the thread with it into the mouth of the operator. An act of mouth suction would in itself be quite insufficient to induce a sufficiently strong air-current through the eye of the shuttle. A sudden and strong inhalation is required. As a result any particles of dust, fluff, dye, thread, size or disease germs, which may be resting in or near the eye of the shuttle, are apt to be inhaled. A weaver working on four looms had to perform this act, known as 'shuttle-kissing', 450 to 500 times a day. Although each weaver had her or his own set of shuttles, these were also 'kissed' by at least the tenter and the overlooker.[93] In order to avoid shuttle kissing, many weavers developed a knack to leave a bit of cotton through the eye of the shuttle. Then they put their cop close onto it, twisted it and drew it through.[94]

A further threat was posed by the need to clean machinery. Although the Factory Act of 1878 prohibited women and young persons from cleaning machinery in motion, both groups of workers persisted in doing so for a number of reasons. In textile factories, fluff settled on the wheels and had to be pulled off on a continuous basis, frequently causing weavers to catch their fingers. Moreover, some cleaning operations, though not involving machinery directly, still required going near or under machines. This was the case when sweeping up. Finally, there was an incentive to start cleaning early or, despite the prohibition applying to women and young persons, do it during the dinner hour. The cleaning of four looms took at least an hour, and although weavers might have been allowed to stop their machines at any time to do so, this inevitably entailed a loss of earnings. Hence they preferred breaking the law and running the risk of being fined when caught by a factory inspector.[95]

Sanitary conditions in weaving sheds were another sore point. Weavers complained of the lack of dressing rooms in which to hang and dry their wet clothes.[96] Moreover, they would have been available to women weavers changing out of their skirts and into their fustian aprons prior to work. The need to do so on the shopfloor and in front of men was deplored at least by some observers, who claimed to voice the view of some of those immediately concerned.[97]

Complaints about sanitary conditions in cotton mills were corroborated by the investigations of female factory inspectors, appointed from 1893 onwards,[98] who had at least their own sensibilities offended by what they found. They deplored the lack of ventilation of most mill lavatories, which moreover opened directly out of rooms and were emptied by their contents being carried through the workshop during working hours. Generally, they found sanitary accommodation dirty and neglected and often situated only a few feet from some of the looms and other machinery.⁹⁹

By the closing decades of the nineteenth century, cotton operatives worked in the most extensively regulated industry by far. Although the law was neither all-embracing nor universally respected, the awareness of the illegality of certain practices reinforced workers' sense of their rights at the workplace and pointed the way to further improvement.

The Composition of the Cotton Workforce

The workforce in the Lancashire cotton industry was divided by age as well as gender. From its inception, as noted above, the factory system had relied on child labour, which also paved the way for government interference in the economy. By continually raising the age at which children were allowed to start work in the mill, factory legislation regulated and thereby institutionalized child labour. In the last quarter of the nineteenth century alone the age of entry was raised from 10 in 1876 to 11 in 1893 and to 12 in 1899.¹⁰⁰ The proportion of children employed in cotton processing reached its height at 15 per cent of the workforce in 1874, dropping to around 5 per cent in the 1890s.¹⁰¹ They were the so-called half-timers, who combined half-day attendance at school with half a day's work in the factory.¹⁰² This system had been established by the Factory Act of 1844. Demand for child labour was greatest in the textile industries of Lancashire and Yorkshire, which employed 80 per cent of all half-timers.¹⁰³ By the 1880s, the majority of half-timers, most of them girls, were to be found in weaving. The half-time system persisted until 1920, having received the consistent support of weavers' unions and their rank and file.¹⁰⁴

In addition, the Lancashire cotton industry was characterized by a marked gender division of labour by department. Because of the unions' ban on members employing female piecers, mule spinning had been turned into an almost exclusively male domain in Lancashire, though not in Scotland.¹⁰⁵ When ring spinning machines began to be introduced into the county's mills from the 1870s, mule spinners washed their hands of this new-fangled machinery, leaving it to be operated by women only. They formed the worst paid and most downtrodden group of workers and were commonly referred to as the 'white slaves' of the industry.

In weaving, by contrast, as noted above, the early factories had been staffed predominantly by women and children. After being joined by men, women had retained their preponderance, which even increased over the second half of the nineteenth century. By 1890, there were 199 764 workers employed in weaving sheds in the region covered by the Northern Counties' Amalgamation. Taking the 47 943 odd hands into account, one is left with 151 821 actual weavers. Of the total number of workers, 9988 (5 per cent) were male half-timers, 15 981 (8 per cent) were female half-timers, 17 979 (9 per cent) were male full-timers under 18, 33 960 (17 per cent) were female full-timers under 18, 47 943 (23.8 per cent) were men over 18, and 73 913 (37 per cent) were women over 18. Taking all age groups together, there were 123 854 (about 62 per cent) females employed in weaving as compared to 75 910 (about 38 per cent) males.[106] By 1907, the figures were 218 521 (about 67.6 per cent) females as compared to 104 696 (about 32.4 per cent) males.[107]

Despite this increase in the proportion of females among the weaving workforce, women's employment in cotton declined relative to the size of the population. This decline was manifest in each age group above 15.[108] White gives the following numbers of cotton workers per million of the population aged 10 and over:[109]

	1880	*1891*	*1901*	*1911*
Men	51 762	49 001	40 561	41 718
Women	61 300	57 542	50 284	50 065

This table yields the following proportional decline for women: 6.1 per cent in the period 1880 to 1890, 12.7 per cent in 1891 to 1900, and 0.4 per cent in 1901 to 1910. The corresponding proportionate decline for men was 5.3 per cent in the period 1880 to 1890 and 17.2 per cent 1891 to 1900, while in the period 1901 to 1910 there was an increase of 2.9 per cent. Between 1880 and 1900, the cotton industry lost in relative importance as an employer of both male and female labour. The decline was most marked for both gender groups between 1891 and 1900, being greater among men than among women. In the preceding decade, though the proportion was lower for both gender groups, the decline was slightly more marked (by 0.8 per cent) among women. Between 1901 and 1910, the decline was virtually halted in the case of women, but actually reversed in that of men. Nevertheless, in neither case was the proportionate level of employment of 1891 regained.

Despite the increasing feminization of the cotton workforce in the decades preceding the First World War, the proportion of women varied with the specific conditions of the labour market in each locality where cotton processing went on. Consequently, as Savage has noted,[110] women's experience of the cotton industry was varied. In most of the cotton towns the industry, despite being the largest employer, was far from monopolizing the labour market. Engineering, mainly catering to the needs of cotton processing, was important, as was coal mining, because the bulk of the cotton industry was concentrated on the south Lancashire coal field, which supplied it with the necessary source of steam power. Both engineering and coal mining were overwhelmingly male industries.

As a result women formed a larger proportion of the cotton workforce in Preston, Chorley and Accrington than in Burnley or Blackburn. Nelson and Colne, by contrast, counted more men than women in their cotton industry in the complete absence of alternative employment in coal mining or engineering.[111] By 1914, around 75 per cent of the workforce in Nelson and its neighbouring villages of Brierfield and Barrowford were employed in weaving. Other sectors of the local labour market did not absorb more than 4.5 per cent of the workforce each.[112] According to the figures for 1901, there was a slight preponderance of males (54 per cent) over females (46 per cent) in the local weaving workforce.[113]

In Blackburn cotton also predominated, though not to quite the same extent. The town's main secondary industry was engineering, geared to the cotton trade and mainly producing textile machinery. In 1881, only 6 per cent of the town's total workforce were employed in engineering, as compared to cotton's 59.7 per cent. This ratio had remained nearly unaltered by 1911. In Rochdale, by contrast, the engineering workforce was half the size of that of cotton, while in Oldham the two were equal in terms of the number of workers employed.[114]

In Bolton, which was predominantly a spinning town, 64.2 per cent of women workers were employed in textiles by 1911. The majority of these (66 per cent) worked in ring spinning and only 31 per cent in weaving.[115] Here the engineering workforce was half the size of that in cotton.[116]

In various cotton towns the proportion of females in the local cotton workforce in 1907 was as shown in Table 1.[117] In each of the places listed, except Blackburn City, the number of females exceeded that of males, yet in different proportions. Blackburn City had an almost equal proportion of men and women in its local cotton workforce. The average proportion of females in Blackburn City and District taken together is 54.15 per cent, and the two also boasted the highest number of females employed in cotton in absolute terms. In Rochdale, Bolton and Stockport, all of which were spinning towns, males and females would largely have worked in different departments of the industry. In Preston, the cotton

Table 1

Place	Males	Females	Proportion of females
Manchester C.	9 271	29 011	75.8
Man. District	20 911	57 524	73.3
Oldham	36 937	43 003	53.8
Rochdale	20 729	22 655	52.2
Bolton	20 558	27 776	57.4
Stockport	18 489	33 817	64.7
Blackburn C.	6 196	6 171	50.0
Bl. District	54 189	75 637	58.3
Preston	14 405	26 486	64.8

industry was predominantly female, as was the case in Manchester, both in the City and the District. In 1894, the greatest proportion of women and girls among cotton operatives had been found in Wigan, Manchester and Salford, yet in none of these towns was the greatest proportion of local women employed in the industry.[118] Only in conjunction with the structure of the local labour market can the proportion of females among the cotton workforce serve as an indicator of the absence of gender segregation at work.

Winstanley has quoted from the 1911 census the details shown in Table 2 indicating the relative importance of cotton manufacture in Lancashire boroughs.[119] Quite clearly, a high female labour participation rate was closely related to the proportion of women employed in the local cotton industry. This is particularly obvious in the case of Wigan, whose labour market was neatly divided between male employment in coal mining and female jobs in the cotton industry.

The cotton industry stood out not only on account of the large number of females employed, but also because of the proportion of married women among them, which was exceptionally high by national standards. In 1894, 32.9 per cent of the women over 18 years of age who were employed in the cotton mills of Lancashire and Cheshire were either married or widowed.[120] Although that proportion had fallen to 28.6 per cent by 1907,[121] it was still far in excess of the national mean of working married women, which had been 5.3 per cent in 1901.[122] In Yorkshire, by contrast, the proportion of married women among all textile

Table 2

	Cotton workers as % of all employed workers		Total female employment as % of all females over 10
	Males	Females	
Blackburn	36.41	74.14	59.19
Bolton	24.99	61.86	43.93
Burnley	40.06	76.84	56.29
Bury	22.63	61.69	50.19
Manchester	4.01	12.42	39.40
Oldham	31.20	69.12	46.08
Preston	25.42	68.16	54.32
Rochdale	28.02	60.03	48.37
Salford	7.29	22.99	38.63
Warrington	0.69	18.89	29.80
Wigan	3.81	46.66	37.19

workers varied in 1911 from 11 per cent in Dewsbury and 12 per cent in Bradford to 9 per cent in Halifax and 7 per cent in Huddersfield.[123] In the silk processing town of Macclesfield in Cheshire, employment rates of married women were more similar to those in the Lancashire cotton industry. In 1901, 33.2 per cent of the married and widowed women were in employment, their proportion rising to 34.1 per cent by 1911.[124] Many of the married women employed in cotton weaving must be assumed to have been mothers of small children. This assumption cannot be quantified.[125] Again local variations were marked, as Table 3 shows.[126]

The proportion of married or widowed women had declined everywhere, the decline ranging from only 1.54 per cent points at Rochdale to 9.4 per cent points at Oldham, with 6.3 per cent points being the average. Furthermore, the percentage of married or widowed female cotton operatives was clearly related to the preponderance of weaving in the local economy, being highest in the weaving centres of Burnley and Blackburn, much lower in the spinning towns, very low indeed in Wigan, and virtually non-existent in Stockport.

Although the variation in these figures suggests that the proportion of married women in employment was related to the structure of the male labour market, this was not the only factor having an impact. Savage has found that in Preston more than two-thirds of the cotton workers with low earnings, mainly weavers and piecers, had a wife in employment on account of the inadequacy of the male wage. The wives of cotton workers commanding higher earnings and those of supervisory workers, such as spinners, overlookers, tapesizers and grinders, had a participation rate which, though lower, was still above the national average. Looked at from the wives' angle, about 60 per cent of married female cotton

Table 3

Married or widowed women as percentage of the female cotton workforce in urban districts with over 50 000 inhabitants		
	1894	1911
Burnley	44.7	36.75
Blackburn	43.1	36.50
Preston	38.3	30.19
Stockport	37.7	—
Bury	35.6	30.20
Oldham	33.4	24.00
Rochdale	29.2	27.66
Salford	28.4	19.93
Bolton	20.5	13.06
Wigan	9.8	8.13

workers had husbands in cotton or metal production, the majority of whom were well paid.[127] Such rates of married women's employment despite good male earnings indicate the need to look for extra-economic factors in order to account for them. This will be done in subsequent chapters.

The majority of the females employed in Lancashire cotton weaving took up work in the mill in their early teens, as half-timers, and many continued in employment after marriage. For them weaving was more than a transitory stage between leaving school and getting married. On the edge of the cotton district, in places like Preston or Wigan, weaving had become overwhelmingly female by the closing decades of the nineteenth century, mainly as a result of 'masculine' occupations absorbing the bulk of the male labour force. In the heartland of cotton weaving, by contrast, in places like Blackburn and Burnley or Nelson and Colne, where the proportion of male and female operatives was roughly equal, women found themselves working side by side with men.

Women Weavers' Wages

Weavers' pay, as noted above, was regulated by price lists, which laid down in minute detail the amount of money due for each exactly specified type of cloth. Piece rates differed according to the class of goods produced, but not by gender. As a result, women weavers were among the highest paid groups of female workers. In 1906, women over 18 were able to attain higher hourly earnings in only two industries, as compared to 87 industries paying female workers less per hour than did cotton weaving. Men, by contrast, could earn more in 65 industries, as compared to 45, where pay per hour worked out less than in cotton weaving.[128] In other words, men weavers worked for a woman's wage.

Female cotton weavers' pay compared favourably, too, with women's earnings in other textile industries. Clara Collet, a university-educated economist who was appointed the first woman labour correspondent of the Board of Trade, in 1893,[129] found that, in the early 1890s, many female weavers in Lancashire earned about 24s. a week all year round, while in Yorkshire 18s. a week was exceptional for a woman and seldom maintained for any length of time. She further ascertained the wages of male and female weavers in Lancashire to be equal on average to those of the best male weavers in the highest paying district of Yorkshire.[130]

The principle of equal piece rates for equal work was far from universal even in textiles. While applying in the Macclesfield silk industry,[131] in the Huddersfield area, for example, female woollen weavers were paid at rates that were 10 to 15 per cent less than men's,[132] and in the Ulster linen weaving industry men appear consistently to have earned more than women.[133] Elsewhere, male and female textile operatives hardly ever performed identical tasks.[134] Lancashire women weavers thus profited both from a higher level of pay in cotton as compared to woollens and from the non-gender-specificity of piece rates. Female weavers themselves felt sufficiently strongly about their right to equal rates repeatedly to take strike action over this issue,¹³⁵ thereby gaining a reputation for insisting on being treated equally with regard to rates of pay.¹³⁶

Although the payment of non-gender-specific piece rates in cotton weaving is commonly acknowledged by both contemporary compilers of data and historians, opinions diverged at the time, and have continued to do so, as to whether equal piece rates translated into equal weekly earnings. There were a number of variables having an impact on weekly pay: the number of looms operated per weaver, the type of cloth woven, the ability to adjust one's own looms so as to avoid machine downtime while waiting for the overlooker and, last but not least, the individual degree of skill. As a result of the differential effect of these variables in any one week, weavers' weekly earnings were subject to marked fluctuation. Wage statistics therefore tend to be based on average weekly earnings calculated over a certain period of time. Wood, for example, one of the standard sources on wages in the cotton industry from 1806 to 1906, based the average weekly wages he listed in one of his tables on six weeks, apparently chosen at random, in 1833, on 26 weeks each for 1840, 1850 and 1860, and on the whole year in the succeeding years except for 1905 and 1906, for which he chose one specific week each.¹³⁷ Moreover, he distinguished between 'average earnings' and 'average earnings for an ordinary week's work',¹³⁸ without specifying the difference. Averages therefore conceal peak earnings attained in particularly good weeks by both male and female weavers.

Each of the variables having an impact on weekly pay was perceived as gendered by the compilers of data. They commonly assumed men to work a larger machine complement than women, to be allocated better-paying classes of goods, to be able, unlike women, to adjust their own looms, and generally by virtue of being male to possess greater strength and stamina, enhancing their productivity and hence their pay. Such preconceptions would ensure that the possibility of women earning equal wages to men was not entertained. Wage statistics relating to Lancashire cotton weaving are therefore distorted by an inherent gender bias, rendering it virtually impossible to determine whether or not, or the extent to which, equal piece rates translated into equal wages.

The distortion is exemplified by a consideration of the impact exerted by the size of the machine complement on weavers' wages. In 1906, weavers' earnings in Burnley varied with the number of looms operated in the following way:¹³⁹

No. of looms	No. of weavers	Average earnings per week
2	42	12s.4d.
3	386	19s.9d.
4	6 005	25s.3d.
6	92	31s.9d.

The size of machine complement per worker varied by location in accordance with the type of cloth in which a particular place specialized. Ashton and Bolton, specializing in fine, high-quality cloth, as well as Oldham and Manchester had a larger proportion of two- and three-loom weavers among their local workforce than did Stockport, Blackburn and Burnley. The latter two, where four-loom weavers predominated, as shown above, specialized in coarse cloth.[140]

Taking each category of weavers for all of Lancashire in 1906, one arrives at the following data:[141]

Category	Male wages	Female wages	Diff.
6 looms	32s.10d.	30s.7d.	2s. 3d.
4 looms	24s.11d.	23s.5d.	1s. 6d.
3 looms	19s. 6d.	17s.8d.	1s.10d.

The fact that the differential was greatest among six-loom weavers appears to tally with presumed gender differences in competence and stamina. Yet, if this were indeed the case, one would expect the diffential to increase in proportion to the size of the machine complement. The fact that the differential was larger among three-loom weavers than among those tending four calls this assumption into question. Age, the impact of which is considered below, may have played a role here.

Nor was there any marked gender difference in the size of the machine complement per weaver. Between 1830 and 1880, the number of looms per operative had been expanding steadily. Thereafter the average 3.3 looms per weaver in 1886 had increased to only 3.44 looms by 1906. According to Riley, for the majority of experienced weavers on normal cloths the standard loom complement stabilized at four. The major exceptions were a sizeable group of six-loom weavers mainly in Burnley and Nelson districts. They were assisted each by a tenter, or learner, and were supposedly always male.[142] Yet as the representation above has shown and the following chapter will corroborate, six looms were by no means confined to men.[143] Wherever certain types of loom, such as large sheeting looms, were the prerogatives of men, the arbitrariness of the allocation became apparent when, during the First World War and the ensuing shortage of male labour, women were set to work on them.[144] Moreover, in 1914, a trade union official from Burnley was quoted in the *Cotton Factory Times* as stating that women worked an equal number of looms with men,[145] a statement corroborated by women weavers themselves.[146]

The Report on Earnings, which referred to 1906, asserted that the gender difference in the size of loom complements had been levelling out. The great majority of men were found to be tending four looms, while women principally tended three to four looms. However, more than 50 per cent of female weavers operated a loom complement of four. As a result, men averaged 4.1 and women

3.5 looms per weaver.[147] This difference may well have resulted from the fact that the loom complement per worker was smaller where work was more skilled and that, as shown above, the centres of the fine trade boasted a predominantly female workforce. Moreover, these ratios yield a non-gender-specific average of 3.8 looms per weaver, which is higher than Riley's quoted above. These data, distorted by a gender bias as they are, do not allow any hard-and-fast conclusion to be drawn. However, they suggest that women weavers, far from being barred from operating the maximum number of six looms, possibly did so, though smaller numbers than men.

Earnings varied, too, between localities. These variations have consistently been explained by reference to the percentage of men among the local weaving workforce. The Return of Rates of Wages of 1889 proposed this explanation on the basis of the data shown in Table 4.[148]

In Table 4, places are ranked in decreasing order by annual wage levels. If the same localities were listed in decreasing order by the proportion of men among the local weaving workforce, the following list would emerge: Burnley, Blackburn, Darwen, Oldham, Rochdale, Ashton, Preston, Bolton, Bury, Stockport, Manchester. The striking difference between both tables shows the proportion of men to have no bearing on local wage levels. On the contrary high annual wages and a low proportion of men among the local weaving workforce point to women's high earnings as the explanation, as was conceded in the Return.

Gibson, too, accounted for local variations in wages by reference to the proportion of men among local weavers. He found that in 1906 weavers were paid 35 per cent more in Burnley, Blackburn and Stockport than in the low paying districts of Oldham, Bolton, Ashton and elsewhere. The high-paying districts of

Table 4

Place	Annual wages	Proportion of men
Burnley	£42	35.4
Darwen	£42	26.1
Preston	£40	20.6
Ashton	£38	20.9
Bolton	£38	19.0
Blackburn	£38	28.6
Oldham	£37	24.9
Rochdale	£36	24.0
Bury	£34	19.0
Manchester	£33	16.0
Stockport	£33	18.2

Burnley, Blackburn and Stockport had 47 per cent, 34 per cent and 14 per cent men respectively, while the low-paying districts of Oldham, Bolton, Ashton and elsewhere had only between 9 and 0 per cent male weavers among their local workforce respectively.[149] This difference in levels of pay may equally be attributable to the adoption of the Uniform List in 1892, which, as argued above, benefited weavers operating fast-running looms and producing inferior qualities of cloth. White, too, has reiterated the argument on the basis of figures for 1911.[150] Yet again the argument fails to tally with the evidence. Were his reasoning correct, Burnley with the highest proportion of men weavers in his list should have had the smallest gender differential in earnings rather than Blackburn.

Furthermore over time and not least under the impact of the Uniform List what gender differential in earnings may have existed was diminished. This is demonstrated by the following table compiled by Savage on the basis of the wage censuses for 1886 and 1906:[151]

Locality	Wage Differential	
	1886	1906
Burnley	1.2%	2.6%
Blackburn	28.3%	2.7%
Preston	22.3%	7.6%
Bolton	8.7%	8.8%

While the gender differential in earnings fell quite dramatically in Blackburn and Preston, by just under 90 per cent and about 65.5 per cent, respectively, in Burnley it more than doubled, while in Bolton it increased very slightly indeed. Again these findings bear no relation to the percentage of men in the local weaving workforce. On the contrary, they appear to make complete nonsense of that causation, because, if the argument held, the gender differential could not have diminished most both in a district with a high proportion of male weavers, such as Blackburn, and in one where the reverse was true, such as Preston.

White has compiled a comparative table (see Table 5) of the wages of male and female weavers by locality on the basis of the Report on Earnings of 1909, which refers to 1906.[152] This may be used to shed light on the impact on wage levels exerted by differences in the age composition between the male and female sections of the weaving workforce.

Table 5 yields in turn the gender differentials in earnings by locality shown in Table 6. Interestingly, the gender differential in earnings was smaller among four-loom weavers, being as low as 8d. in Blackburn and Burnley, than among all weavers. This may be explained by differences in the age composition of the workforce by gender, something that only Clara Collet investigated systematically. As noted above, the majority of half-timers in weaving were girls, who, as they gained in age and skill, would still deflate women weavers' average wage levels

Table 5

	Men		Women	
	4 looms	All	4 looms	All
Ashton	23s.10d.	21s.11d.	21s. 6d.	18s. 1d.
Oldham	—	—	21s.33d.*	17s.11d.
Bolton	24s.10d.	25s. 0d.	22s.10d.	18s. 9d.
Leigh	—	—	20s. 0d.	17s. 7d.
Manchester	—	—	20s. 0d.	16s. 0d.
Stockport	23s. 3d.	22s.11d.	22s. 2d.	21s. 0d.
Preston	24s.10d.	23s. 9d.	23s. 1d.	20s. 5d.
Blackburn	25s. 5d.	24s. 9d.	24s. 9d.	23s. 6d.
Accrington	24s. 6d.	22s. 5d.	23s. 4d.	20s.11d.
Burnley	25s.11d.	27s. 7d.	25s. 3d.	24s.11d.
Bacup	24s. 4d.	24s. 0d.	23s. 0d.	20s. 4d.
Rochdale	23s. 4d.	23s. 4d.	22s. 7d.	19s. 8d.

* *sic* in White (1978)

on account of their larger proportion as compared to male adolescents. This effect is demonstrated by Table 7, which refers to 1886.[153] As this comparison shows, the inclusion of the wages earned by females under 18 working full-time deflates adult women weavers' average weekly wages by between 11d. and 2s. 1d.

Rather than demonstrating the impact on wage levels exerted by the proportion of men among the local weaving workforce, these tables indicate that local variations were related to the department of the industry which predominated in a

Table 6

Place	4-loom weavers	All weavers
Ashton	2s. 4d.	3s.10d.
Bolton	2s. 0d.	6s. 3d.
Stockport	1s. 1d.	1s.11d.
Preston	1s. 9d.	3s. 4d.
Blackburn	8d.	1s. 3d.
Accrington	1s. 2d.	2s. 6d.
Burnley	8d.	2s. 8d.
Bacup	1s. 4d.	3s. 8d.
Rochdale	11d.	3s. 8d.

Table 7

District	Average Weekly Wages of Women and Girls	
	Full-timers	Women above 18
Burnley	18s. 2d.	20s. 1d.
Darwen	16s.10d.	18s. 5d.
Blackburn	16s. 5d.	18s. 4d.
Preston	15s. 5d.	17s. 5d.
Todmorden	15s. 3d.	16s. 8d.
Ashton	15s. 0d.	16s. 7d.
Bury	14s. 8d.	16s. 3d.
Oldham	14s. 1d.	16s. 0d.
Stockport	13s. 5d.	14s. 9d.
Rochdale	13s. 5d.	14s. 4d.
Bolton	12s. 1d.	14s. 2d.
Manchester	11s.11d.	13s. 2d.

given locality. In the spinning district weavers' wages were lower than in the weaving district. Gibson concluded from this that there appeared to be a tendency for the family wage of workers to equalize itself among the different districts, enabling families to earn something approximating a living wage even where the wages of one or the other family member might have been below average.[154] In other words, variation was confined to the relative contribution men, women and children made to the family income, with possibly dramatic repercussions for relations of authority between family members.

Living standards among the Lancashire cotton workforce were determined by a family wage economy, in which families relied for survival on the pooled earnings of their members. According to Chapman, a weaver's family had to have a greater number of its members in paid work, including a larger proportion of its children, than a spinner's family. Moreover, the family labour group was greatest where work was coarsest and heaviest and wages lowest.[155] Wives would be able to abandon factory employment only when their earnings were made up for by children's wages. Hence the bulk of females employed in weaving were in the age brackets 15–24 and 25–44, as the example of Burnley demonstrates. Here 56 per cent of all women over the age of 10 were in employment in 1911.[156] In that year, females formed the following proportions of the workforce in each age group:[157]

Age group	Males	Females	Prop. (app.)
10–14	1520	2036	57.3
15–24	3988	8194	67.3
25–44	5230	6787	56.5
45–	3108	1047	25.2

Despite the inconsistencies in the statistical evidence, prohibiting any clear-cut conclusions to be drawn, the consensus among historians of the Lancashire cotton weaving industry appears to be that women's weekly earnings were lower than men's, though much less so than in other trades. Closer inspection reveals this consensus to rest on shaky foundations. Patrick Joyce's highly influential work on cotton employers' paternalism is a case in point. His uncritical reliance on claims made by others is all the more serious, forming as they do one of the linchpins of his own argument. He begins by noting that weaving was highly unusual among all textile crafts in that men and women were paid the same rates and worked alongside each other. This equality threatened to undermine male authority both at work and in the home. Yet male weavers' dominance was assured, Joyce has maintained, by variations distinguishing male from female labour. These variations served to symbolize the inequality of the sexes, proclaiming it to the cotton community at large.[158] The variations remain unspecified in the main body of the text, but the accompanying footnote refers the reader to a piece each by Joanna Bornat and Jill Liddington.

The former has noted in the article referred to that, in Colne Valley in West Yorkshire, 'the facts of life at work were such that women received roughly 10 per cent less in wages'. This gender differential was legitimized by men's ability to lift their finished pieces of cloth off the loom, which did nothing to alleviate women's resentment at being so blatantly discriminated against.[159] It is not at all clear what impact conditions in the Yorkshire woollen industry are supposed to have on the Lancashire cotton industry. What is more, this passage in Joanna Bornat's article only serves to highlight the specificity of Lancashire cotton weaving in paying non-gender-specific piece rates, noted by Joyce himself.

Jill Liddington, Joyce's other authority, has argued in the article referred to that because of the way looms were allocated and adjusted and the – unspecified – criteria by which weavers' piece rates were calculated, women earned about 4s. less per week than men. She has cited as her authority an article by Ada Nield Chew.[160] This tells the story of Mr and Mrs Bolt, who work as weavers in the same mill, and are paid the same rate. Each of them minds four looms and they are doing exactly the same work. On the particular pay day referred to in the article, Mr Bolt receives 26 shillings, while his wife's earnings amount to only 20 shillings 'because for four or five days she had in bad warps, and could not get on, owing to continual "floats" and "smashes"'.[161] The difference in earnings between husband and wife is attributed to bad luck on her part, with no indication given that this was the result of systematic discrimination of women workers. The outcome of a week's work could just as well have been the other way round, and the author's opting for the wife as the victim of unfortunate circumstances may have been actuated by her wish to pander to her readership's presumed notion of what was the proper distribution of power and authority between husband and wife.

Jill Liddington herself must have been unconvinced, because in *One Hand Tied Behind Us*, for which that article was a preliminary study, she has somewhat tempered the previous statement, pointing instead to a controversy over the reality of equal pay in Lancashire weaving sheds. She now relates the 4s. extra earned by men to their working a larger number of looms than women, whose narrower looms moreover yielded a lower rate. She has referred to Alice Foley, a Bolton weaver and trade union activist (discussed more fully in Chapter 6), stating that only men did the highly paid heavy work of weaving counterpanes on very large wide looms. Apart from Alice Foley's testimony, Jill Liddington has cited Barbara Drake and the Webbs as taking opposite sides in the controversy over equal pay.[162] Alice Foley's observation, while no doubt correct, referred to the specific situation in Bolton, where there was indeed a division of labour by gender between male counterpane weavers on broad looms and female weavers on looms of ordinary width (more fully discussed in Chapter 6).

In her study, *Women in Trade Unions*, Barbara Drake, by contrast, was reluctant to rely uncritically on commonly available wage statistics. She cast doubt on the figures produced by the Board of Trade for 1906, which showed a difference in the amount of weekly earnings between men and women and which have been extensively quoted from above. The difference was attributed to delays caused by women having to wait for the overlooker to adjust their machines and to assistance required from a learner, paid out of the weaver's wages. Barbara Drake was unconvinced, asserting:

> It is possible, however, that other conditions were not exactly equal, and that differences could have been discovered in the cloth as well as a difference in age, which was twenty years and over for men, but only eighteen years and over for women. In some establishments, where the operatives are assisted by labourers in removing the full 'spools' from the sheds, the extra wage cost is similarly charged against them; but this charge would almost certainly be compensated for to the weaver by increased output and additional earnings on the looms. Men and women, moreover, enjoy the same assistance. A difference in output between men and women cotton weavers is not at present remarked by trade unionists, or by employers.[163]

By contrast, 20 years previously, in their *Industrial Democracy*, the Webbs had noted:

> The piecework list of prices, to which all workers must conform, applies to men and women alike. But it is interesting to observe that the maintenance of a Standard Rate has resulted in a real, though unobtrusive, segregation. There is no attempt to discriminate

between women's work and men's work as such. ... But, taking the cotton-weaving trade as a whole, the great majority of the women will be found engaged on the comparatively light work paid for at the lower rates. On the other hand, a majority of the men will be found practically monopolizing the heavy trade, priced at higher rates per yard, and resulting in larger weekly earnings.[164]

Yet such clear segregation of jobs by gender – men monopolizing the heavy trade and women crowding into the light trade – was nowhere to be found in Lancashire, with the possible exception of Bolton. On the contrary, as shown above, women formed a particularly large proportion of weavers where high-quality goods were produced. In fact the Webbs quite erroneously presented Lancashire cotton weaving as exemplifying those trades which, instead of excluding women, had opted for a strict segregation of tasks by gender, a course of action the Webbs found highly commendable. Their main concern was not the extent to which the principle of 'equal pay for equal work' might have been put into practice, but rather the threat posed to wage levels by women undercutting men. Hence they recommended the adoption of non-gender-specific rates of pay in conjunction with strict segregation of tasks by gender.[165]

The issue of equal pay for equal work had been exercising at least Sidney Webb for some time. Making use of his contacts with working men and women members of the Fabian Society, he assembled a large amount of data on male and female wage rates in a wide range of industries. From this evidence he concluded that women employed in manufacturing industries earned from one-third to two-thirds of the amount received by men. Regarding the comparison of piece rates, he found the main difficulty to lie in the fact that there were only a very few instances of men and women doing precisely similar work, one of these being Lancashire cotton weaving. In 1891, he wrote:

> Perhaps the clearest case of similar work is that of the Lancashire cotton weavers, where men and women often perform exactly the same work side by side in the same shed, under practically the same Factory Acts restrictions. Here the piece-work rates are the same for women as for men, and clever women often get through more work, and thus earn higher weekly wages than men.[166]

It is not clear what had intervened in the six years between the publication of this article and that of *Industrial Democracy* inducing Webb to renege upon both his former recognition of the absence of gender segregation and his statement of possible wage equality between men and women weavers in the Lancashire cotton industry.

The near equality of wages was suggested by a table Webb had compiled (our Table 8) from the Board of Trade Return for 1889.[167] Interestingly, in his table the differential ranged from 1d. in Todmorden to 1s.4d. in Stockport, being much smaller than is suggested by any of the preceding tables. What inequality in earnings between men and women weavers there was Webb attributed to the delays caused by women having to wait to have their looms adjusted, while men were able to do that themselves.[168] In an attempt at generalization, he wrote:

> It should be noted that in all these instances of equal remuneration for equal work, both sexes are practically equally restricted by the Factory Acts; there are strong Trade Unions for both; both sexes have been at work in the industry for a long period; and the influence of competition appears to be very little checked by economic friction of any kind.[169]

His list of conditions allowing non-gender-specific rates to be paid was echoed almost verbatim 20 years later by Dorothea Barton[170] and in the 1980s by Hunt.[171] Webb, too, was clear about the relevance of the family wage economy in Lancashire, where, he maintained, the combined weekly earnings of husband and wife amounted to the same as an engineer's or iron-moulder's weekly pay.[172]

His conclusion, tentative though it was, reveals the desperate attempt to pinpoint 'objective' reasons for women's lesser pay. These he saw in their lower productivity and their lower standard of living.[173] Quite clearly, Webb was unable or unwilling to acknowledge discrimination on the basis of gender. In fact he openly denied even the possibility by asserting, 'The problem of the inequality of wages is one of great plurality of causes and intermixture of effects, and we might not improbably find that, as is often the case, there is no special "women's question" in the matter.'[174]

Further doubt on the validity of traditional sources on wages is cast by Janet Greenlees.[175] Interestingly, she has also found female investigators to be more open on the whole to the possibility of men and women earning equal pay than male investigators, as is borne out by Clara Collet[176] and Barbara Drake. Janet

Table 8

District	Men	Women
Burnley	21s. 7d.	21s. 4d.
Darwen	22s. 2d.	20s.11d.
Preston	21s.11d.	20s. 9d.
Blackburn	21s. 0d.	20s. 8d.
Ashton	21s. 5d.	20s. 4d.
Oldham	—	19s. 9d.
Todmorden	19s. 5d.	19s. 4d.
Rochdale	19s. 7d.	19s. 0d.
Bury	19s. 2d.	18s.11d.
Stockport	19s. 8d.	18s. 4d.
Manchester	—	17s. 9d.

Greenlees's analysis of wage data taken from the few surviving mill records and covering the period from the late eighteenth century to the 1860s shows the wage gap between male and female wages to have been consistently lower and occasionally reversed from that cited by most historians. She takes the smaller gender wage gap as an indication that women were more highly valued as workers than merely for their cheapness and availability.[177]

Male weavers' recognition of the similarity of skill levels between men and women as the basis of equal earnings following the transition to the factory can be traced back at least to the beginning of the nineteenth century, when a male handloom weaver from Bolton stated before a parliamentary committee in 1808 that 'women's talent is equal to men's when the work is not too heavy; we have some women whose talent is equal to any man's in the middle kind of work'.[178] Trade union officials, too, were convinced of women's capacity to earn as good wages as men. According to a unionist from Ashton, 'a woman would not go to work for nothing, anymore than a man, and, as a rule, they will fight as hard to maintain wages as men'.[179] And Joshua Wilkinson of the Northern Counties' Amalgamation equally stated: 'A female is as good a weaver as a man, in fact in most cases better.'[180] Consequently, '[a] woman can earn as much as a man, perhaps more'.[181] This official was echoed by one of the Webbs' correspondents, who focused on skill as the chief determinant of wage levels by maintaining that '[a] clever woman will earn more than a slow man'. And Mary Haslam from Bolton, where she was actively involved in the women's suffrage movement, though not a weaver herself, stated in a letter to Beatrice Webb: 'Women weavers are frequently preferred, and in fine work, earn more than the men on account of their more nimble fingers.'[182] While uncritically subscribing to the belief in women's natural endowment for particularly intricate jobs, at the same time she revealed great pride in female weavers' ability to make a contribution to the national economy that was both valuable and valued.

Conclusion

The Lancashire cotton weaving industry was characterized by a large proportion of females among its workforce, many of whom spent a sizeable portion of their lifetime toiling in the mill, starting in their early teens and continuing long after getting married and starting a family. True, married women's factory employment was necessitated by the inadequacy of male weavers' wages for the support of a family. Hence the notion of a male bread-winning wage had no currency in weaving communities. Instead, wives were expected as a matter of course to contribute what amounted to about half the family income, at least until their share was made up for by children's wages. Given the marked degree of homogeneity characteristic of most weaving communities,[183] where the bulk of the population, male and female, young and old, worked in the mill, and neighbourhood and shopfloor largely overlapped in terms of personnel, neither the high labour participation rate of women nor the large proportion of wives among them was perceived as something out of the ordinary.

In the heartland of the weaving district, women found themselves working side by side with men, operating the same type, and frequently the same number, of looms, for which they were paid equal rates. Depending on the individual level of skill, it was possible for a female weaver to earn the same, if not more, than her male counterpart. These characteristics of the labour process in weaving point to the possible existence of extra-economic incentives for women to stay on in paid employment, an issue that will be investigated in the following chapter.

Notes

1 See Farnie (1979, p.7).
2 See Rose (1996a, pp.10ff); see also Burgess (1975, p.231).
3 See, for example, Marrison (1996). Farnie, however, confines usage of this term to the Edwardian boom years, see Farnie (1979, p.327).
4 See Marrison (1996, pp.224–63); for the increase in foreign competition, see also Farnie (1979, esp. ch.5).
5 See White (1978, p.17).
6 See Robson (1957, p.4).
7 See Lazonick and Mass (1984, p.2).
8 See Jones (1933, p.277).
9 See Clapham (1938, p.66).
10 See Robson (1957, pp.332–3).
11 See Farnie (1979, p.24).
12 See Lazonick (1986, p.181).
13 See Tyson (1968, p.120).
14 See White (1978, p.17).
15 See Farnie (1979, pp.180, 185).
16 See Robson (1957, p.4).
17 See White (1982, p.210).
18 See Marrison (1996, p.264).
19 For the inter-war period, see Dupree (1996); for the final decline since 1940, see Singleton (1991; 1996).
20 See Marrison (1996, p.239).
21 See Jenkins (1979).
22 See Busfield (1986, p.184).
23 See Rose (2000, p.165).
24 Similarly, the ring spinning companies set up in Rochdale in the early 1880s made use of the cultural characteristics and technical competence of the local workforce, which looked back upon a long tradition of throstle spinning, from which ring spinning had evolved; see Toms (1998, pp.11–2).
25 See Jewkes (1930, p.195).
26 See Jewkes (1930); see also Jewkes and Jewkes (1966).
27 See Farnie (1979, p.306).

28 See Longworth (1987, p.58).
29 See Kenny (1982, p.51).
30 Ibid., pp. 45, 46–7.
31 See Bennett (1951, pp.95–7).
32 See Trodd (1978, pp.17–8).
33 See Rose (2000, p.172).
34 See Farnie (1979, p.296).
35 According to an investigation of Oldham public limited companies, only a few shares were held by cotton operatives themselves; see Smith (1961).
36 See Toms (1998).
37 See Kenny (1982, p.57).
38 See Farnie (1979, p.286).
39 The founding date of this mill contradicts Rose's contention that the crisis brought on by the Cotton Famine stifled all attempts at cooperation in weaving, because firms run along cooperative lines lacked resources; see Rose (2000, p.164).
40 According to Trodd (1978, p.255), the mill was equipped with 338 looms.
41 According to Trodd, (ibid.), there were 125 worker shareholders. This would have required each of them to hold shares of an average value of over £11 for the above figure to be attained.
42 See Bennett (1951, pp.99–101); see also Trodd (1987, pp.255–6).
43 See Mark-Lawson (1987, p.204).
44 See Fowler and Fowler (1984, p.2).
45 Ibid., p.3; see also Mark-Lawson (1987, p.206).
46 See Marsden (1884, p.58).
47 See Savage (1988, pp.206, 211).
48 See Rose (2000, pp.159, 161).
49 See Turner (1962, pp.384, 387).
50 This reasoning was made explicit by a manufacturer in his correspondence with the Webbs, see *Webb Collection* XLVII, pp.270–71. For the general recognition of this principle, see, for example, *CFT*, 27.11.1903, p.1. Elsewhere, male and female textile workers rarely performed identical tasks, nor were they paid the same rates. For the gender gap in wages among the workforce of Courtauld's silk mills in Essex, see Lown (1990, pp.105ff). For a particularly notorious Belgian example of a cotton manufacturer, Voortman in Ghent, giving preference to female and juvenile labour as a deliberate cost-cutting strategy, see Scholliers (1995; 1996). In the German textile industry, too, both jobs and machines were largely gendered, making for a gender gap in earnings. Interestingly, in times of conflict when factory owners deployed female workers as wage cutters, male textile workers resorted to demanding equal pay for equal work in order to retain their jobs; see Canning (1996, p.297).
51 See Turner (1962, pp.128, 200).
52 See Kirk (1985, p.278).
53 For an enumeration of these variables and their bearing upon labour input and pay, see British Association for the Advancement of Science (1887); see also Chapman (1904, pp.265–6).
54 See Biernacki (1995).
55 See Chapman (1904, p.266). For an appraisal of Chapman as a historian of the cotton industry, see Farnie (1978).
56 See Savage (1988, p.214).

57 See Turner (1962, p.389).
58 See Commission on Labour, *PP*, 1892, XXXV, p.170.
59 See Hopwood (1969, p.188).
60 See Commission on Labour, *PP*, 1892, XXXV, p.183.
61 See Kirk (1985, p.278).
62 See Cole (1962, p.207).
63 See Chapman (1904, p.236).
64 See Clegg *et al.* (1964, pp.240, 245).
65 For masters' associations, see McIvor (1983; 1996).
66 See McIvor (1996, p.69).
67 See McIvor (1983, pp.37, 104).
68 See Toms (1998, pp.12–13).
69 See Chapman (1900–1901, pp.77–8). The Association's activities were favourably reported in employers' journals; see, for example, *Textile Mercury*, 16.2.1901, pp.129–30.
70 See Joyce (1980, p.64).
71 See Porter (1967, p.59).
72 See McIvor (1996, p.143).
73 See McIvor (1983, p.156).
74 See White (1982, p.219).
75 See White (1978, esp. ch.8).
76 See Hopwood (1969, p.188).
77 See Chapman (1904, pp.92–6); see also Wood (1910, p.5), Jones (1933, p.103).
78 See Clapham (1932, p.418).
79 See Tuckwell and Smith (1908, pp.127ff).
80 For an incisive critique of the half-heartedness of this attempt to curb fining, see Ford (1900, p.175).
81 See Clegg *et al.* (1964, pp.240ff).
82 See Commission on Labour, *PP*, 1892, XXXVI, p.177; see also Employment of Women, *PP*, 1893–4, XXXVII, Pt. I, p.665.
83 See Summary of Returns, *PP*, 1909, LXXIX, p.854.
84 See Wikander *et al.* (1995, p.8).
85 See, for example, Walby (1986, esp. pp.108–29).
86 For the gendered language of factory legislation, see Gray (1993), also Rose (1996b).
87 See Lewis and Rose (1995, p.93), also Rose (1996b).
88 See Harvey (1909, pp.10–11).
89 For an example of a mill owner at Preston summonsed at the instigation of a factory Inspector for contravening this Act, see *CFT*, 6.5.1904, p.7. The summons was dismissed, because the defendant's solicitor had persuasively argued that employers had a right to expect their employees to observe the provisions of the Act and not lay them such traps.
90 See *Manchester Guardian*, 29.12.1908, GTC 5/11; see also McCarthy (1953, p.15).
91 See Lancashire Textile Project, respondent AF2, p.19; respondent AC9, p.18.
92 For the failure or inadequacy of guards to prevent shuttles from flying out, partly with the connivance of workers, see Harrison (1993, pp.262–3). For different types of guards, see *CFT*, 23.2.1906, p.4.
93 See *PP*, 1912–13, XXVI, p.83.
94 See Mrs. J.H., Tape 692, MSU TLSL.

95 See, for example, *Manchester Guardian*, 10.1.1913, GTC 13/13; see also *Lancashire Post*, 16.10.1913, GTC 13/45; Harrison (1993, pp.263–4).
96 See, for example, *CFT*, 29.5.1914, GTC 5/77; see Report of Cotton Cloth Committee, *PP*, 1897, XVII, pp.140, 144, for weavers' approval of dressing rooms.
97 See, for example, *Daily Dispatch*, 27.11.1912, GTC 5/67.
98 For the struggle for, and history of, the female factory inspectorate, see McFeely (1988). A rather self-congratulatory account of its early years is given by Dame Adelaide Anderson, Chief Woman Inspector during most of the period covered by her book; see Anderson (1922).
99 See Employment of Women, *PP*, 1893–4, XXXVII, Pt. I, p.664. For the important function, completely ignored by the investigator, of lavatories as the site of unsupervised socializing during working hours, see Messenger (1988, p.163).
100 See Sandiford (1907, pp.320–21).
101 See Winstanley (1996, p.131).
102 For the history of the half-time system and its relevance to the cotton industry, see Bolin-Hort (1989), also Challand and Walker (1995).
103 See Sandiford (1907, pp.319–20).
104 See Bolin-Hort (1989, pp.118, 209, 228, 240).
105 See Turner (1962, p.128).
106 These percentages have been calculated on the basis of the figures quoted by Amalgamation officials before the Commission on Labour, *PP*, 1892, XXXVII, p.18. The figures had been extracted from the 1890 factory returns by Thomas Birtwistle, member of the Amalgamation's central committee; see *PP*, 1892, XXXV, p.172.
107 See Summary of Returns, *PP*, 1909, LXXIX, p.854.
108 See Report by Miss Collet, *PP*, 1894, LXXXI, Pt. II, p.855.
109 See White (1978, p.15).
110 Savage (1988, p.205).
111 See Farnie (1979, p.301).
112 See Hill (1997, p.27).
113 See Ross (1991, p.39); see also Fowler and Fowler (1984, p.4), Mark-Lawson (1987, p.215).
114 See Beattie (1992, p.19).
115 See Frost (1988, pp.7, 9, 15).
116 See Beattie (1992, p.19).
117 The proportions have been calculated on the basis of the figures given in the Summary of Returns of 1907; see *PP*, 1909, LXXIX, p.855.
118 See Report by Miss Collet, *PP*, 1894, LXXXI, Pt. II, p.854.
119 See Winstanley (1996, p.123). It should be noted that his figures include the bleaching, dyeing and finishing trades.
120 See Report by Miss Collet, *PP*, 1894, LXXXI, p.883.
121 See Summary of Returns, *PP*, 1909, LXXIX, p.858.
122 See Savage (1982, p.10).
123 See Bornat (1988, p.225).
124 See Norris (1988, p.198).
125 Clara Collet, who subjected the available statistics on the employment of women to close analysis in order to identify the factors accounting for the high proportion of married women employed in the cotton industry, used the category 'married women

in employment' as proxy for 'mothers in employment'; see *PP*, 1894, LXXXI. The need to do so is caused by the way in which data were collected and analysed in the relevant period. Census data relating to women were classified according to age group and marital status. In order to establish the percentage of married women weavers with children under the age of 10, one would need to refer to census enumerators' books, which record occupation and marital status, as well as number and age of children per household. On the basis of this information, however, it is impossible to establish whether all women who reported themselves as weavers were actually in employment or had temporarily left their jobs with the intention of returning to them at some later stage. Detailed information of this kind is only available from local studies, which have so far been confined to the middle decades of the nineteenth century, yielding the following figures. In Blackburn, Ashton, Oldham, Burnley, Chorley, Haslingden and Preston, the proportion of married women operatives (not all of them necessarily weavers) with children under one year of age ranged in 1851 from 14.95 per cent to 27.45 per cent, the average being 21.03 per cent; see Hewitt (1953, pp.136–7). In Preston more specifically, 23 per cent of all wives with children worked, and 20 per cent of all wives with children under the age of 10 worked away from home in 1851; see Anderson (1971, p.71). In Oldham, finally, over one-third of local women with children aged 11 or under went out to work around mid-century; see Foster (1974, p.97).
126 See Report by Miss Collet, *PP*, 1894, LXXXI, p.889; Winstanley (1996, p.130). The percentages for 1894 were calculated by Clara Collet on the basis of factory returns, the compilation of which depended on the collaboration of the firms asked to supply the requisite information. For the pitfalls involved in using the factory returns, see Jenkins (1978). The percentages for 1911 were calculated on the basis of that year's census figures, which are arguably more accurate.
127 See Savage (1987, pp.74, 78).
128 See Jewkes and Gray (1935, p.15).
129 For Clara Collet's life and her professional achievements, see Groenewegen (1994b).
130 See *PP*, 1893–4, XXXVII, Pt. I, p.664.
131 See Norris (1988, p.194).
132 See Bornat (1988, p.210).
133 See Messenger (1988, p.144).
134 See note 50.
135 See, for example, *CFT*, 16.11.1888, p.5; see also Report on Strikes and Lock-Outs, *PP*, 1889, LXX; White (1982, p.220).
136 See, for example, a statement by the General Secretary of the Spinners' Amalgamation, *CFT*, 14.12.1888, p.6.
137 See Wood (1910, p.77).
138 Ibid., pp.38ff.
139 See Firth (1986, p.85).
140 See Report on Earnings, *PP*, 1909, LXXX, p.30.
141 This table has been calculated on the basis of Report on Earnings (note 140), pp. 33–4.
142 See Riley (1981, p.9). Thomas Stuttart, of James Stuttart & Sons, cotton spinners, appearing as a witness before the Royal Commission on the Depression of Trade and Industry, also maintained that women weavers seldom managed more than four looms as compared to men's four, five or six, see *PP*, 1886, XXI, p.171.

143 See also complaint about a shed at Rawtenstall, where women worked six looms as compared to the four which were standard in the district (*CFT*, 31.1.1890, p.5). See also the case of two women weavers working five looms each when this was fairly uncommon even for men: Lancashire Textile Project, respondent AK2, side 1, p.9.
144 See, for example, Roberts (1981), respondent H8P, p.24.
145 See *CFT*, 29.5.1914, GTC, 5/77. This statement, which was made in the context of a campaign for the further shortening of hours, may have to be taken with a grain of salt. In order to arouse public sympathy, trade unions focused their propaganda on the plight of married women weavers, who, they claimed, were overtaxed by having to attend to their domestic duties on top of working the same number of looms as men. The possibly accurate statement of men and women working the same number of looms was here presented as a fact to be deplored.
146 See, for example, *CFT*, 29.8.1913, p.1.
147 See *PP*, 1909, LXXX, p.33.
148 See *PP*, 1889, LXX, p.851.
149 See Gibson (1948, p.61).
150 See White (1978, p.40).
151 See Savage (1988, p.214).
152 See White (1978, p.33).
153 See Report by Miss Collet, *PP*, 1894, LXXXI, p.909.
154 See Gibson (1948, pp.61, 67). This point was also made in the Report on Earnings; see *PP*, 1909, LXXX, p.29.
155 See Chapman (1904, p.158).
156 See Trodd (1978, p.34).
157 See Firth (1986, p.30). The age brackets have been amended from his, which are erroneously defined as 10–15, 15–25, 25–45.
158 See Joyce (1980, pp.112–13).
159 See Bornat (1977, p.117).
160 See Liddington (1977, p.33).
161 *The Englishwoman*, 1912, p.40.
162 See Liddington and Norris (1985, p.95).
163 Drake (1984, pp.121–2).
164 Webb and Webb (1897, pp.500–501).
165 Ibid., p.501.
166 Webb (1891, p.640).
167 See ibid.
168 See ibid.
169 Ibid., p.645.
170 See Barton (1921–2, p.118).
171 See Hunt (1981, p.103).
172 See Webb (1891, p.645).
173 See ibid., p.649.
174 Ibid., p.659.
175 These include, among others, Wood (1910), which is often referred to as an authoritative source on wages in the cotton industry. Janet Greenlees's warning apart (see Greenlees, 1999, p.185), his method of compiling and presenting wage rates by locality and job category without any regard to gender render his data useless for the purposes of this study.

176 This is in line with Clara Collet's concern, displayed throughout her numerous investigations, for integrating the subject of women's work into the general corpus of labour economics. She did so by most careful compilation and analysis of statistics, the results of which enabled her effectively to refute many of the biased contemporary views on women's paid employment, which were often based on very slender evidence; see Groenewegen (1994b, pp.153, 163).
177 See Greenlees (1999, pp.184–6).
178 Report and Minutes of Evidence on Cotton Manufactures, *PP*, 1808, vol. 2, p.127, quoted in Clark (1997, p.120).
179 See Commission on Labour, *PP*, 1892, XXXV, p.168.
180 See ibid., p.183.
181 See ibid., p.19.
182 See *Webb Collection*, XLVII, p.79.
183 The degree of locational homogeneity of the cotton communities was surpassed only by the mining communities; see Burgess (1975, p.244).

Chapter 3

The Trouble with Weaving: Deriving Satisfaction from Work

The large number of females employed in the weaving sheds of Lancashire diligently attended their looms in order to make a contribution to family income that, as they knew only too well, greatly helped first their parents and subsequently themselves as mothers of a family to make ends meet. Although the need for females to carry on in paid employment for the best part of their lives was generally acknowledged by the cotton community, the tenacity with which women weavers clung to their jobs cannot be attributed to penury alone. They uniformly considered themselves to be performing a skilled trade that took considerable time to master. Their self-perception, however, clashed with the comparatively low esteem in which they were held by outsiders, including many historians,[1] who regarded weaving as semi-skilled. As one engineer, who had been working in a weaving mill for some considerable time asserted, one of the big troubles about weaving is that it has never been recognized as the skilled job which it undoubtedly is'.[2]

This clash of perceptions was closely linked to the fact that the vertical specialization which had come to characterize the cotton industry by the closing decades of the nineteenth century, as shown in the preceding chapter, was overlaid with a gender division of labour. The industry's two major processes, spinning and weaving, were ranged quite differently with regard to the level of skill involved. Mule spinning was the virtually exclusive domain of men often dubbed 'barefoot aristocrats'.[3] Though working in their bare feet in order to keep a grip on floors slippery with oil dripping from machinery, their wages were substantial enough to elevate them to the ranks of the 'labour aristocracy'. This term is used here merely to denote groups of workers whose skill gave them considerable control over the labour process as well as an income high and regular enough to sustain a life style deemed 'respectable'. A closer investigation of the reasons why different levels of skill were believed to be required by spinning and weaving respectively points to factors outside the labour process.

Definitions of Skill

Skill is most commonly thought of as denoting those faculties and abilities that a particular job requires from the worker performing it and which are acquired during a period of training, either formal or informal. Thus the degree of mechanization or automation that a particular job has undergone would affect the requisite level of skill as well as the degree of control workers may have over the labour process. Because of the scarcity of their labour, workers in the possession of skill are able to claim above-average wages and enjoy relative job security, which in turn forms the material base on which a respectable life style can be built. Skill thus has repercussions beyond the shopfloor. In particular, it forms a chief component of masculinity, enabling the worker enjoying this attribute to support his family out of his wages with only limited recourse to the earnings of his wife and children.

With the erosion of legal checks on the supply of labour for a particular trade,[4] unions succeeded in appropriating control over the intake of labour in highly organized trades. This enabled them, moreover, to fend off the impact of mechanization on those workers who had seen some or most of their skills being transferred to machines. It is the policy of controlling labour supply in combination with the dwindling into insignificance of any empirical basis of skill in the requirements of the labour process that is commonly referred to as the social construction of skill. With regard to the Lancashire cotton industry, Turner has put the classic case by arguing that

> 'skill' itself is not a factor wholly independent of collective organization. Not merely do individual skills tend to dissolve in the absence of trade unionism (or some similar collective regulation) but – as in the cases of the self-actor spinners ... – many 'skills' are actually the product of trade unionism itself, instead of *vice versa*.[5]

Turner here refers to the transition from the partially hand-driven spinning mule to the fully steam-driven self-actor that had taken place from the 1830s onwards. The development of the self-actor had chiefly been motivated by employers' wish to undermine the strong position of the skilled spinner through further mechanizing the mule. The ostensively named self-actor seemed to have achieved this, reducing, as its advocates claimed, the spinner's work to mere machine tending.[6]

Despite this apparent deskilling as a result of technological innovation, as Turner has argued, spinners were able to press for high wages thanks to their union strictly controlling entry to the trade. Each spinner had two piecers, or learners, to help him operate a set of two mules, for which he paid them out of his own wages. Piecers' promotion to the pay and status of spinner was not consequent upon their having gained proficiency at their trade, but depended, as noted in Chapter 2, upon a pair of mules becoming available as a result of a spinner leaving his employment.[7]

As is implied, though not spelt out, in Turner's argument, it was their high degree of unionization that had enabled spinners significantly to shift the relations of power between labour and capital in their favour. Moreover, employers' willingness to collude with spinners' social construction of skill, as More has pointed out in his critique of Turner,[8] can be attributed to the overall wage bill remaining unaffected, because piecers were paid a time wage out of spinners' earnings, which were based on piece rates. Yet More agrees with Turner in pointing to spinners' strategic position in the labour process rather than any job-related abilities as accounting for their position as skilled workers.

With regard to a number of trades other than spinning, however, More has insisted on the actual requirements of skill, anchored in the labour process, without which construction of skill would not have been possible. He has demonstrated the persistence of different levels of skill by pointing to the willingness of employers to provide genuine training, particularly in those industries in which mass production techniques were not economically viable. This was the case where the good produced was always changing and thus required knowledge of a whole range of techniques among the workforce. Alternatively, the product's market position, for example in the case of producer goods, meant that only small numbers of a complex product were required, inducing employers to rely on a high level of skill among their workforce rather than on complex and hence costly machinery. Trade union insistence on extended periods of training, More has further argued, can be attributed to their wish to prevent an overstocking of the labour market as a way of safeguarding members' long-term job security.[9]

In a different vein, Mary Freifeld has cautioned against taking claims about deskilling at face value. She has convincingly argued that the self-actor, in contrast to the claims made by its inventor, rather than deskilling the labour process led to a recomposition of skill. It was the high degree of variability of raw cotton, in conjunction with the imperfections of machine functionings, that required the spinner to keep on fine-tuning the self-actor to the job in hand.[10]

It therefore appears more appropriate to see skill as the result of the interplay of requirements based on the labour process, social construction and the relations of power between labour and capital in a given trade. This view also tallies with the Victorian understanding of the term. Victorians saw as skilled those workers who had mastered difficult working techniques in industries in which that was worthwhile, that is in which the demand for labour endowed with those skills exceeded the supply. This in turn gave these workers a considerable degree of control over the labour process. With skill constituting itself in the contested terrain between capital and labour, as Harrison has stressed,[11] skill content has to be established for each trade individually.

In order for this to be done, gender has to be taken into account, too. In a seminal article, Anne Phillips and Barbara Taylor have argued that skill is an ideological category expressing the gender hierarchy in capitalist industry.[12] The gender-specific attribution of skill and the uncritical equation of many male jobs with skilled work that this entailed was, according to these two authors, a response to the actual deskilling that occurred in the course of industrialization. The preservation of male dominance in the gender hierarchy through the monopolizing of skill by men formed an important weapon in the struggle between unionized workers and employers over labour process control.[13]

The Skill Content of Weaving

What measure of skill did work on a mechanical loom require? Contemporaries dealing with the technical development of the machine were in no doubt. Richard Marsden for one, a City and Guilds examiner of spinning and weaving and a prolific writer on both subjects, maintained in 1895 that the mechanical loom had meanwhile been so perfected as to reduce the job of the weaver to tending a fully automated machine.[14] This belief, incidentally, echoed the claim that had been made for the self-acting mule some decades earlier, but has been shown to be untenable. The view of weaving as mere machine tending has persisted into the present. In a circular argument, this assumption simultaneously serves to explain the large presence of women in the industry.[15]

Yet this belief needs to be balanced against the fact that Lancashire cotton operatives, precisely because they looked back upon the longest tradition of mechanization in the country, had been socialized into factory work over several generations, thus boasting a high level of what Maxine Berg has termed 'factory skills', that is workers' ability to reproduce a limited number of operations accurately and speedily.[16] Though not specifically related to the job in hand, these skills were indispensable for the smooth running of production. Occasionally even employers would acknowledge the proficiency of Lancashire operatives, attributing it to their having been bred to the factory.[17]

In addition, weavers required specific skills, which were to do with the nature of both the material and the machinery they were dealing with. As a natural product, which is subject to almost infinite variation, cotton requires a high degree of experience-based knowledge and ability to be processed. What is more, the many variables having an impact on cotton processing render it impossible clearly to specify each stage of the process. These variables relate to the widely varying character of the yarn, which in turn depends on the quality of the raw cotton used in spinning.[18]

Furthermore, there is a large number of types of cloth that cotton can be woven into and which place varying degrees of strain on the yarn used. Ideally, the quality of the yarn should improve in proportion to the quality of cloth desired. Yet, in order to cut down on production costs in both spinning and weaving in the face of stiffening competition from abroad, master spinners and manufacturers, as noted in Chapter 2, resorted to inferior primary products without reducing the requirements on the quality of the end product,[19] relying on their workers' skill to compensate for any deficiencies of the material supplied. Weavers obviously resented having their job made even more arduous or having to sustain a drop in wages as a result. Especially in times of depression, complaints about so-called 'bad material', often culminating in strike action, would proliferate.[20] On one occasion the inferior quality of the yarn supplied to weavers induced one correspondent of the *Cotton Factory Times* to answer the question, 'May weaving be classed as skilled labour?' as follows: 'Well, we happen to know that just at present it requires the greatest skill and tact of the oldest and best of weavers to produce something like a decent piece of cloth.'[21]

Apart from the yarn supplied, the machines, too, had their peculiarities, because Victorian machines, as Savage has noted,[22] were tailor-made rather than mass produced. Looms were neither very sophisticated nor working at optimum efficiency. Hence it was up to the weaver to obtain the best possible results from a deficient machine by constantly readjusting it to the job in hand. Accordingly, to be mechanically minded among weavers meant to know one's looms.[23] There were no two looms that were identical; each of them had a 'personality' of its own.[24] Weavers, who were strongly identified with their set of looms,[25] as Priscilla Ross has noted, tended to personalize them, because, as one weaver put it, 'you were with them more than with your husband'.[26]

Coping with the idiosyncrasies of the machinery required a high degree of competence in the use of the production technology. Furthermore, the demands on cloth quality increased, too, so that particular labour-saving tricks, which resulted in a certain unevenness of the cloth, ceased to be tolerated.[27] Clinging to the set of looms one had become familiar with helped, here, to decide how best to avoid a thin place in the weft whenever a shuttle was changed. As one weaver explained: 'Oh it's definitely easier if you've got your own looms, yes. I mean, you get to know how them looms are and what's what with them, so to speak.'[28] This increase in the demands made on quality occurred at the same time that machinery was speeded up. In the 1830s, 90 to 112 picks per minute had been the norm, yet by the 1880s looms were running at up to 400.[29]

In weaving, the technical difficulties and hence the demands made on workers' skill increased from the production of plain, coarse cloths through fine cloths to those with complicated patterns and mixed warps. It is significant that those places specializing in the production of high-quality goods, such as Preston, Bolton and Chorley, also had the largest proportion of females among their weaving workforce, as demonstrated in Chapter 2. Certainly, within the industry high requirements of skill did not act as an impediment to the employment of women.

Women Weavers' Skill Consciousness

Women weavers themselves had developed a self-image of being skilled workers. Weaving, as one of them asserted, 'is a trade, it is not something that you could just walk into. It had to be learnt. In fact I don't think you actually learn everything about it.'[30] Her words were echoed by another weaver, who maintained: 'My mother used to say that you could be in weaving and still learn ... It was a skilled job if it was done proper.'[31]

Becoming a good weaver therefore required taking an interest in the job. As one weaver explained: 'Weaving is a thing that you've either got to like or you don't like – there's no in between, if you're not interested in it, well I wouldn't advise anybody to go into it because it's not easy to learn.'[32] Those who failed to master the trade succumbed to the strain engendered by payment according to output and, provided they could afford to do so, left the mill.[33] Others held out, but in the absence of any satisfaction derived from their job the disagreeable aspects of work in the mill impinged on them, making them suffer from the heat, the humidity and the need to sweep up without stopping one's machines.[34] Yet others were only reconciled to the objectionable aspects of their job by the prospect of earning good wages when all their looms were running smoothly.[35]

Competent weavers, by contrast, derived pleasure from doing their job, and doing it well. They enjoyed watching the pattern form in the cloth being woven[36] and expressed a strong preference for fancy over plain weaving.[37] Making more demands on their skill, it rendered their job more interesting.

Weavers prided themselves on their ability to do something else besides minding their looms, such as reading a novel.[38] The socialist weavers of Nelson, often dubbed 'Little Moscow',[39] had a reputation for managing to finish reading the morning paper before the eight o'clock breakfast break.[40] Crocheting was another popular pastime indulged in during dinner breaks,[41] while waiting for new beams to be put into one's looms,[42] or watching one's looms running.[43]

Given this degree of self-determination on the basis of full mastery of the labour process, Lancashire weavers scorned the idea of going into domestic service, where they would be at the beck and call of a demanding mistress.[44] As a contemporary observed, '"service" to the independent Lancashire factory girl was a form of employment deeply tainted with the stigma of genuine servitude. No self-respecting girl would go into "service".'[45] Shop work was equally disdained.[46]

Male weavers would retire from their jobs in the mill at some point between 50 or 60 years of age, depending on the class of goods produced in their district. They would open a small shop or start some other little business. Their savings, accumulated from a lifetime's earnings, coupled with assistance from their families, would ensure their livelihood for the remainder of their days.[47]

Women, by contrast, abandoned work at the mill only when children were old enough to substitute for their mother's wages, as shown in Chapter 2. Many would shift to cash-generating activities performed in their own homes, providing services for factory women, such as taking in their children or their washing.[48] Yet this did not happen as a matter of course. The attraction of weaving expressed by one woman as 'I couldn't keep out of the mill somehow, you know, I always wanted to go',[49] proved equally strong in the, admittedly extreme, case of a 79-year-old weaver from Burnley. At the height of her powers and assisted by her son, she had been tending six looms, enjoying the respect and admiration in which co-workers held weavers operating a machine complement of this size.[50] Obviously, six-loom weavers were recruited from among the ablest and toughest workers, qualities that were perceived to vary by individual but not by gender. In that particular weaver's old age, the roles had been reversed. Now her son was running six looms with his mother's assistance. This was clearly not an old woman driven to the factory by penury. Not only was her son, who would have been earning top-level wages from his set of looms, living with her, but she also received an old age pension.[51] Acting on inclination, this woman would presumably have concurred with a weaver asserting that she 'always wanted to go in the weaving, I don't know why, but I always, and I love my work and I was more relaxed at work than what I was at home, I really enjoyed my work, as I say, it was no trouble to me'.[52] These women's self-esteem and pride were clearly associated with the skill involved in their job, about which they spoke with a fluency and confidence that testified both to their expertise with the industrial processes they described and to their familiarity with formal relations of employment.[53]

In their accounts, women weavers appropriated characteristics which in the discourse of the contemporary labour movement bore unequivocally masculine connotations.[54] Regardless of how they might have been viewed by others, the women spoke of themselves as skilled workers who, by mastering up to six looms, had learnt a trade requiring a high degree of skill. Their personal testimonies represent a process of discursive self-determination in a double sense. Not only did they divest certain concepts of their gender-specificity by appropriating as feminine what was usually thought of as masculine, they also subverted the gender discourse of the labour movement, in which the housebound working-class woman was ubiquitous, by constructing for themselves the identity of skilled workers whose competence was equal to men's, as their weekly earnings testified. Their self-representation, strikingly deviant from the dominant understanding of working-class femininity, was embedded in, and derived its acceptability from, the cultural values shared by the weaving communities of which the interviewees formed part.[55] The great value placed by the community on competence at work for men and women alike is also apparent in the way skill in weaving was acquired.

The Acquisition of Skill

Implanting in their daughters' minds the wish to become a weaver was an important objective working-class parents in the cotton-weaving district aimed at in the upbringing of their female offspring. Practical preparation for factory work, rather than any encouragement to look forward to a life of domesticity, was part and parcel of girls' preparation for adulthood.

Children had their earliest experience of the inside of a shed long before reaching the age at which they could legally be employed as half-timers. The factory, as the site of waged work, was not sealed off from the residential area around it, of which it formed the focus, the sound of its bell setting the rhythm of everyday life in the entire neighbourhood. It was customary for young children to take breakfast and dinner to neighbours in the mill as a way of earning a few pence.[56] What they were able to observe in the shed filled them with fear and fascination alike.[57] Although the clattering noise of the machinery appeared to them insupportable, and hardly any of them failed to notice the need for weavers to resort to lip-reading in order to communicate with each other, the precision of workers' rapid yet exact motions among the confusion of swiftly moving mechanical devices filled the youngsters with admiration, making the attainment of such competence appear a desirable goal.

Particularly keen girls who had set their minds on becoming weavers might watch grown-ups at work through the windows of the shed.[58] But for all children preparation for the job began in the family. Older family members would deliberately prepare younger ones for their entry in the factory, for instance by demonstrating particularly frequent and complicated processes,[59] such as shuttle changing. By the time youngsters entered the mill they would already be familiar with most aspects of the labour process, including the people they were likely to encounter on the shopfloor.[60]

Skill in weaving was not acquired in the course of a formal apprenticeship, but through training on the job, which was the same for boys and girls. Only in the insignificant branch of band weaving was a five-to-seven-year apprenticeship maintained. This was, moreover, an almost exclusively male domain.[61] Once children were old enough, the vast majority of them would start half-time in the mill. In the rare case of individual deviation from this pattern, pressure was brought to bear by family and peer group alike. The attraction of being with one's peers weighed heavily in favour of the mill, as compared to any other kind of job,[62] and only a few were self-assured enough to make themselves conspicuous by refusing to conform to what was regarded as the normal career pattern.[63] If community norms failed to produce the desired behaviour,[64] girls aspiring to jobs outside the mill would have been told, in the manner of this mother, that they 'had big ideas and the sooner they were knocked out of [them] the better'.[65] Aspirations thus thwarted were bound to taint weavers' attitude towards their jobs.[66]

Family members who were fully-fledged weavers were instrumental in procuring jobs for youngsters in the first place.[67] They would 'speak for' their younger relatives, thereby vouching for them in terms of behaviour and, possibly also, talent for the job. Authority to hire rested with the overlooker, or tackler, as he was known in Lancashire.[68] His familiarity with the weaving community enabled him to select particularly skilled weavers for work in his section of the shed.[69] The assumption among tacklers appears to have been that weaving skill ran in the family and that kin of good weavers were likely to turn out competent workers, too.

The initial stage of learner lasted for a few weeks. Only once they had mastered certain basic skills, which the more talented ones managed in as little as three months,[70] were learners promoted to tenters, or weavers' assistants, and they then began to receive wages. Learning consisted mainly in closely observing the experienced worker, with only the piecing of threads being actually taught.[71] Around 1890, half-timers, who split their time between school and factory, earned 1s.3d. to 1s.6d. per week on average, and up to 2s.9d. when they were particularly talented.[72] Small though they might appear, these earnings were eagerly awaited by the youngsters' families. In 1886, one Preston mill was reported as making its tenters undergo a kind of apprenticeship before being allowed to manage a pair of looms of their own. Six young girls were put on a 12-loom range with a young man acting as a tutor, whom each of them had to pay 3s. out of her weekly earnings.[73] The indignant tone of the report is presumably accounted for by the element of extra exploitation involved in this set-up, which would have been deeply resented by parents waiting for the extra income brought home by their children.

The prospect of earning a wage and the awareness of its relevance to family income, coupled with the corresponding adjustment of the new wage earner's standing within the family, in many cases sugared the bitter pill of submitting to factory discipline. In exceptional circumstances the youngest family member might take home the biggest wage. This particular girl did not tip up her earnings until the whole family had congregated around her,[74] thus making sure she would be given the recognition due to the family's chief earner that week.

While the actual amount of pay may have varied over time, the proportionate level of earnings remained the same. The time wage, which did not change for months, if not years,[75] was paid to the full-timers by the weaver for whom they worked.[76] This set-up was markedly similar to the spinner–piecer relationship in the spinning department of the industry. Spinners were notorious for driving their piecers to increase output and pocketing the extra income.[77] In weaving, by contrast, the tenter's wage remained unchanged regardless of any reduction in the weaver's pay.[78] This is why young workers were often treated roughly by their more experienced colleagues,[79] whose wages might suffer from learners' lack of experience. If a tenter made too many mistakes, thereby impairing the weaver's earnings more than he or she was willing to tolerate, he or she would have them sacked.[80]

Weavers held a position of authority over their tenters, which was open to abuse. Tenters might be made to sweep another weaver's looms on top of their own,[81] or in clear contravention of factory legislation to do the cleaning while the machinery was in motion.[82] Though a certain measure of corporal punishment may have been accepted without complaint,[83] weavers could face dismissal for physically abusing their assistants.[84]

Tenters would defer to the age and skill of their instructors, consistently referring to the females among them as 'missus'[85] and running all kinds of errands for them. There was always the danger of tenters being exploited as cheap ancillary labour instead of being properly instructed. A correspondent of the *Cotton Factory Times* upbraided weavers in the following terms:

> I firmly believe that in their early training they should be taught discipline. I contend, however, that the discipline is the work of the weaver who takes a young person to teach. Give them a thorough grounding in the technicalities of the trade, and then they would not be much troubled afterwards in the warehouse [penalized for turning in inferior work] ... The fault lies sometimes with the weaver ... some of whom seem to take little or no interest in their tenters, beyond using them for the donkey-work and errand going. This is not weaving, and weavers ought to feel that when they take tenters they are in a sense responsible for teaching them all the details of the trade.[86]

Given the marked degree of authority enjoyed by the experienced worker, some tenters claimed to be 'frightened to death' of the weaver they worked for and understandably tried to be paired up with one they liked.[87] Weavers with a reputation for being particularly capable were also sought after by tenters.[88] Often this would be a relative. Analysing data from Croston, a small weaving village near Preston, Savage has found that in 1891, of the 37 tenters employed at a particular mill, 31 appear to have been related to weavers employed by the same firm. Fifteen tenters even appear to have been related to a weaver working under the same overlooker. At another mill in the same village, of the 22 tenters employed, 18 were related to a weaver, with 15 of them working under the same overlooker as their weaver relative. Most of these links existed between women and children: 29 of the tenters from both mills were related to a female weaver, and only 12 to a male weaver. Eight tenters had both a male and a female relative working at the same mill.[89]

Although the weaver–tenter dyad need not be gender-homogeneous,[90] many girls were initiated into the art of weaving by mothers, aunts or other female relatives.[91] The transmission of skill thus often occurred along the female line of a family. The job of the instructor was not confined to teaching the tenter the skills of the trade.[92] Apart from sharing with the mother in the upbringing of the learner, the job comprised teaching shopfloor mores, such as the employee's duty vis-à-vis the employer[93] and ways of seeking redress in cases of unfair treatment by involving the union.[94]

After about two years, a tenter could count on being allocated the first two looms of her or his own.[95] Again, working near an experienced relative was an advantage, ensuring as it did that, if need be, there would be someone at hand willing and able to help.[96] With promotion to a set of looms of one's own began a new stage in the aspiring weaver's career, the corresponding rise in wages marking the passage to adulthood. This was openly acknowledged by one weaver stating that that was 'a very great day in the young weaver's life, the Lancashire equivalent of the young girl's coming-of-age'.[97] Hence it is no wonder that many a veteran of the trade was able in old age to recall the exact amount earned on the first set of looms of her own.[98] Over time, and with experience gained, the number of looms allocated to an individual weaver increased,[99] until, after about six or seven years, four looms were mastered.[100]

Gender Competition

In weaving, male and female workers, to the extent that they were producing identical cloth on identical machines, needed to have the same skills and abilities relating to the labour process. This was acknowledged by remuneration on the basis of non-gender-specific piece rates. It was this lack of labour process-based distinctions between men and women that incited male workers to seek other ways of distinguishing themselves from the women with whom they were working side by side on the shopfloor.

Physical strength was one attribute believed to differ between genders. True, the technological development of the loom, by automating the movement of the shuttle and the healds, had shifted the demands made on workers from physical exertion to increased attention and a speed-up of the requisite motions,[101] but physical strength had not become completely obsolete. Setting on the loom without causing flaws in the material, for instance, required a degree of exertion which could damage workers' health.[102] Thus the invention of patent brakes, which facilitated setting the loom on, was hailed by the *Cotton Factory Times* as an improvement of particular importance for women and young workers,[103] despite the fact that men were by no means immune to injuries from the exertion required.[104]

Even though physical strength did not lend itself to clearly distinguishing between male and female workers, on many occasions the higher degree of resilience in men to the pressure exerted by the need to drive oneself in order to meet production targets was at least implied. Thus one union official maintained: 'It is the women and girls who suffer. She struggles against her strength in competition with the most expert male weavers.'[105] Men weavers thus believed, but could not always prove, themselves to be the more productive workers because they were male.

Women weavers' awareness of the lack of resilience imputed to them comes across particularly clearly in their evidence on steaming. Possibly acting on union instruction, the overwhelming majority of the male weavers interviewed by the Cotton Cloth Committee, set up to investigate the effects of this practice, expressed their strong opposition to steaming, even declaring that they would rather sustain a drop in wages than carry on working with steam. By contrast, the majority of the female witnesses claimed not to mind steam being injected into the sheds where they were working.[106] Part of their supposed indifference was certainly to do with the fact that steaming helped weaving inferior types of yarn by preventing frequent breakage of threads. The following instance typifies the statements made by female weavers called as witnesses before the Commission on

Humidity and Ventilation investigating the issue of steaming again in the early 1900s. On being asked whether the humidifier had made her ill, one weaver replied: 'No, it is not much that does. I can stand anything. I have not lost a day yet from being ill.' Her feigned indifference to steaming did not prevent her from stating that many weavers at her shed complained about the humidity of the atmosphere and were off sick with influenza.[107] In this way she managed to present herself as strong and resilient while at the same time making a stand against steaming.

Apart from gender-specific competition between male and female weavers, there was permanent conflict between male weavers and overlookers, or tacklers. These formed the best paid group of workers in weaving, receiving a commission on the earnings of the weavers in their charge, called poundage, which amounted to 5 to 7 per cent.[108] Tacklers thus had a vested interest in the productivity of the weavers in their section of the shed, trying to increase this by all means in their power. Hence they were traditionally unpopular.[109] As they were known to compete with each other over good weavers,[110] it made sense for them to assign machines and jobs in accordance with a given weaver's level of skill rather than favour men throughout in a blatant display of male collusion. This specific organization of the labour process in weaving thus lends further weight to the assumption made in the preceding chapter that it was perfectly possible for a female weaver to earn the same or even more than her male counterpart engaged in weaving the same kind of cloth.

Overlookers were supposedly skilled mechanics maintaining the looms in their care in good working order as well as performing managerial tasks. Their maintenance work comprised putting beams into looms, gaiting them up for the particular kind of cloth to be woven as well as giving weavers all the information they needed for weaving the required kind of cloth. Their managerial tasks encompassed allocating looms to weavers and deciding when weavers were ready to be promoted to a larger number of looms, or, in the case of tenters, to a set of looms of their own. Apart from being responsible for hiring and discharging weavers, they had to enforce discipline on the shopfloor. In Preston, for instance, one tackler looked after about 80 looms worked by between 25 and 30 weavers.[111]

The prerequisites for tackling were supposed to be thorough knowledge of loom mechanics and the types of cloth that can be woven on different kinds of looms, mechanical skills, the ability, if need be, to teach weavers certain aspects of their trade, as well as physical strength required to carry heavy beams to looms.[112] Tackling was an exclusively male domain. In the words of a contemporary, 'Of course they were always men, because nature made this work unsuitable for women in many respects.'[113] What this expert presented as natural was the fact that, characterized as it was by the exercise of authority coupled with mechanical skill and physical strength, the tackler's job bore all the hallmarks of a masculine occupation.[114] This belief was shared by many a female weaver, citing the requisite mechanical knowledge, the strength required for lifting the heavy warp beams and the need to get down on the floor and become dirty as reasons why women could not be tacklers.[115]

The power tacklers wielded over the weavers in their section was open to abuse, including sexual harassment.[116] Women refusing them sexual favours risked losing their jobs. Nevertheless, this did not generally prevent the women concerned from suing their assaulters.[117] Close supervision of shopfloor behaviour to prevent sexual harassment was seen as part of a factory owner's duty,[118] but dismissal of the guilty party would often only follow on a verdict of guilty.[119]

Women weavers' ability effectively to defend themselves against overbearing overlookers was clearly circumscribed by the possibility of finding alternative employment. Yet tacklers' behaviour, too, was subject to a number of restraining forces, as Shani D'Cruze has pointed out.[120] Control may have been exercised, albeit inconsistently, by employers keen to maintain shopfloor discipline, by the law informed by dominant motives of social order embodied in the rational self and the bourgeois family as well as by kin and family desiring respectability. Sexual harassment was in clear breach of weaving communities' code of sexual conduct, and women, as potential victims, were not prepared to condone such behaviour.[121] It provoked particular anger when performed by tacklers, adding as it did to resentment of overlookers' exalted position. This became apparent in the strikes engendered by some tacklers' conduct towards the women weavers in their charge.[122] Women themselves found a certain degree of protection from unwanted sexual advances in being part of a large group.[123] Yet the sensationally distorted perception of 'factory morality' derived more from the unease caused contemporaries by the 'indiscriminate mingling of the sexes' at the workplace, and particularly by the shift in authority over females from male kin to male strangers, than from pervasive sexual exploitation of women weavers.[124]

Insisting on the characteristics of tackling as male prerogatives was even more important in view of the fact that in weaving the gender-specific allocation of these characteristics was far from clear-cut. As has been shown with regard to training, women were in a position of authority over their male and female tenters. Their authority extended beyond tasks related to the labour process.[125] The special mechanical knowledge and skills of tacklers were anything but undisputed, because their abilities did not necessarily differ either in degree or kind from those of their weavers. Their only privilege was access to tools and spare parts.[126] When carrying out maintenance work, tacklers relied on their experience and their senses, rather than subjecting looms to any systematic check for faults.[127] As tacklers' experience was based on years of working as weavers, it comes as no surprise that most weavers were able to carry out many repairs on their looms themselves.[128] Correspondingly, tacklers expected to be called to looms only in difficult cases, leaving minor repairs to be performed by weavers. Furthermore, they counted on weavers noticing the slightest indication of any faults in their looms and putting them right before greater damage might ensue.[129]

Although this was expected of male and female weavers alike, it was generally claimed by overlookers that women, because of their lack of mechanical knowledge, were unable to set up and tune their looms for the different types of cloth to be woven. The practical refutation of the belief that women were unable in principle to understand mechanics came only in the inter-war period, when some women officially trained to be tacklers.[130] Yet this did not stop the claim that female weavers usually did not bother to acquire mechanical knowledge from being repeated as late as 1930.[131] Even if they had wished to do so, women would have had no chance. The implementation of the Technical Instruction Act of 1889 led to curricula specified along gender lines. While young men were taught weaving and pattern-making, young women learned cooking and dress-making.[132] Nor were women entitled to scholarships for Technical Colleges, which, with regard to the Manchester one, drew forth a strong protest from the local Women's Trade Union Council in 1903.[133]

Despite these obstacles placed in their way, women could not help but discover from extensive experience how the looms at which they spent their days were operating. This is why they were indeed able to carry out repairs and tune the machines themselves.[134] Moreover, there was a strong incentive for doing so, because it helped reduce pay cuts by keeping machine downtime low.[135] It also made for some measure of independence of tacklers, who in a blatant display of power liked to keep their weavers waiting. Some weavers therefore devised ways of luring reluctant tacklers to their looms, for instance by offering them biscuits as a reward.[136] Finally, independence in these matters protected them from tacklers demanding sexual favours in return for repairs.[137]

Tacklers' Masculine Prowess

Promotion to tackling was the only career step male weavers could take without leaving the industry, and becoming a tackler was the ambition harboured by many.[138] In the absence of any alternative employment in the heartland of cotton weaving, tackling was the only escape route out of an occupation felt by many men to be demeaning on account of its feminine connotation and the virtual impossibility effectively to mark themselves off from the large number of female colleagues. Compared to the frustration engendered by being trapped in a feminine job, tackling held out the prospect of affirming workers' masculinity. As a male weaver wrote retrospectively:

> How I admired the tackler for his strength, his aloofness, his skill, his almost mystical knowledge of looms which enabled him quickly to discover the cause of faulty weaving and to master cantankerous and rebellious looms ... I admired his masculine gruffness as he scowled at weavers who came to him [to fetch him to their looms when he was busy] ... At that time he was my ideal of perfect manhood, and I could scarcely contain my admiration for his prodigious strength when he lifted in the new beams full of warp;

pulled the hand-tree turning over the loom without the aid of the strap and pulley – the knotted muscles of his hairy arm standing out, his jaw set, his lips forming an expression of scorn and contempt for the recalcitrant loom he would presently master ... [I would] stand and dream of the day when I would be a tackler myself and wear a waistcoat full of keys.[139]

For some the tackler, in his display of physical strength, craft 'mystery' and authority, was the perfect incarnation of masculinity. Yet tackling was a well-guarded preserve. By 1890, overlookers had achieved nearly 100 per cent unionization, enabling them strictly to limit access to their job. The number of apprentices was not to exceed 5 per cent of the total membership of a particular overlookers' association. Preference was given to tacklers' male kin,[140] in Colne, at least, to the extent of occasionally waiving the rules laying down the permitted number of apprentices in favour of an overlooker's son. Around 1910, the overlookers' associations of Colne and Preston[141] reserved the right to give permission to learn, while in Burnley, by contrast, the right to choose the man to be trained rested with employers. In order to be accepted, the prospective apprentice had to pay an initiation fee to the union, which ranged from 10s. in 1890 to 40s. in 1914, and needed the approval of at least two-thirds of the overlookers at his mill.

During the first two years, the apprentice would learn to weave all types of cloth on all the looms to be found at his mill. In the third year he would be attached to an overlooker, learning to set up and maintain looms. On completion of the apprenticeship, the overlooker would be placed on less than a full complement of looms until he had gained experience. Eventually, he became responsible for 50 to 100 looms, depending on the class of goods produced.[142]

With their tight control of labour supply, the levying of an initiation fee, and not least the secrecy with which they surrounded themselves,[143] overlookers' unions were clearly modelled on the highly exclusive craft unions. The secrecy of the organization reinforced the aura of mysticism attached to the tackler's job in a bid clearly to mark overlookers off from weavers.

Tension on the Shopfloor

Demarcation remained a contentious issue. Relations between male weavers and overlookers were fraught because, although their specific skill was anything but obvious, tacklers were placed in a position of authority. In their anti-tackler polemics, male weavers would demand that factory hierarchy reflect actual skill levels by being placed above tacklers,[144] not least because, they claimed, the latter were superfluous anyway.[145]

Tacklers' mechanical competence was cast into doubt by male and female weavers alike.[146] Although a tackler's interference with a loom might exacerbate rather than improve matters,[147] the blame would always be placed on the weaver.[148] Moreover, weavers would put the skills of any new tackler to the test. In order to cope, new hands relied on experienced overlookers showing them tricks.[149]

Tacklers were the favourite butt of weavers' jokes, which clearly acted to defuse the tension bound to build up in the tackler–weaver relationship and which derived from the closeness and familiarity that characterized the relationship between workers and their overlooker. Weavers' jokes depicted tacklers as habitual liars, lazy and damned.[150] Yet by the 1920s they were increasingly portrayed as simple or 'gormless',[151] as the Lancashire dialect had it. According to a popular saying, 'tacklers were weavers with the brain's [sic] taken out'.[152] According to the editor of the column 'Mirth in the Mill', which had become a regular feature of the *Cotton Factory Times* in 1907, only one in 10 jokes were sent in by female readers.[153] Although the claim is impossible to verify, as only a few contributors used their full names, the preponderance of men would corroborate that the particular humiliation felt by male weavers vis-à-vis overlookers was vented in a proliferation of jokes. Overlookers' popularity hit a particularly low ebb whenever they proved willing to replace weavers who had struck work.[154]

The conflict between these two groups of male workers over the issue of skill was heightened by the presence of female workers in the shed and the gender competition this involved. In this respect the Lancashire setting differed markedly from other centres of the textile industry. In the Dundee jute industry, for instance, male tenters, or sub-foremen, were placed in a position of authority over weavers who were exclusively female.[155] It was hard enough for male weavers to submit to the authority of a group of men whose claim to power and better pay on account of a higher level of skill was anything but undisputed. Humiliation was added to bitterness by the fact that there was no difference between them and their female co-workers when it came to subordination to tacklers. The existence of tacklers, male weavers felt, placed them in the same rank as girls,[156] the comparison revealing the slight on their manhood that they perceived.[157]

At the centre of the tensions between tacklers and male weavers thus stood the issue of male respectability, which was inextricably linked with the possession of skill and authority. In this vein a correspondent of the *Cotton Factory Times* complained in 1885 that the position of weavers, and male ones in particular, under present conditions was anything but respectable. The remedy he advocated was officially to allow men weavers to maintain their own looms. Furthermore, he suggested that they could be placed in a position of authority over their female co-workers.[158] This would render tacklers superfluous, and the wages thus saved could be used to improve weavers' pay.[159]

Others believed that tacklers were necessary only because there were women and children employed in weaving.[160] This belief implied not only that women, like children, were unable to carry out some of the tacklers' tasks themselves, but also that they stood in particular need of supervision and discipline. Still others claimed that employers had allowed tacklers to monopolize certain skills in order to be able to employ women and children at lower rates than men.[161]

In relation to tacklers, male weavers saw themselves as being in the same position as their female co-workers. Thus they were forced to search for other ways of at least partially restoring their masculine dignity. One possibility was to make the protection of female weavers' virtue their particular concern. This was somewhat double-edged, however, because, lacking ways of sanctioning tacklers' behaviour, their reproaches would imply admission of their own lack of power.

The frequent complaints about tacklers' rough language and tyrannical behaviour towards female weavers[162] served to undermine both the former's competence as professionals and their personal qualities as human beings.[163] The assumption was that only those tacklers lacking in skill were forced to resort to intimidation.[164] Their meanness of character was believed to show in their not daring to behave towards men in the same way, because the latter would put up resistance.[165]

It is significant that, while abounding with instances of women who complained about driving, sources also show that female weavers did not submit to tacklers quietly. On the contrary, there are numerous instances of women militantly opposing tacklers whose behaviour they found objectionable,[166] including sexual harassment,[167] and whose ability to put up resistance was not confined to the shopfloor.[168] Competent weavers in particular were fairly immune to retaliation from tacklers, who relied on good weavers for their own income.[169]

Instances of women's resistance did not change the way in which they were consistently portrayed as victims. With regard to the behaviour of tacklers, it was the literally patriarchal authority of men as the protectors of their womenfolk that was at issue. In this vein one correspondent of the *Cotton Factory Times* asked how tacklers would feel if the author were to use obscene language to their wives and sisters.[170] And another correspondent expressed amazement at the apathy of those men whose female kinfolk were exposed to such treatment and language on the shopfloor.[171]

Female Work Culture

One of the chief sources from which women's resistance to overbearing superiors flowed was the strength of numbers. The factory-based organization of weaving assembled in one place a large number of women spending a great deal of time in each other's company. In view of the centrality accorded by weavers to paid work, it comes as no surprise that there should be indications of something approaching a female work culture, which revolved around female solidarity inside and outside the mill. The notion of work culture, according to Kathleen Canning, implies the possibility of a relatively autonomous sphere of action on the job that workers create as they distance themselves from the structure of production and the authority of employers.[172]

Solidarity, the linchpin of work culture, was ambiguous in that it not only created niches of autonomy on the shopfloor, but was also deployed to enforce conformity. As in the neighbourhood, so in the factory, the proximity and overlap of neighbours and co-workers acted as an effective means of exerting social control, especially, though not exclusively, as regards sexual mores. Any woman suspected of having a sexual relationship with a married man met with strong disapproval, while common-law unions, though frowned upon, were tolerated. Smoking or the use of cosmetics was deemed 'fast', nor were any concessions made to personal vanity, as the following incident shows.

The Lancashire 'mill girl', an appellation applied regardless of age, was known nationwide by the shawl she donned on her way to and from work. One day Alice Foley, a weaver in Bolton (discussed more fully in Chapter 6), exchanged her shawl for a shabby sailor hat discarded by her sister. When one day she returned unexpectedly to her looms, she came upon a procession of laughing women parading round the alleys, the leader holding aloft the hat on top of a sweeping brush. Yet censure was tempered by good-naturedness, for during the afternoon several of her co-workers offered her a toffee or an orange as their way of saying, 'Sorry, old pal, if we have offended, but, for goodness sake, do come off that stilt.'[173]

Shopfloor mores were enforced by group pressure, too. Keeping to oneself in order to maximize one's output was frowned upon, and any attempt to disown a faulty cut, attributing it to another weaver so as to evade a fine, was quashed by close group supervision.[174] Furthermore, the workplace afforded numerous opportunities for mutual support. The tightest bonds formed between those working in close proximity to each other, because, given the level of noise in a weaving shed, communication at a distance was impossible. Weavers alerted each other to ends about to come out at their looms[175] and shared fines to lighten the financial loss of the weaver thus penalized for faulty cloth.[176] Particularly skilled weavers would also undo a friend's faults for them, while the woman thus helped attended their looms.[177]

When an operative fell ill, she would be seen safely home by the woman working next to her, who lost in earnings owing to the time spent away from her looms. Conversely, when some member of an operative's family died and she was summoned to the watch-house to be told the sad news, her sympathizing co-workers kept her looms running.[178] Though unable to spare her the bereavement, they were at least able to minimize her financial loss.

Women also helped each other cope with the dual responsibility of caring for a family and holding down a job. They would regularly bring their family troubles to the shopfloor, telling colleagues about family rows[179] and possibly asking each other's advice. One weaver, who rushed home during the half-hour morning break to breastfeed her baby, which regularly made her five minutes late, could rely on the woman working next to her to set on her looms for her and to stop them if anything went wrong.[180] In view of the many joys and sorrows shared, it is no wonder that, on leaving the mill, a colleague of long standing was sure to be given a present as a token of remembrance.[181]

Women devised a variety of ways to break the tedium of work. Despite the noise level, they used to sing while tending their looms[182] and, if they were lucky, one of them might have an instrument and play a few tunes during the dinner break.[183] Although tacklers usually had no compunction in enforcing discipline on the shopfloor,[184] young workers appear to have enjoyed some measure of liberty in recognition of their need for some respite from the strictness of work discipline. As one weaver recalled:

> we had some terrific friendships you know, and things like the dinner hour was really great for the young ones, we would get together and sit around the mill lodge and we'd joke and generally just lark about and sometimes, and this was fantastic, we'd sneak into the rooms where they kept all the cotton wool and throw ourselves around in the cotton and we'd be making a right din and sooner or later a strict voice would come and shout 'what's going on in there?' and we'd go really quite [sic], it's funny though, no one ever came looking for who was making the noise, they would just shout and I think a lot of that was because they understood that young people can get carried away.[185]

Everyone joined in celebrating Christmas and birthdays. On such occasions workers would give themselves special treats, the expense for which was shared. Collecting the necessary money could have sexual overtones. Men who had been kissed unawares had to pay into the kitty.[186] Weddings were accorded special relevance, marking as they did a status passage in the female life cycle. When a co-worker was about to get married, weekly collections of money were made[187] to buy a present and to meet the expenses of the footing that was expected on such an occasion. The traditional wedding present to a colleague was a large new chamber-pot, which was first tied to the machinery high above the bride's loom for all to see and subsequently attached to the front of the bridal carriage.[188] Everyone would be regaled with special food and drink, including alcohol, the consumption of which on mill premises was usually prohibited.[189] Yet, in recognition of the special occasion, this prohibition as well as tacklers' authority were waived,[190] the men retiring from the scene of the party. They might be given a special treat, too,[191] to ensure their withdrawal.[192]

Once the event had become women only, weavers decked themselves in fancy costume, and the party began. The bride would be draped in a curtain or a white sheet, and in anticipation of her 'walking down the aisle', she would be led in a procession down the alley running along the centre of the shed.[193] Some of the women might dress up as men, imitating masculine behaviour[194] as a way of subverting male dominance by flaunting gender difference. Coupled with men's exclusion from these parties, such behaviour denied men's power to control their behaviour. There might have been some dancing,[195] and the elder women would tell ribald jokes, sending the younger ones giggling with embarrassment.[196] A woman's closest colleague might be chosen as bridesmaid,[197] testifying to the way in which relationships at work overlapped with those in private.[198]

These events, as Sallie Westwood has argued with regard to women hosiery workers, circumscribed though they were by the factory regime and management's authority, testify to the strength women derived from collective action. This enabled them to force management to back off from any interference in women's celebrations of what they considered high points in the female life cycle.[199] Furthermore, these occasions bear witness to women weavers' ability to reclaim work time and factory space for uses of their own, frustrating any attempt on the employers' part fully to regiment their workforce.[200] Finally, the organization of such informal activities focusing on the female life cycle, and the manifold ways in which women 'brought their families to work',[201] acted as strong bonding devices among groups of female weavers,[202] empowering them to resist.

These informal parties further testify to women weavers' ability to reappropriate space and time designed for the generation of profit to purposes of their own, which were far removed from the exigencies of production. For the women staging them these celebrations were a means of proclaiming the way work and family meshed in their lives. The fact that they were able to do so openly rather than surreptitiously testifies to the acknowledgment of this interconnection on the part of management. They appear to have valued women as workers too much even to attempt to frustrate their desire to demonstrate that life is not all work, but also play, including at the workplace.

The Family as the Unit of Production

As Tamara Hareven has observed with regard to the Amoskeag Manufacturing Company in New Hampshire, 'Work in the mills provided an experience of partnership and sociability which was organized along sex lines, but which nevertheless carried a family ambiance into the workrooms.'[203] 'We were one big happy family,' is how one weaver summed up the quality of the relationships formed at work.[204] Many actually found themselves working in the company of kin. That was true for many tenters, as shown above, but applied more generally as well. Sheds often were a 'commune of neighbours, friends and close relatives'.[205]

In the cotton-weaving district of Lancashire, families not only pooled their earnings, but also carried on operating as a unit of production in the factory environment. Members of one family would try and obtain employment at the same mill.[206] Not least as a result of the recruitment patterns in weaving described above, overlookers were aware of kinship ties among their workers. They would place relatives in close proximity to each other,[207] but also victimize entire families for the wrongdoings of one of their members.[208] Alternatively, the family themselves would strive to be reunited at some other mill on the dismissal of one of their members.[209] Obviously, working in the company of relatives afforded some measure of protection from the onslaught of management authority,[210] yet standing up for kin at work entailed the risk of losing one's job.[211]

Although the family units to be found on the shopfloor need not be gender-homogeneous, in places with a majority of females among the weaving workforce, such as Preston, they often were. Given that the process of schooling newcomers in the rules of the shopfloor was part and parcel of the instruction youngsters received from their elders, and that solidarity and mutual support were salient features of women's experience of work in the mill, Savage's emphasis on patriarchal control exerted by tacklers in collusion with husbands and fathers over female weavers in Preston appears exaggerated. The examples of interventions in the labour process by male kin on behalf of female relatives, culled from the records of the Preston Weavers' Association,[212] need to be balanced against the examples, at least equally numerous, of mothers intervening on behalf of daughters. Moreover, it was mothers, rather than tacklers, whom daughters referred to as the ultimate authority on matters of work discipline.[213]

Conclusion

Skill is no objective measure of requirements based on the labour process, but the result of a social process of construction, in the course of which, in quite an arbitrary manner, particular aspects of a given job are singled out to buttress, or undermine, the claim of a particular group of workers to performing a skilled job. It therefore appears misguided to concentrate solely on the characteristics of a given task in order to determine the level of skill it requires. It is at least equally important, if not more so, to take into account the social status of the workers performing the job.[214] In Lancashire cotton weaving, gender-specific connotations dominated in the construction of skill. This is particularly apparent where the construction becomes fractured, as in the demarcation between tacklers and male weavers as well as between male and female weavers.

The criteria of physical strength and technical competence failed objectively to mark off the tasks of tacklers from those of weavers, but as components of the contemporary notion of masculinity they were appropriated by males. Conversely, by emphasizing these job characteristics in combination with social control in the labour process, men were able to claim tackling as their preserve.

While these gender-specific connotations of a given task succeeded in distinguishing tacklers from female weavers, they failed to do so with regard to male weavers. These seriously questioned tacklers having any specific labour process-based skills and abilities and frequently refuted them in practice. Thus tacklers' demarcation from male weavers turned out to be a social construction, based as it was on the effective limitations imposed on access to this trade by virtue of a high degree of unionization. This is one important reason why tacklers also succeeded in retaining their monopoly on certain managerial tasks such as the hiring and dismissal of weavers.

Gender-specific criteria, though of a different kind, were relevant to the distinctions made between male and female weavers. Here recourse to labour process-based skills and faculties made no sense, with all weavers carrying out the same tasks. This equality in the labour process strengthened male weavers' bid to distinguish themselves from their female co-workers. In north-east Lancashire, the heartland of weaving, the lack or smallness of any wage differential between men and women posed a serious threat to male dominance. In their quest for difference, male weavers had recourse to the contemporary belief in the essential difference between men and women. In harmony with the prevailing notion of femininity, they portrayed female weavers as physically inferior and less resilient on the whole and emphasized their need of protection from sexual assault.

The predominance of the gender-specific connotation of skill is further underpinned by a comparison between spinning and weaving. All the elements on which rested spinners' claim to skill – such as authority over helpers and the requirements imposed by the highly variable character of both the material and the machinery involved in the job – were present in weaving as well. Yet the large contingent of women in the weaving workforce precluded the recognition of these elements of skill. Weaving was labelled semi-skilled, because women proved capable of performing the job.

Oblivious to the low esteem in which weaving was held by outsiders, while expressing the values shared by their communities, female weavers consistently spoke of themselves as skilled workers having mastered a trade, thereby laying claim to attributes intimately linked with masculinity. They deployed them to fashion for themselves an identity of women workers whose competent tending of machines and ability to produce faultless cloth formed the prerequisites of a desired level of pay. Acutely aware of the significance of their earnings to family income, they were quick to draw the analogy between themselves and male workers who laid claim to a respectable life style on the basis of skill.

Women took pride in their ability to make an important contribution to family income on the basis of their competence at work. This combined with the satisfaction derived from performing a complicated job well and the delight they took in mixing with other women on the shopfloor to induce women weavers to enjoy working in the mill. They were not the downtrodden victims suffering from double subordination by industrial capitalism and male hegemony. Proud of their work-based skills and counting on the support from female co-workers, they held their own both against the dictates of economic exploitation and the impact of male dominance.

Notes

1   For a critique of historians superimposing their own ranking of particular jobs on the subjects of their investigation, see Stephenson and Brown (1990).
2   Lancashire Textile Project, respondent AIP, p.7.

3   See Fowler and Wyke (1987).
4   See, for example, Derry (1931–2).
5   Turner (1962, pp.193–4).
6   See Marsden (1884, p.230); see also Ellison (1968, p.32). For an appraisal of Ellison as a historian of the cotton industry, see Farnie (1978).
7   See Turner (1962, p.128); see also Lazonick (1979).
8   See More (1980, esp. ch.7).
9   Ibid.
10 See Freifeld (1986).
11 See Harrison (1985, p.9).
12 See Phillips and Taylor (1980).
13 For a French example of gender-specific definitions of skill to fend off the encroachments of industrial capitalism by the knitters of Troyes, see Chenut (1996). For case studies of the ways in which skill as a gendered category operates to objectify the gender division of labour, see de Groot and Schrover (1995).
14 See Marsden (1895, p.173).
15 See, for example, More (1980, pp.229–30); for the application of this argument to Yorkshire woollen weaving, see Busfield (1988, p.74).
16 See Berg (1985, p.265).
17 See, for example, Andrew (1887, p.11); see also *Textile Manufacturer*, 15.1.1902, p.2.
18 The almost infinite variations of the cotton fibre continue to exercise the minds of scientists concerned with designing highly sophisticated computer-aided methods of determining cotton quality as a prerequisite for adjusting automatic spinning machinery accordingly; see Frey and Schleth (1994), Harig et al. (1994).
19 See White (1982, p 211); see also *CFT*, 1.3.1907, p.7.
20 See, for example, *CFT*, 5.12.1890, p. 5; also Commission on Labour, *PP*, 1892, XXXVI, p.352.
21 *CFT*, 5.12.1890, p.5.
22 See Savage (1982, pp.17–18).
23 See Ross (1991, p.66).
24 Personal communication to the author from a female weaver employed at Quarry Bank Mill industrial museum at Styal, Cheshire.
25 See also Lancashire Textile Project, respondent AH10, p. 11.
26 See Ross (1991, p.66).
27 See, for example, *CFT*, 26.4.1929, p.1.
28 Lancashire Textile Project, respondent AF2, p.19.
29 See Ellison (1968, p.37).
30 See Roberts (1981), respondent H7P, p.33.
31 See ibid., respondent T4P, p.5.
32 Bolton Oral History, tape 5, p.4.
33 See, for example, ibid., tape 27b, p.5.
34 See Mrs H.G. Tape 656 MSU TLSL; see also Roberts (1981), respondent B9P, p.19; respondent C5P, p.46; respondent D2P, p.27; respondent G1P, p.109.
35 See, for example, Roberts (1981), respondent W4P, p.40.
36 See, for example, Mrs M.H. Tape 640 MSU TLSL.
37 See, for example, Roberts (1981), respondent B1P, p.7.
38 See, for example, Mrs T.T. Tape 668 MSU TLSL; see also *Reynolds Newspaper*, 28.6.1914, GTC 5/83.

39 See Hill (1997), p.86.
40 See White (1982, p.214); see also *Reynolds Newspaper*, 28.6.1914, GTC 5/83.
41 See, for example, Roberts (1981), respondent H8P, p.32.
42 See, for example, ibid., respondent L1P, p.45.
43 See, for example, ibid., respondent C2P, p. 10; see also *Reynolds Newspaper*, 28.6.1914, GTC 5/83.
44 In Essex, by contrast, domestic service lured an increasing number of women away from employment in Courtauld's silk mills towards the end of the nineteenth century; see Lown (1990, p.61).
45 McCarthy (1953, p.151).
46 See Brooks (1926, p.131).
47 See Commission on Labour, *PP*, 1892, XXXVI, pp.176, 184.
48 See Roberts (1982a, pp.49–52).
49 See Mrs J.H. Tape 692 MSU TLSL.
50 See Early Recollections, Fanny King, *DDX*, 978, p.1.
51 *CFT*, 29.8.1913, p.1.
52 Bolton Oral History, tape 5, p.4.
53 These findings are corroborated by the interviews conducted by Miriam Glucksmann with women weavers who had entered employment in the 1920s and 1930s; see Glucksmann (2000, p.55).
54 See, for example, Alexander (1984), Rose (1986b, 1988), Thompson (1988), McClelland (1989).
55 In her study of women's reminiscences of the Second World War, Penny Summerfield has emphasized the determining influence upon the way a narrative is told of the cultural values shared by the public to which it is addressed; see Summerfield (1998, p.20). This influence has been discernible in the material produced by women cotton workers to the extent that one assumes the respective interviewers to have been representatives of the communities the interviewees lived in rather than outsiders.
56 See, for example, North-West Sound Archive, 23a, 23c; see also McCarthy (1953, p.45), Schulze-Gävernitz (1892, p.147). For an appraisal of Schulze-Gävernitz as a historian of the cotton industry, see Farnie (1978).
57 See, for example, Bolton Oral History, tape 28A, p.2.
58 See, for example, Grimshaw, Burnley Central Library, *G3*, p.4.
59 See Roberts (1981), respondent A1P, p.7; respondent H7P, p.2; see also Roberts (1986, p.38).
60 For a US example where this was true, the Amoskeag Manufacturing Company in Manchester, New Hampshire, see Hareven (1977a, p.200). For the evidence on which this article is based, see Hareven and Langenbach (1979).
61 See Commission on the Depression of Trade and Industry, *PP*, 1886, XXII, p.72.
62 See, for example, Roberts (1981), respondent H2P, p.2; respondent P2P, p.6.
63 See, for example, ibid., respondent O1P, p.2.
64 For a general consideration of the impact of communities on local labour markets in historical perspective, see Whipp (1985).
65 Mrs T.T. Tape 668 MSU TLSL.
66 See, for example, Roberts (1981), respondent H7P, pp.4, 33.
67 See, for example, *CFT*, 6.2.1885, p.4; see also Roberts (1981), respondent H7P, p.34.

68 For detailed information on overlookers in weaving I am indebted to Dermot Healey, who has made available to me an unpublished typescript.
69 See Lancashire Textile Project, respondent AH10, p.14; see also Savage (1985, pp.181–2).
70 See Commission on the Depression of Trade and Industry, *PP*, 1886, XXII, p.71.
71 See Roberts (1986, p.61).
72 See Schulze-Gävernitz (1892, p.146).
73 See *CFT*, 23.4.1886, p.5.
74 See Mrs M.H. Tape 640 MSU TLSL.
75 See *CFT*, 1.3.1907, p.1.
76 See *CFT*, 16.3.1906, p.5.
77 See Lazonick (1979).
78 See Commission on Labour, *PP*, 1892, XXXV, p.183.
79 See, for example, *CFT*, 26.5.1905, p.8; see also Roberts (1981), respondent A3P, p.3; respondent B1P, p.11; respondent B2P, p.20; respondent T5P, p.12; respondent H2P, p.2.
80 See, for example, Bolton Oral History, tape 5, p.5.
81 See, for example, *CFT*, 24.4.1891, p.7.
82 See, for example, *Lancashire Post*, 18.4.1906, GTC 13 I/4.
83 See, for example, North-West Sound Archive, 27a.
84 See, for example, Preston Weavers: Complaints, *DDX*, 1089, 19.5.1909, p.309.
85 See Bolton Oral History, tape 5, p.4; see also North-West Sound Archive, 5; Roberts (1986, p.48).
86 *CFT*, 18.9.1913, p.5.
87 See, for example, Bolton Oral History, tape 5, p.4.
88 See, for example, Brooks (1926, p.125).
89 See Savage (1981, p.14).
90 See, for example, Preston Weavers: Complaints, *DDX*, 1089, 14.11.1904, p.24; 30.5.1905, p.43; 5.7.1906, p.105; see also Roberts (1981), respondent H2P, p.2.
91 See, for example, Roberts (1981), respondent A1P, p.6; respondent A3P, p.6; respondent C5P, p.46; respondent T4P, p.5.
92 See, for example, Kenny (1994), case 5, p.6.
93 See, for example, Preston Weavers: Complaints, *DDX*, 1089, 31.12.1906, p.135.
94 See, ibid., 12.6.1906, p.101.
95 See Commission on the Depression of Trade and Industry, *PP*, 1886, XXII, p.71. Of course the period spent at any one stage varied by individual, see, for example, North-West Sound Archive, 5.
96 See, for example, Roberts (1981), respondent T4P, p.5; see also Lancashire Textile Project, respondent AO2, p.2. For experienced weavers helping recently promoted colleagues so that their cuts passed quality control, see *CFT*, 6.2.1891, p.7. For the abuse this practice could give rise to see, for example, *CFT*, 8.1.1891, p.5.
97 McCarthy (1953, p.16).
98 See, for example, North-West Sound Archive, 1988.0094.
99 See Commission on the Depression of Trade and Industry, *PP*, 1886, XXII, pp.71–2.
100 See Savage (1982, p.18).
101 See Fowler and Fowler (1984, p.2).
102 See *CFT*, 17.8.1888, p.4.
103 See *CFT*, 13.3.1885, p.6.

104 See, for example, *CFT*, 17.8.1888, p.4.
105 See *CFT*, 10.4.1903, pp.4–5.
106 See Committee on Cotton Cloth Factories, *PP*, 1897, XVII, p.22 and *passim*.
107 Committee on Humidity and Ventilation, *PP*, 1909, XV, p.699.
108 See Biernacki (1995, p.152). According to Schulze-Gävernitz (1892, p.146), this percentage amounted to 1s.4d.
109 See Tippett (1969, p.93).
110 See, for example, Lancashire Textile Project, respondent AH10, p.14.
111 See Savage (1985, p.179).
112 See Marsden (1895, p.476).
113 Ibid.
114 This belief was universal in the textile industry. The only exceptions in the Scottish jute industry, for example, were shifting mistresses, whose authority was confined to supervising boys and girls, see Gordon (1991, pp.28–9). In the German cotton industry, too, the occasional forewoman was confined to all-female shops; see Canning (1996, p.226).
115 See, for example, Roberts (1981), respondent A1P, p.52; see also North-West Sound Archive 1988, 150.
116 See, for example, *CFT*, 22.6.1888, p.4; 29.11.1889, p.7; 8.7.1904, p.6; Employment of Women, *PP*, 1893–94, XXXVII, Pt. I, p.664; see also Lambertz (1985).
117 See, for example, *CFT*, 8.7.1904, p.6; but see *CFT*, 22.6.1888, p.4; 29.11.1889, p.7, for cases in which no action was taken by the victim.
118 See, for example, Employment of Women, *PP*, 1893–94, XXXVII. Pt. I, p.664; Marsden (1895, p.485).
119 See Employment of Women, *PP*,1893–94, XXXVII, Pt. I, p.664.
120 See D'Cruze (1998, p.108). Her analysis of cases of sexual violence involving mill workers is marred by her lack of familiarity with conditions in weaving mills and her premise that such cases demonstrate the overlap of the gendered nature of familial and workplace authority. For a more detailed refutation of the assumed fit between male authority in the home and at the workplace with regard to weavers, see Chapter 6, below.
121 Shani D'Cruze has found evidence of working-class women and children in the industrial towns of Lancashire refusing to submit silently to sexual violence and relying on the support of local women in the endeavour; see D'Cruze (1993).
122 See, for example, Employment of Women, *PP*, 1893–94, XXXVII, Pt. I, p.664. The cases mentioned in this source have also been investigated by Lambertz (1985, esp. pp.34–6).
123 See Lambertz (1985, p.37).
124 See, for example, Clarke (1899, pp.83–5); see also sermon by one Father Day, *CFT*, 13.6.1914, p.4; see also McCarthy (1953, pp.17–18). For an implicit refutation of the allegation that immorality was rampant among factory operatives, see, for example, *CFT*, 12.3.1909, p.1.
125 See *CFT*, 6.2.1885, p.4.
126 See, for example, Savage (1985, p.181).
127 See Lancashire Textile Project, respondent AC9, p. 24; see also Tippett (1969, pp.74–5).
128 See Savage (1985, p.181); see also Preston Weavers: Complaints, *DDX*, 1089, 16.9.1907, p.183; see also Roberts (1981), respondent G1P, p.51; respondent H1P, p.7.

129 See, for example, *CFT*, 22.2.1929, p.1.
130 See Lewis (1984, p.178).
131 See *CFT*, 25.4.1930, p.1.
132 See *CFT*, 9.10.1891, p.5.
133 See *CFT*, 29.5.1903, p.6.
134 See Savage (1985, p.181); see also *CFT*, 27.2.1885, p.8; 25.4.1930, p.1. For a particularly striking example of a female weaver's tackling skills, see Ross (1991, p.71).
135 See, for example, *CFT*, 10.12.1886, p.7.
136 See, for example, Foley (1973, p.52). For a particularly recalcitrant tackler, see Preston Weavers: Complaints, *DDX*, 1089, 29.7.1905, p.62.
137 For an example of a complaint about a tackler which implied that his favouritism had sexual overtones, see *CFT*, 6.7.1888, p.5; see also Lambertz (1985).
138 See, for example, Lancashire Textile Project, respondent AD8, p.16.
139 Holt (1939, pp.37–9).
140 See, for example, Lancashire Textile Project, respondent AC10, p.13.
141 See Firth (1986, p. 57) and Savage (1987, p.81).
142 See Turner (1962, p.274); see also Firth (1986, p.56 and *passim*).
143 See Firth (1986, p.98).
144 See *CFT*, 10.12.1886, p.7.
145 See *CFT*, 6.2.1885, p.6.
146 See, for example, *CFT*, 14.12.1888, p.5.
147 See, for example, Preston Weavers: Complaints, *DDX*, 1089, 1.6.1904, p.10.
148 See North-West Sound Archive, 1990, 2A.
149 See Lancashire Textile Project, respondent AC10, p.2.
150 See Fowler and Wyke (1995, pp.38–9). For an extensive treatment of the way in which humour was deployed in the *CFT*, see Cass (1996, pp.215–35).
151 See also McCarthy (1953, p.18).
152 Lancashire Textile Project, respondent AC16, p.26; see also Roberts (1981), respondent B9P, p.6.
153 See Fowler and Wyke (1995, p.13).
154 For a particularly notorious example of overlookers taking the employers' side in a strike, see Hall (1975, p.21).
155 See Gordon (1987–8, p.30).
156 See *CFT*, 18.9.1885, p.7.
157 For the humiliation felt by a Swiss weaver on account of being placed on a par with women, girls and boys by the piece rate, and declaring this parity to be unnatural, see Kunz (1942).
158 See *CFT*, 2.10.1885, p.7; for a rather sceptical response, see *CFT*, 9.10.1885, p.7.
159 See *CFT*, 6.2.1885, p.5.
160 See *CFT*, 12.6.1885, p.7.
161 See *CFT*, 18.9.1885, p.7.
162 See, for example, *CFT*, 26.11.1886, p.5; 31.12.1886, p.5; 21.10.1904, p.5.
163 This is also borne out by the analysis of British workers' complaints about overlookers carried out by Biernacki (1995, pp.184–5).
164 See *CFT*, 13.2.1885, p.8; see also Roberts (1981), respondent C1P, p.42.
165 See *CFT*, 18.12.1891, p.1.
166 See, for example, *CFT*, 28.8.1885, p.5; 16.10.1885, p.4; 23.5.1890, p.5; 31.8.1906, p.4.

167 See Lambertz (1985).
168 See note 121, above.
169 See, for example, Mr C.R. Tape 113 MSU TLSL.
170 See *CFT*, 22.2.1889, p.4; 10.9.1897, p.1.
171 See *CFT*, 11.7.1890, p.4.
172 See Canning (1996, p.285).
173 Foley (1973, pp.58–9).
174 See, for example, Preston Weavers: Complaints, *DDX*, 1089, 29.6.1906, p.103; 1.3.1909, pp.295–6.
175 See, for example, Roberts (1981), respondent C2P, p.10.
176 See, for example, ibid., respondent T4P, p.18.
177 See, for example, Preston Weavers: Complaints, *DDX*, 1089, 7.12.1907, p.205.
178 See Foley (1973, p.60).
179 Ibid.
180 See Miss E.B. Tape 655 MSU TLSL.
181 See Foley (1973, p.76).
182 See, for example, Smith (1933, p.18).
183 See Roberts (1981), respondent A3P, pp.6–7.
184 See ibid., respondent W4P, p.4.
185 Kenny (1994), case 5, p.6.
186 See Mrs D.W. Tape 667; Mrs T.T. Tape 668 MSU TLSL.
187 See Roberts (1981), respondent A1P, p.9.
188 McCarthy (1953, p.18).
189 See Foley (1973, p.58); see also Roberts (1981), respondent A1P, p.9.
190 McCarthy (1953, p.18); see also Roberts (1981), respondent A1P, p.9.
191 See Roberts (1981), respondent A1P, p.9.
192 The custom of women-only parties was not specific to Lancashire cotton weaving. In the Ulster linen industry, for example, the occasion to celebrate was not necessarily an impending wedding, but, at least among Catholic workers, St Patrick's day; see Messenger (1988, p.190).
193 See Foley (1973, p.58).
194 McCarthy (1953, p.19).
195 See Roberts (1981), respondent A1P, p.9.
196 See Foley (1973, p.58).
197 See Roberts (1981), respondent B2P, p.20.
198 For colleagues going on holiday together, see, for example, ibid., respondent B1P, p.16.
199 See Westwood (1984, pp.89–90, 101).
200 For a discussion of the struggle between employers and workers engendered by conflicting values and motivations concerning the purpose of production, see Behagg (1995). Conditions in German factories have been investigated in a similar vein by Lüdtke (1980) and with particular regard to the textile industry by Machtan (1981).
201 See Lamphere (1985), who has investigated ways in which women workers 'bring the family to work' as constitutive of specific work cultures, either resistant or compliant.
202 For similar instances in a different industry of women workers celebrating all-female parties and generally having a good time with each other, all of which led them to value highly their companionship at work, see Phillips (1994).

203 Hareven (1977, p.198).
204 See Roberts (1981), respondent B1P, p.16.
205 McCarthy (1953, p.18).
206 See, for example, Cookson, Burnley Central Library, G3, p.18; see also Lancashire Textile Project, respondent AC5, p.2; respondent AO1, p.41.
207 See, for example, Lancashire Textile Project, respondent AB3, p.5.
208 See Preston Weavers: Complaints, *DDX*, 1089, 29.1.1906, p.83; 14.2.1906, p.84.
209 See, for example, *CFT*, 23.6.1886, p.5.
210 See, for example, Preston Weavers: Complaints, *DDX*, 1089, 15.10.1904, pp.21–2.
211 See ibid., 28.5.1906, p.99.
212 See Savage (1982, p.11 and *passim*).
213 See, for example, Preston Weavers: Complaints, *DDX*, 1089, 21.7.1909, p.332.
214 See also the rather tentative hints in Boot (1995).

Chapter 4

The Weaver's Rest: the Ultimate Escape from Weaving

In the Lancashire cotton weaving industry the labour process offered no opportunity for anchoring differences of gender as a way of bestowing on them some seemingly objective quality. Male and female weavers, as Chapter 3 has shown, were working side by side, operating identical machines and producing the same types of cloth, the making of which was remunerated according to non-gender-specific piece rates. Nor, as also argued in Chapter 3, did skill serve as a marker of difference. Labour process-based faculties and abilities varied, it is true, but they did so individually and no doubt by age and experience, but not by gender. Precisely because of the lack of any labour process-based differentiation, male weavers sought other ways of distinguishing themselves from their female co-workers, as becomes clear in their use of gender in the campaign against driving in weaving sheds. This campaign was organized around the suicides of young female weavers. Though affording trade unions the welcome opportunity of stereotyping women as victims of overbearing circumstances, the suicides at the same time throw into relief the extent to which female weavers' identity revolved around their ability to perform a skilled job.

The Driving Evil

'Driving' was the term employed in Lancashire cotton weaving to denote methods of bringing extra pressure to bear on workers to increase output. Given that weavers were paid by the piece, there was a strong incentive to drive themselves as hard as they could to maximize earnings. The need to do so became so deeply ingrained that not even in old age would they slacken their efforts to produce more than the average amount of cloth per week.[1] In the words of Patrick Joyce, in the cotton communities, 'Work got under the skin of everyday life.'[2] The term 'driving', however, was reserved by cotton operatives and their unions for ways of pressurizing over and above the method of payment. The association with slave-driving that the term evoked only served to underline its pejorative meaning. In Lancashire, the person identified as the slave-driver was the overlooker or tackler. Occasionally, the similarity between tacklers and slave-drivers was made explicit when a group of weavers would present a particularly authoritarian overlooker with a whip.[3]

Tacklers, whose function and position in the labour process have been described in the preceding chapter, had a vested interest in increasing productivity, because their wages, as also noted in Chapter 3, were directly related to the output of the operatives in their charge. Conversely, tacklers had a profound influence on weavers' earnings, because their readiness to attend to defective machines and their competence in setting them right determined the length of time a faulty loom stood idle, thus reducing the weaver's pay. Furthermore, overlookers' power to allocate beams to looms deeply affected both the arduousness of the weaver's task and the amount of money to be earned. While it made economic sense to put the beams with the best quality material, making for smooth weaving, into the looms of the ablest workers – a practice giving rise to the frequent allegation of favouritism[4] – the degree of respect a tackler was able to command from the weavers in his set depended crucially on what they perceived as fairness and justice in his dealings with them as well as the independence he managed to maintain vis-à-vis the employer. Obviously, the overlooker was sandwiched between masters' intent to extract maximum output from their workforce and the workers in his charge, whose obstinacy and even open rebellion when feeling ill-treated could make life for him very difficult indeed.[5]

While other branches of the cotton industry, such as the card and spinning rooms, were largely self-managing, in weaving the mechanical tasks and, even more so, the managerial functions involved in overlooking had come to form a specialist occupation in the wake of industrialization. The technical intricacies of the power loom as compared to its manually driven predecessor were believed to be beyond the abilities of the workers, especially since the influx of newcomers into the trade in the early nineteenth century had eroded the general command of mechanics among hand loom weavers. The managerial duties involved in overlooking followed from the need to break the workforce into factory discipline. It was only in the course of the twentieth century that overlookers shifted over from being employers' agents to the side of the operatives, a shift accompanied by the shedding of supervisory functions and concentration on mechanical specialization.[6]

When, in the closing decades of the nineteenth century, British industry began to feel the effects of foreign competition, as noted in Chapter 2, master spinners and manufacturers responded with cost cutting by means of supplying low-quality cotton or yarn, which caused a larger number of breakages when spun or woven. The resulting intensification of operative labour, however, was not spread evenly. In spinning, the adult worker, who stood in the position of subcontractor to his two assistants, called piecers, supervised and paid them a time wage out of the earnings based on the team's weekly output. When pressure mounted, spinners were able to pass onto piecers a large part of the extra work without the extra earnings,[7] as argued in Chapter 3. This kind of driving found its limits in the fixed time wages paid to piecers, who, unlike weavers, lacked any immediate interest in productivity levels, leading them to respond to intolerable pressure with go-slows.[8]

In weaving, apart from payment by the piece, it was the specific organization of the labour process that lent itself to increasing productivity without incurring the costs involved in investment in new machinery[9] or rationalized management techniques resorted to elsewhere.[10] Maintaining the quantity and quality of output per weaver, despite the supply of inferior yarn in addition to the continual speeding-up of looms,[11] was possible through ruthless exploitation of the overlooker's position, which enabled him to pressurize the weavers in his charge into intensifying their labour. The interconnection between driving and rising competition, both at home and abroad, was recognized by employers.[12] Indeed, driving intensified in the years prior to the First World War as a direct consequence of declining mill profitability.[13]

The most common method of driving was the slate system, usually combined with the posting up of wages. This involved the overlooker going round the weavers in his charge and noting down their weekly output on a slate, which gave him the opportunity of admonishing those whose output was lagging behind. Subsequently, the wage list was displayed in a prominent place in the shed for all weavers of that particular section to see how they ranked with regard to output.[14] Usually, the name of the weaver who had emerged bottom of the list was circled in red or otherwise highlighted.[15] At some mills the slate was even carried round the weaving shed to invite contempt from co-workers.[16] Thus moral pressure was exerted on less able weavers to bring their output up to average. Moreover, as they were entitled to hire as well as to discharge weavers, tacklers had the power of sanctioning alleged slackness beyond exposing operatives by means of the published wage list.

The Darwen Suicide

Complaints about driving were regularly aired at shop meetings or in the columns of the *Cotton Factory Times*. In 1892, union officials appeared before the Royal Commission on Labour to give evidence on driving in weaving sheds,[17] but the practice continued unabated. In the summer of 1901, however, an opportunity presented itself publicly to expose the evil complained of for so long. On 18 June of that year, a 17-year-old female weaver from Darwen had taken poison following her dismissal for not getting sufficient work done. At the inquest, the coroner's investigations established this as the cause of her suicide. In summing up, he condemned the driving system in the strongest terms, declaring that he

> considered it was a most extraordinary and arbitrary way of dealing with the workpeople, and it was surprising that the firm could get anyone to work for them under those conditions ... This is the worst case of driving in cotton mills that I have ever come across, and I come across a great many. I must say that morally, though perhaps not legally, I think the girl's death lies on John West, the tackler, and on the manager and master of the Olive Mill [where she had been employed].[18]

Seizing on the coroner's forthright condemnation of the driving system, the Northern Counties' Weavers' Amalgamation called on its constituent bodies to hold public meetings on driving in weaving sheds, instructed its Central Committee to take the requisite steps to have this grievance abolished, and assured the Darwen society in particular of its willingness to support them in their struggle against the practice.[19] At the public meetings duly called all over the Lancashire weaving district, driving was not only unanimously condemned, but was also demonstrated to vary by locality and even to be superable.

One crucial variable appeared to be tacklers' pay. Where driving was worst, poundage tended to be lowest.[20] Conversely, where tacklers received a fixed wage, as at Colne and Nelson, driving was rare,[21] and the slate had been abolished.[22] At Wigan, only one shed was reported to resort to the posting up of wages.[23] This is particularly significant, because at Wigan, as demonstrated in Chapter 2, weaving was almost exclusively female, with men chiefly working in the local coal-mines. Blackburn and Burnley, by contrast, were notorious for driving, which, in the case of the latter, was attributed to the preponderance of smaller mills, built and run on borrowed money.[24] This was an allusion to the room-and-power system, which, as shown in Chapter 2, was not confined to Burnley.

Throughout its anti-driving campaign, the Weavers' Amalgamation was at pains to emphasize that it was not waging a struggle against particular mills or particular individuals but trying to eradicate a system endemic in the industry as a whole.[25] This did not stop the owners of the mill from which the dead weaver had been dismissed repudiating publicly the coroner's indictment of their conduct, in an attempt to whitewash their reputation. Furthermore, they forced the weavers employed under the same tackler as their dead co-worker to sign a statement exonerating him from all objectionable conduct.[26]

The weavers' unions consistently employed the Darwen suicide to drive home to the cotton operatives the need for strong organizations as a prerequisite to combating driving successfully.

> The weavers of Lancashire [read one such appeal] ought to need no further stimulus than the simple record of the Darwen tragedy to rouse them to a determination to abolish all the elements of such a cruel and heartless system. A great and beneficial change could very soon be effected if weavers unitedly applied themselves to that end, and it will be to their lasting discredit if they allow the present opportunity to pass without securing such conditions of employment as will secure them a living under more pleasant and 'human' conditions than has been their lot in the past.[27]

Furthermore, the case was taken to the Joint Standing Committee of Employers and Operatives, which, as set out in Chapter 2, had been established so as to prevent workplace conflicts from escalating into strikes. Although employers conceded that driving did exist, no remedy could be agreed upon.

As both parties were aware that the organization of the labour process was not the only source of pressure, the blame for driving could not be pinned on tacklers alone. Young workers were under strain, with parents eager to see increases in the wages contributed to the family income, which depended on earnings other than those of the husband or father to be adequate. Thus they would urge their children to ask to be allocated extra looms as soon as possible as a way of boosting wages.[28]

In the case of 24-year-old Kate Ashling from Facit, familial pressure was at least a contributory factor in her suicide. She had not enjoyed weaving and wanted to go back to throstle spinning, but was prevented by her sister because of the better wages paid in weaving.[29] Other families could afford to be more lenient.[30] Their ability to sympathize with children under pressure at work was clearly circumscribed by their financial circumstances. Despite the association of cotton weaving and female suicides in some parents' minds, even those wishing to protect daughters from such risk would overcome their misgivings on account of the good wages to be earned.[31]

As children's pay was crucial to the family income, parents made sure that their offspring gave satisfaction at work. It was common for children who started work in the mill to learn the trade by tenting for a parent or relative, as shown in Chapter 3. In this way the child's progress in weaving could be closely monitored and assistance given when required. Unless working at the same mill as their children, parents would delegate supervision to some trustworthy individual of their acquaintance.[32] In this way relatives or friends acted as buffers between young weavers' performance at work and managerial requirements. Thus the foster parents of the Darwen weaver who had committed suicide complained at the inquest about the manager having failed to inform them that the firm, where they were employed, too, were dissatisfied with their foster daughter's performance and dismissed her straight away. This would imply that, had they received such information, they would have tried to find ways of helping her improve, perhaps by showing her some tricks of the trade. Moreover, they were aware that tacklers had been instructed to ensure that their weavers attained the productivity target set, and had warned their daughter to do her best.[33]

By pointing to sources of pressure outside the workplace, based on cotton weavers' family economy, employers managed to sidestep demands for a fixed wage for tacklers. Moreover, unionists themselves were far from unanimous on this issue. While some wanted poundage to be abolished as lying at the root of driving,[34] others were afraid that tacklers would then lose the incentive of maintaining their looms in good shape, much to the detriment of the weavers concerned.[35] Moreover, it was feared by some, employers would be more likely to drive their tacklers even harder if these were paid a standing wage. This argument effectively removed the blame from tacklers and pinned it on employers, thus enabling the weavers' unions to invite overlookers to join their fight against the driving system.[36] In the end, the Joint Standing Committee of Employers and Operatives recommended that both the slate system and the publishing of wages be abolished and that the power of dismissal be transferred from tacklers to managers.[37]

Gendering Exploitation

What makes the campaign that evolved around the Darwen suicide particularly interesting is the way in which the allegation that driving was inherent in the weaving industry meshed with the way in which both cause and effects of the campaign were being gendered. While it is true that women predominated among the weaving workforce, as demonstrated in Chapter 2, the point the unions were consistently making – that they were not hounding particular individuals, but fighting to have an entire system abolished – implied that all weavers, regardless of gender, though not of age, were subject to driving.[38] Yet when spelt out, the misery caused appeared to differ significantly along gender lines. Thus the secretary of the Blackburn Weavers' Association was reported as saying at an anti-driving meeting in that town that 'the system had sent hundreds of young lads to the army, and it caused hundreds of young girls to throw themselves away, body and soul, rather than contend with the conditions which prevailed'.[39]

That this implied not only suicide but also prostitution was made clear by a statement from a leading official of the Preston weavers' union.[40] The allegation that the factory system was driving women into prostitution harked back to the 1840s, when the Chartists had used it as an indictment of industrialization.[41] In both cases the argument achieved an inversion of cause and effect, in that the exploitation inherent in the capitalist mode of production was submerged by women's supposed unfitness to cope.

Focusing on the youth of driving victims, by contrast, made sense in a trade in which skill increased in proportion to experience gained, as demonstrated in Chapter 3. Thus the particular vulnerability of the young was reflected in the age of those committing suicide. While acknowledging differences of stamina and adeptness in the weaving workforce, the unions felt that these were adequately accounted for by the piece rate system and should therefore not be made the cause of dismissal.[42] However, the unions' perception of these differences was clearly gendered, with stamina, and possibly also adeptness, being seen as attributes of maleness and closely linked to men's ability to maintain a family on their wages. Thus David Shackleton, secretary of the Darwen weavers' union, claimed that the 'disgrace of discharge' was felt particularly keenly by weavers who were heads of families.[43] At Accrington, by contrast, the local Weavers' Friendly Society, which operated outside the trade union movement, acknowledged that dismissal could be very hard for young people, too, when their earnings were crucial for keeping their families in relative comfort.[44]

Financial considerations did matter in an industry in which the difference between men's and women's wages was minimal as a result of all being paid the same piece rates. As a consequence, male weavers were unable to support their families out of their wages alone, a state of affairs under which weavers' union officials, and Shackleton in particular, smarted, and which he chose to ignore in his anti-driving rhetoric. Wages, however, could not be separated from skill, which determined not only the amount of pay a weaver took home at the end of the week, but also her or his standing both in the shed and in the community at large. Hence weavers' abhorrence of the slate, on which each of them might be exposed as failing to reach average output, the implication being both that dismissal was looming and that this weaver was lacking in skill.

Throughout the campaign, driving was consistently portrayed as being primarily directed at female weavers. The *Yorkshire Factory Times* had followed the events in the wake of the Darwen suicide closely, although, or possibly because, driving was virtually unknown in the woollen industry.[45] One of its comments, which reiterated the points made by various cotton unionists, read as follows:

> The worst of it is, too, that its cruel effects for the most part fall on the weaker vessels – our mothers and sisters and daughters – and actually make life for so many of them not worth living, as here demonstrated. Perhaps the most aggravating and disgraceful feature of the Darwen case is that a mere girl of seventeen or eighteen is ruthlessly cast adrift because she fails to earn more than 22s. a week ... A possible predilection for suicide affords no justification for mercilessly thrusting our weaker and more sensitive sisters to the wall, unless our Christianity is a mere cloak to assume on occasion.[46]

Through this depiction of women as the primary victims of driving, appeal was made to men's chivalry (a term actually used in the article) to come to their female co-workers' aid by shielding them from this evil. One Preston official capped this standard line of argument by stating: 'When women and girls get home after the factory's loosed they are so exhausted that they are not fit for much, and we are not likely to have a strong race of operatives in the coming generation.'[47]

Ultimately, this remark implied, driving jeopardized Britain's leading role as an industrial nation through the detrimental effects it had on women's reproductive capacity. This unionist thus agreed with contemporary concern about the 'fitness of the race' that had emerged as a result of the poor physical condition of many of the recruits to the Boer War, still fresh in people's minds.

The Darwen suicide gained publicity that extended well beyond Lancashire. It was reported by the Women's Trade Union League in its *Women's Trades Union Review*, which backed the demand for a fixed wage for tacklers.[48] In her series of articles entitled 'Victims of Our Industrial System: The Cotton Workers of Lancashire', written for *Young Oxford*, a monthly magazine devoted to the Ruskin Hall Movement, Ada Nield Chew, at that time working as an organizer for the Women's Trade Union League, also took up the issue when dealing with cotton weaving. After deploring the ubiquity of driving, she attributed both the high rate of suicides and the large number of inmates in Lancashire asylums to the perpetual strain under which weavers had to work. Whilst suicides, she alleged, were 'so common that they are passed over without comment', the public had been roused by the Darwen case and the spirited remarks made by the coroner. Using language much stronger than that of either coroner or union officials, she portrayed the incident as an indictment of a system in which class and gender intermingled, thus victimizing female weavers both as women and as workers.

> What can be more degrading [she asked] than that men should make money as a result of driving women to the point of suicide and madness? If things were called by proper names occurrences such as that just related would be termed murder. But our commercial system makes even murder legitimate and we call it by another name and tell ourselves that it cannot be helped.[49]

Industrial Manners

The effectiveness of the unions' anti-driving campaign can be gauged from the employers' response, voiced in one of their publications, the *Textile Mercury*. What put the employers on edge was the impression given by the unions that their campaign had won them public support. Employers were particularly concerned that union propaganda might result in legislation to curb driving, which they held to be indispensable for exerting social control and for increasing productivity. They were thus at pains to show that tacklers and the managerial powers conferred on them were necessary to ensure discipline on the shopfloor. The slate system, they contended, was a safeguard against operatives being cheated in the reckoning up of their wages.[50]

There was one grievance, however, the existence of which employers did acknowledge, and that was tacklers' rudeness towards female weavers.[51]

> Tacklers are too often rough and coarse in their language [the *Textile Mercury* claimed] and many women of gentle and refined natures must suffer considerably when they are harshly spoken to by such men. It is even possible that some timid and hysterical[52] girl might, in mental terror, and not knowing what she was doing, do as the girl in Darwen is alleged to have done – commit suicide exactly as school-children occasionally do in very similar circumstances. All this, however, while wholly regrettable, is to a great extent inevitable.[53]

Thus, playing down the sad incident at Darwen by infantilizing women, employers took up a grievance frequently voiced by female weavers, trying to deflect the unions' campaign against driving into one for the improvement of 'industrial manners'. This allowed employers, moreover, to turn the whole affair into an attack on weavers, from whose ranks the vast majority of tacklers were recruited.

> Would it not be well for the weavers' unions [they asked] to institute schools for teaching good manners and helping on the development of a higher state of refinement, so that when their male members are promoted to be tacklers they may carry with them these better feelings into their new sphere of labour?[54]

What the employers' mouthpiece glossed over in this piece as 'industrial manners' was one particular constellation in which gender conflict in the weaving industry came to the fore. Whenever a female weaver was confronted by a tackler, a cloth-looker – whose job involved inspecting finished pieces of cloth for faults – or a manager and required to account for the quality of her work, she found herself entangled in two types of power relationships being superimposed on and reinforcing each other, with the man representing both male and managerial authority and the woman having to try and hold her own despite being doubly disadvantaged, both as a woman and as a subordinate worker. In the words of one female weaver, overlookers 'were the men to fear'. Some of them were real bullies, and 'anyone who was timid, those men could put the fear of God in them, they could and they did, too'.[55] Yet it may be precisely because some women at least refused to be intimidated that male figures of authority resorted to particularly coarse and rough language to lend force to their authority. Nellie Devine, who had been a weaver for 26 years[56] when called to give evidence on fining before the Truck Committee, as a representative of the Oldham Weavers' Union, on the committee of which she served for at least 10 years,[57] remarked when making her statement: 'It is not every woman who can defend herself before the manager in the warehouse, especially as some of the people are not kind in their remarks and try to frighten the weaver who speaks in her own defence.'[58]

What is remarkable therefore is not that some women failed to stand up to figures in whom coalesced the power of men and of management, but that some women obviously required an extra measure of intimidation to become subdued. As one tackler was reported by a weaver as having said to her on one occasion: 'Thou has [sic] been a weaver long enough, thou should never tell a tackler what to do.'[59] Women did stand up to male figures of authority they believed to be acting unfairly, as the following incident shows. At a mill where a tackler was bullying a girl over not turning off enough cloth, an older female weaver reprimanded him for his attitude. She also spoke up against the manager, who had apparently been called in to support the tackler. When he started swearing at her, she threatened to bring the factory inspector in.[60] This woman obviously knew how best to defend herself, and one is intrigued to know to what extent her pluck was a function of her age,[61] her skill and standing as a weaver and perhaps also as a married woman.

The Accrington Suicide

The campaign around the Darwen suicide failed to bring about any improvement in weavers' working conditions. The only concession unions had been able to wring from employers was a readiness to deal with any authenticated case of driving that might be brought before them by the union officials.[62] Such an opportunity presented itself nearly two years later, when the Darwen incident was replicated, except that this time the scene was Accrington, and luckily the young woman who had tried to drown herself[63] was rescued by a passer-by. Thus she was able to testify that her attempted suicide had been due to her tackler threatening to dismiss her unless her performance improved. When her case was taken to the Joint Standing Committee, there was no denying that it had been caused by driving.[64] This forced employers to change tack and, while acknowledging that driving did exist, they individualized the issue by attributing it to particular tacklers who were overbearing, and shifted responsibility for it to weavers clamouring for more looms than they were able to cope with.[65] Union officials and employers alike felt that young weavers were promoted to looms of their own before attaining proficiency at their trade,[66] following the introduction of compulsory schooling. This should have had the effect of delaying adolescents' promotion to a full complement of looms by about three to four years. Most weaving families, however, were unable to hold out so long without substantial extra income. Hence the pressure brought to bear by parents on children to move on to a full set of looms by the age of 18, although the period of training on the job had been considerably curtailed.[67] Otherwise, the same arguments as in the Darwen case were repeated by unionists and the public at large, portraying women as particularly vulnerable to driving[68] as a result of their being naturally disadvantaged in the competition with men.

In July 1903, the *Women's Trades Union Review* published an article on driving by Annie Marland Brodie, an ex-Lancashire cotton worker who had gone on to become a Women's Trade Union League organizer. In her article, extracts of which were reprinted in the *Cotton Factory Times*,[69] she exposed one of the methods employed by tacklers to increase output. She cited the example of a female weaver who, although already topping the wage list of her set, was asked by her overlooker to make 1s. more per week so that he could use her to drive his other weavers even more. 'This working woman,' wrote Annie Marland-Brodie, 'to her everlasting honour, refused to make this slavery of the loom more severe, and ended by smashing the "wages slate" into atoms.' Such spirited conduct the author attributed to this woman's staunch trade unionism, which set an example she wished to see emulated by women everywhere. After pointing out what each of the three parties involved in driving – weavers, overlookers and employers – could and should do to bring this practice to an end, she went to the root of the matter by advocating the abolition of payment by the piece in weaving as the surest way of eradicating the driving evil.[70]

This remedy, however, was anything but popular with Lancashire weavers.[71] For this reason, and because of the fundamental nature of the change involved, unions shied away from pressing for a time wage.[72] Weavers' opposition to a fixed wage presumably stemmed from the idea that piece rates allowed them to exercise some degree of control over their earnings. Given the way in which rates were set, this was certainly an illusion in the case of most operatives, but may have contained at least a grain of truth for the fittest and ablest. This would go to show how piece rates, apart from putting pressure on workers to exert themselves, also operated towards eroding solidarity at the workplace.

In 1903, the agitation focused on the poundage system, which the unions were determined to have abolished, even hinting at the possibility of a general strike to achieve their goal.[73] Moreover, attempts were made to gain the support of the overlookers' union by portraying tacklers as resentful of a system that placed the onus of ensuring maximum productivity on them.[74] Tacklers themselves tried to alert weavers to their own predicament, which arose from their ambivalent position in the labour process. Thus they presented themselves as 'sandwiched between the devil and the deep blue sea' and 'creatures of circumstances', who were themselves pressurized by employers to drive their weavers.[75]

In an interview with the *Cotton Factory Times*, James Tattersall, the secretary of the National Association of Powerloom Overlookers, was at pains to refute the allegations levelled against tacklers in the columns of that paper by arguing that any action on the part of tacklers to the detriment of their weavers would also have adverse effects on themselves. He came out strongly against poundage, adducing as the only reason why it was favoured by some that 'it cannot be said they have not earned the wages received'. Moreover, he tried to lend his argument more weight by pointing to the USA. Unlike the employers, who made competition from the United States the excuse for the persistence of driving,[76] Tattersall used the comparison to show that the fixed wage paid to overlookers in the USA did not impair the industry's performance.[77] This rapprochement led in 1906 to the unions of both groups of workers joining the Northern Counties Textile Federation in order to minimize friction between both trades and to work jointly for the substitution of a fixed wage for poundage.[78]

Unfortunately, incidents such as those at Darwen and Accrington were anything but uncommon. These two cases had been singled out by the weavers' unions, because each time driving had been irrefutably established as the cause of these desperate deeds. The only other detailed report about a female suicide that it has been possible to cull from the pages of the *Cotton Factory Times* during the period under consideration received a great deal of attention, because it involved two people, an 18-year-old weaver and her 12-year-old sister. While the inquest established dismissal for failing to give satisfaction at work as causing the elder sister to drown herself, there was considerable doubt about the younger sister having joined her voluntarily.[79]

The *Cotton Factory Times* abounded with reports about weavers' suicides.[80] Some of these concerned male weavers, all of whom had taken their own lives for reasons unrelated to work and mainly to do with illness.[81] What appears to have played an important role in male suicides, apart from the physical pain involved in some cases, was men's despair at their inability any longer to provide for their families and the erosion of their masculinity that this loss of the role of provider entailed. Disease or some kind of physical impairment was also present in a few female suicides, but as contributory rather than sole causes, in that they undermined even further women's efforts to attain the productivity targets set.[82]

Fining

In the unions' anti-driving campaign, women featured exclusively as victims. Yet even female weavers celebrated for their pluck failed to break the mould, as the example of an earlier campaign against fining demonstrates. Fining, though usually classed separately, was also a form of driving. Most fines, imposed much to the chagrin of weavers, were aimed at maintaining discipline at work. Operatives were penalized for being late, leaving looms too long, failing to send a notice within a specified time when being absent, or even for being found working during meal hours by a factory inspector.[83]

Apart from being fined for breaches of factory discipline, it was common for weavers to have a certain amount deducted from the price to be paid for a particular piece of cloth, when that cloth was found to be faulty. By fining weavers for cloth judged to be defective, employers aimed to combine pressure on workers to increase output with ensuring the quality of the goods produced. Owing to their lack of experience, young weavers were more likely to be fined for defective cloth than older and more experienced ones.[84] Opposition to fining derived not only from the arbitrariness of the penalties imposed, but also from the fact that hardly ever were allowances made for the conditions under which faults had occurred. Fining placed the blame on the weaver regardless of possible defects of the machinery or the quality of the yarn supplied. Obviously, weavers who had already lost out through having their work rendered more arduous through bad yarn or having spent hours unpicking a flaw in the cloth resented being fined on top.

The power relationship played out in fining was noted by a half-timer working as a cloth-looker's clerk. Though male, he was more inclined to defer to female weavers on account of the age difference and therefore more sensitive to the power exerted by his master. 'I never quite got used,' he wrote retrospectively in his autobiography, 'to the sarcastic way in which the cut-looker spoke to these women, who were often old enough to be my mother, or even in some cases, my grandmother, and I greatly disliked docking off the sixpences and shillings.'[85]

When, by contrast, cloth-lookers had male weavers up to the warehouse to account for flaws in their cuts, they were deprived of the gender element of their authority and hence, rather than confront their subordinates openly, were reported to resort to hypocrisy and deviousness,[86] or even to let them off scot-free.[87] This kind of male collusion not only helped introduce a differential between male and female wages, but also to make male weavers appear to be the more skilled workers. When fining did occur, male weavers felt the slight on their competence as well as the financial loss keenly. As one male weaver said, with reference to the 1940s, when the practice still persisted: 'It would make you cry … I've nearly come away in tears.'[88]

Trade unions had pressed for cotton weaving to be exempted from the 1896 Truck Act, as noted in Chapter 2, in order to retain the right of examining whether or not a fault in the cloth was attributable to the weaver. As long as they failed to have fines abolished altogether, unions insisted that every fine be made a question of examination and proof. This appeared to be particularly necessary in view of the arbitrariness involved. Union officials alleged that some of the cloth-lookers inflicting penalties were expected to produce a certain amount in fines during the week. They would further cite the examples of firms which had abolished fining without suffering any deterioration of quality in their products, to refute employers' claims that fining was the only way to ensure quality production. Moreover, they pointed out that some managers actually condoned faulty weaving by allowing operatives to calculate whether they would lose less money by mending the flaw and suffering a setback in wages or by leaving it in and paying a fine.[89]

Making a Stand against Fining

In 1886, the arbitrariness of fining was highlighted by the case of 22-year-old Martha Ann Kilburn from Rochdale. This weaver had had a very bad warp in, which had caused her a great deal of trouble. When she had finally managed to get the last piece of cloth from this warp off, the cut-looker found it damaged. While not disputing that the cloth was faulty and willing to be fined for it, she refused to buy the whole piece at market value and take it home with her. Though in clear contravention of the Truck Act, this was the custom at the firm where she was employed. She then decided to give notice and leave that mill, whereupon she was summoned for breach of contract. Although the magistrates found against her despite the flimsiness of the case, she still refused to pay as much as a farthing. About a month later, she was summoned again and ordered to pay damages, the costs of the first trial as well as the costs of the summons in the second case. The employer decided not to enforce the order for a month, obviously hoping she would give in. Still she refused to pay. As no action was taken at the expiry of that month, it was generally assumed that the matter had been dropped. A few days later, however, she was arrested, to serve seven days in prison in lieu of the fine. On her release she was celebrated by union officials and weavers as a heroine who had stood up for her principles and suffered martyrdom rather than relent.

At a large public meeting, at which she was presented with a clock as a testimonial of the weavers' esteem, the speeches made by the union officials as well as the resolutions adopted showed that the Kilburn case was used to improve unionization among Rochdale weavers and to induce them to join the Northern Counties' Amalgamation. Furthermore, the point was driven home that working men could and should send at least one of their number to sit on the magistrates' bench so as to balance the manufacturing interest represented there and thus prevent the recurrence of such biased verdicts as had been passed in the Kilburn case.[90]

The central issue around which speeches revolved was the abuse to which fining lent itself. Weavers were painfully aware that their trade was one of the few in which fining was practised at all.⁹¹ John Andrews, the editor of the *Cotton Factory Times*, attributed this, in accordance with his paper's policy,⁹² to the predominance of women in cotton weaving, whom he believed to be naturally less able than men to put up any resistance to such abuse,⁹³ despite the fact that he spoke at a meeting convened to celebrate an instance of such female resistance. He went on to underpin his contention by citing the recent case of a 15-year-old girl who had drowned herself on account of two bad warps she had had in. By thus placing Martha Ann Kilburn in the context of a succession of females ground down by overbearing forces, he portrayed her as quite exceptional, if not unique. Thus even her case was marshalled to emphasize the victimization of women.

Despite some success at local level,⁹⁴ the need for efforts by the weavers' unions to have all methods of driving abolished persisted at least into the inter-war period. As late as 1927, Martha Ann Kilburn's spirited conduct was remembered, when a fine imposed on a 24-year-old female weaver for faulty cloth caused her to commit suicide.⁹⁵ This incident was used by the unions to set off another campaign for the legal prohibition of fining, echoing that of 1913, when a bill had been promoted by the Weavers' Amalgamation for the abolition of all fines⁹⁶ which had come to nothing.⁹⁷

Exploiting Gender

The aims pursued by the parties involved in the anti-driving campaign were obvious enough, and all of them used gender, though in different ways and to different ends. Employers echoed the prevailing infantilization of women to play down the detrimental effects of driving by likening female suicides to children acting rashly on the spur of the moment. The Women's Trade Union League, too, deployed gender to further its own objectives. It highlighted female suicides in order to drive home to women the need to organize. And Ada Nield Chew, a League organizer and a socialist, used these incidents in order more forcefully to condemn an economic system so competitive as ruthlessly to weed out those unable to keep up. Unlike Annie Marland-Brodie, who, by advocating unionization, appealed to women actively to further their own interests, Ada Nield Chew portrayed them as helpless victims of an overbearing system of exploitation.

Weavers' unions, finally, incorporated the three cases described into their own agenda. They wished to enhance unionization, improve working conditions and change managerial structures in a way they believed would benefit weavers. By doing this, they were simultaneously working at a differentiation of the workforce along gender lines. Precisely because of any lack of distinctions based on the labour process, male weavers were eager to mark themselves off from their female co-workers, portraying themselves as having more stamina, more skill and more resilience. True, presenting women weavers as the victims of ruthless exploitation was an effective publicity ploy and certainly helped win public opinion and politicians[98] over to the union point of view, according as it did with contemporary notions of femininity and the prevailing feminine imagery of suicide.[99] But in the very male world of trade unionism, too, the portrayal of women as victims helped affirm the masculinity of male weavers compelled to work in a predominantly female trade.

Male operatives and union officials in particular used the anti-driving campaigns to enhance their self-image, portraying themselves as less vulnerable to pressure and hence both obliged and able to come to the support of their victimized female co-workers by agitating against the driving evil. While the cases at Darwen and Accrington were seized upon both to condemn driving and to demonstrate how women, quite unlike men, were crushed by it, even Martha Ann Kilburn was made to serve the same purpose by being celebrated as an exception rather than as in any way representative of women's frequent resistance to the damaging effects of their working environment.

While not denying the hardship women suffered from the pressure placed on them to perform well, it is argued here that female weavers' suicides, rather than resulting from any lack of resilience or abundance of sensitivity believed to be ingredients of an assumed female nature, were the outcome of the specific opportunities offered women in the weaving industry. Weaving was seen by those involved in it as a skilled trade, as demonstrated in Chapter 3, and female weavers were proud of possessing the abilities and faculties required to process yarn of infinite variations of quality into cloths of the most intricate patterns. Furthermore, the large number of female weavers who carried on working after marriage was attributable, not only to economic necessity, but also to women's unwillingness to give up a job from which they derived some degree of personal satisfaction, as also argued in Chapter 3. True, on account of the piece rate system, female weavers were under enormous pressure, if they wanted to maintain a certain level of pay and retain their jobs. Yet each penny women carried home at the end of the working week gave them a feeling of satisfaction with their own ability to earn on the basis of the skill they had at their command.

Those weavers, both male and female, who were reprimanded for not getting off enough work would try and find alternative employment. They might transfer to older mills equipped with more worn-out machinery, where the pace of work was slower.[100] Where this was not possible owing to the highly localized way in which cotton weaving had specialized, there were far fewer alternative employments open to women than to men, unless they were prepared to sustain a severe drop in wages.

Moreover, reprimands for slackness undermined weavers' reputation both at work and in the community at large. The hiring of weavers was left to tacklers precisely because they were supposed to be able, on the basis of their intimate knowledge of the local community, to pick the best weavers from among those presenting themselves at the factory gate in search of employment.[101] Thus, when his daughters were discharged from a weaving shed for alleged bad work, their father insisted on an apology from the manager, because he would not have his daughters defamed.[102] And at the meeting convened in honour of Martha Ann Kilburn, the union officials present took great care in their speeches to emphasize her proficiency at her trade. By portraying her as an expert weaver, they not only enhanced her reputation as a skilled worker, but also showed up the arbitrariness of fining.

Conclusion

It is suggested here that the suicides by young female weavers were desperate acts committed by women who had given up all hope of ever establishing a reputation for being skilled workers. The preceding chapter has shown women weavers discursively laying claim to the masculine attribute of skill. This analysis of suicides by female weavers has demonstrated the significance of skill as a core element of their identity. Failure to develop this quality, as their suicides dramatized even more convincingly than their discourse, was tantamount to failure in terms of personal development. Precisely because women weavers' identity revolved largely around their jobs – an issue explored further in Chapter 6 – failure to achieve such a level of competence undermined these women's self-confidence and self-esteem. Lacking the opportunity of establishing themselves in an occupation as skilled and well paid as weaving, some of them saw no alternative to committing suicide.[103] It was the availability of such alternative employment to men which acted as a buffer against the effects of driving on male weavers. In fact, a man could not but enhance his reputation as a worker by leaving the predominantly female job of weaving.

Failure to become an expert weaver brought in its wake severe losses, not only in financial terms, but also in terms of personal development. In fact, the two were inseparable. The more a woman excelled at weaving, the better her income, the higher her reputation, and the greater her satisfaction, not least because she successfully measured up to men. The same logic lay at the base of male weavers' and unions' consistent portrayal of women as victims. This approach helped them to construct gender difference and thus to contain the threat posed to their masculinity by the labour process-based equality with their female co-workers. Thus difference emerges as the key element structuring relations between men and women, its overriding importance becoming particularly clear in conditions where it is constructed in the face of gender equality.

Notes

1. See, for example, *CFT*, 7.12.1913, p.5.
2. Joyce (1980, p.97). He has used this observation to explain cotton workers' willingness to submit both to authority at the workplace and to increased workloads. In the context of this study, however, it is seen more favourably as an indication of the centrality of paid work to women weavers' identity.
3. See, for example, *CFT*, 17.9.1889, p.5.
4. For the sexual implications of favouritism, see Lambertz (1985).
5. See Melling (1980, p.191).
6. See Turner (1962, p.159).
7. See Lazonick (1979, p.253).
8. See Lazonick (1981c, pp.503–4).
9. See Copeland (1909).
10. See Melling (1980, pp.194ff).
11. See Ellison (1968, p.37).
12. See Commission on Labour, *PP*, 1892, XXXV, p.258; see also 'A Manager's Views', *CFT*, 1.5.1903, p.4.
13. See Firth (1986, p.71).
14. For a US example of the posting up of wages, here even on a daily basis, and interestingly relating to the exclusively male workforce in the spinning room, see Blewett (1990, p.171).
15. See, for example, *CFT*, 5.1.1900, p.6.
16. See Firth (1986, p.72).
17. See *PP*, 1892, XXXV, p.17 and *passim*.
18. *CFT*, 21.6.1901, p.7.
19. Ibid.
20. See Commission on Labour, *PP*, 1892, XXXV, p.155.
21. See *CFT*, 28.6.1901, p.5.
22. See *CFT*, 21.6.1901, p.5; see also *Webb Collection*, XLVII, p.185.
23. See *CFT*, 28.6.1901, p.5.
24. See Commission on Labour, *PP*, 1892, XXXV, p.17.
25. See, for example, *CFT*, 21.6.1901, p.5; 28.6.1901, pp.5 and 7.
26. See *CFT*, 21.6.1901, p.5.
27. *CFT*, 21.6.1901, p.1.
28. See, for example, *CFT*, 5.7.1901, p.4. See also *CFT*, 26.5.1905, p.8, for a 13-year-old tenter who attempted suicide after the weaver she was tenting for had told her mother that the girl was unfit to tent.
29. See *CFT*, 28.6.1901, p.4.
30. See, for example, *CFT*, 30.10.1908, p.1.
31. See, for example, Bolton Oral History, tape 28A, p.10.
32. See, for example, Committee on Truck Acts, *PP*, 1908, Cd.4443. lix, p.395.
33. See *CFT*, 21.6.1901, p.7.
34. See, for example, *CFT*, 21.6.1901, p.5; see also Commission on Labour, *PP*, 1892, XXXV, p.154.
35. See *CFT*, 21.6.1901, p.1.
36. See *CFT*, 28.6.1901, p.7.
37. See *CFT*, 12.7.1901, p.1.

38 See, for example, the article that opened the debate about the issue in the *CFT*, which deplored the existence of 'a system which has been the cause of so much misery to thousands of young men and women in the country' (*CFT*, 21.6.1901, p.1).
39 *CFT*, 28.6.1901, p.7.
40 See *CFT*, 21.6.1901, p.5.
41 See Schwarzkopf (1991, p.40).
42 See *CFT*, 21.6.1901, p.1.
43 See *CFT*, 21.6.1901, p.5.
44 See *CFT*, 26.7.1901, p.6.
45 The absence of driving in the Yorkshire woollen industry cannot be accounted for by the proportion of women workers, who had come to predominate in weaving; see Busfield (1988, p.64).
46 *CFT*, 21.6.1901, p.5; see also 21.6.1901, p.1; 12.7.1901, p.8.
47 *CFT*, 21.6.1901, p.5.
48 See *Women's Trades Union Review*, January 1902, p.3, *WTUL papers*.
49 *Young Oxford*, September 1901, p.435.
50 See *Textile Mercury*, 6.7.1901, p.4.
51 See, for example, *CFT*, 26.11.1886, p.5; 31.12.1886, p.5; 21.10.1904, p.5.
52 The use of this term, commonly employed to denote the general instability and lack of resilience of the female system, both physical and psychological, emphasizes the employers' intention to play down the Darwen suicide by making it appear the result of some mental derangement on the part of the victim.
53 *Textile Mercury*, 6.7.1901, p.5.
54 *Textile Mercury*, 13.7.1901, p.26.
55 Roberts (1981), respondent A1P, p.8.
56 See Committee on Truck Acts, *PP*, 1908, Cd.4443. lix, p.427.
57 See Liddington and Norris (1985, p.98).
58 Committee on Truck Acts, *PP*, 1908, Cd.4443. lix, p.428.
59 Roberts (1981), respondent H1P, p.8.
60 See ibid., respondent C1P, p.42.
61 For the example of a 67-year-old weaver acting as 'spokeswoman on any occasion of moment', see *CFT*, 7.2.1913, p.5.
62 See *CFT*, 10.4.1903, p.1.
63 Drowning appears to have been the method preferred by female suicides. In the third quarter of the nineteenth century, in all of England and Wales, 33 per cent of female suicides drowned themselves, while 25 per cent hanged themselves, 17 per cent used poison and 13 per cent cut their throats. During the last quarter of the century there occurred a shift among female suicides towards poisoning themselves; see Bailey (1998, p.141).
64 See Records of the Joint Committee, 8.1903, *DDX*, 1274/13; see also Records of the Northern Counties' Amalgamation, Reports of General Council Meetings, 4.4.1903 and 16.5.1903, *DDX*, 1274/14.
65 See *Textile Manufacturer*, 15.5.1903, p.146.
66 See *CFT*, 12.7.1901, p.8.
67 See *CFT*, 12.7.1901, p.1.
68 See, for example, *CFT*, 10.4.1903, p.5; 24.4.1903, p.4; 8.5.1903, p.5; 29.5.1903, p.5.
69 See *CFT*, 10.7.1903, p.8.
70 See *Women's Trades Union Review*, July 1903, pp.5–7, *WTUL papers*.

71 See, for example, *CFT*, 12.7.1901, p.8.
72 See, for example, *CFT*, 10.7.1903, p.8.
73 See *CFT*, 24.4.1903, p.4.
74 See *CFT*, 24.4.1903, pp.4–5.
75 See *CFT*, 1.5.1903, p.4.
76 See, for example, 'A Manager's Views', *CFT*, 1.5.1903, p.4.
77 Ibid.
78 See General Union of Associations of Loom Overlookers, *Almanack and Guide*, 1907. This regional federation had been preceded by some local federations, as in Burnley in 1892 and in Blackburn in 1902; see Trodd (1978, p.302).
79 See *CFT*, 14.5.1886, p.5.
80 See, for example, *CFT* 3.12.1886, p.5; 6.12.1891, p.7; 11.12.1891, p.6; 5.7.1901, p.4.
81 See, for example, *CFT*, 28.6.1901, p.4; 15.8.1913, p.6. This tallies with the results yielded by Olive Anderson's analysis of suicide, according to whom suicide was closely related to ill-health and, in the case of men, the aggravation of the problems of old age; see Anderson (1987, pp.63, 65).
82 See, for example, *CFT*, 15.8.1913, p.6; 29.8. 1913, p.5. Apart from the fact that the relevant Coroner's Inquest Records are no longer extant, newspaper reports have been found to give more detailed accounts of the context in which suicides occurred than the transcripts of the proceedings of the Coroner's Court; see Davies (1991, p.104). The non-existence of the relevant records, coupled with the recording of suicides up to 1911 under the heading of 'violent deaths' and 'uncertified causes' by the Registrar-General, obviate any quantitative analysis of suicides for the period under consideration. Even assuming *CFT* reporting about male weavers' suicides concealed driving as the main cause, this would only go to corroborate the analysis that women were deliberately portrayed as victims.
83 See Committee on Truck Acts, *PP*, 1908, Cd.4443.lix, p.270; see also Employment of Women, *PP*, 1893–4, XXXVII, pt. I, p.663. For an, admittedly excessive, list of 'cloth faults' liable to fining, see *CFT*, 26.2.1909, p.1.
84 See Committee on Truck Acts, *PP*, 1908, Cd.4443. lix, p.396.
85 Brooks (1926, p.125).
86 See, for example, *CFT*, 11.6.1886, p.5.
87 See, for example, *CFT*, 4.7.1890, p.4.
88 Ross (1991, p.110).
89 See Committee on Truck Acts, *PP*, 1908, Cd.4443. lix, pp.391ff.
90 See *CFT*, 29.1.1886, pp.1 and 5; 12.3.1886, p.4; 19.3.1886, p.6.
91 For the practice of fining in home work see Lewis (1984, p.61).
92 See, for example, *CFT*, 4.12.1885, p.1; 16.11.1888, p.1.
93 *CFT*, 19.3.1886, p.6; see also 4.12.1885, p.1.
94 See, for example, *CFT*, 7.12.1906, p.4, and 6.6.1913, p.6 for Darwen, and 17.1.1908, p.3 for Accrington.
95 See *CFT*, 27.5.1927, p.2.
96 See, for example, *CFT*, 29.8.1913, p.5; 21.11.1913, pp.1 and 5.
97 See *CFT*, 13.5.1927, pp.1 and 3; 10.6.1927, p.2; see also *Liverpool Weekly Post*, 30.7.1927, p.7.
98 See, for example, United Textile Factory Workers' Association, Report of the Deputation to the Home Secretary, 26.2.1914, p.8, quoted in Fowler and Wyke (1993, p.33).

99 As more women were confined for insanity than men and suicide was seen as a direct product of mental derangement, Victorians believed suicides to be more common in women than in men. Additionally women, considered lesser beings, were regarded as lacking the will-power and courage required to resist suicidal impulses; see Davies (1991, p.94). The persistence of such beliefs can be traced in Ada Nield Chew's article on driving in *Young Oxford*; see note 49.
100 See Miss E.B. Tape 655 MSU TLSL.
101 See Savage (1985, p.181); see also Lancashire Textile Project, respondent AH10, p.14.
102 See *CFT*, 13.2.1891, p.4.
103 This is further corroborated from a comparative perspective. In his study of suicides in Victorian Hull, Bailey has found that males and females in the 15 to 24 age cohort had the lowest average rate of suicide, which moreover declined over the Victorian period. In the 1890s, however, the rate for females in that cohort rose noticeably so that, in the closing decades of the nineteenth century, the female suicide rate exceeded the male one in age group 15 to 19, while at all other times the reverse was true. Significantly, in the case of female suicides, economic motives were quite uncommon; see Bailey (1998, pp.166, 177).

Chapter 5

Making a Bid for a Family Wage: the Struggle around the Automatic Loom

In the Lancashire cotton weaving industry, the opening of the twentieth century saw the harbinger of potentially momentous change in the shape of a new piece of essential production technology, the Northrop loom. Though expensive to acquire, it held out the promise of enhancing the performance of the industry in Lancashire, which had come increasingly to feel the pinch of international competition, as argued in Chapter 2. Yet this did not make adoption of the loom a foregone conclusion. Manufacturers and trade unions, as well as male and female weavers, judged the machine variously to present a great opportunity, a grave danger or a total irrelevance. These judgments and the actions they set in motion were shaped by economic calculations, political considerations of the distribution of power between employers and unions and the constraints imposed by the specific organization of the industry. In all of these areas, the gender division of labour and power was central to the conditions of the industry as they had evolved since the onset of mechanization. As a consequence, gender played a crucial role in the ways in which the implementation of change was both attempted and resisted.

The Powerloom

Cotton weaving had remained untroubled by technological innovation since 1784, when Edmund Cartwright had invented the first, admittedly crude and short-lived, powerloom to operate in an early kind of factory environment.[1] After a series of necessary modifications[2] the machine was ready for use in the nascent weaving sheds by the third decade of the nineteenth century.[3] Yet it was not until the early Victorian years that powerlooms were installed on a large scale, with implementation receiving a further boost from the technical improvements made in the mid-1840s.[4] Subsequent modifications left the design of the Lancashire loom, as it became known, fundamentally unchanged, while enabling it to operate faster.[5] Concurrently, the machine was being adapted to weaving increasingly finer varieties of cloth of more even quality.

These technical modifications enabled manufacturers to expand the machine contingent assigned to one weaver. In the 1840s, two looms had been operated by one adult weaver with the help of two juvenile assistants. By the 1880s, one worker operated between four and six looms,⁶ in the latter case relying on the assistance of a tenter.⁷ Growth of output was thus the result of a combination of technological improvement and an intensification of labour. As a consequence of mounting loom speed, weavers were having to replace exhausted bobbins with full ones in the shuttle at ever more frequent intervals, and to piece up a growing number of warp threads breaking under the strain of fast-running looms. Both operations required the machine to be stopped.

The Automatic Loom

The need to stop machines in order to change shuttles acted as an incentive on inventors to design a loom that ran continuously as a way of increasing output. Following a number of abortive attempts, some of which dated back to the first half of the nineteenth century,⁸ the first viable so-called 'automatic loom' was finally ready to be marketed by 1894. It had been developed in the USA by James Northrop of the firm of George Draper & Sons and boasted a mechanism replacing exhausted with full bobbins in the shuttle with the machine running at full speed. In addition, an accurate warp stop motion was attached to the loom, which stopped the machine automatically on the breakage of a warp thread, thus relieving the weaver from the need to monitor closely the loom for broken threads.⁹ Weaving had to wait until after the Second World War for the next innovation, the shuttleless loom, to make its appearance.¹⁰

Unlike previous alterations to the Lancashire loom, the automatic, as Mass has pointed out,¹¹ truly represented an innovation, requiring as it did the labour process to be fundamentally reorganized in order for its labour-saving and hence cost-cutting potential to be exploited to the full. This involved both expanding the machine assignment per weaver and confining the tasks of the loom operative to weaving proper, while delegating all operations accidental to weaving to ancillary labour hired to oil and clean the looms, take finished cloth to the warehouse, fetch weft and fill the batteries from which empty shuttles were replenished. Furthermore, to prevent the resulting growth in productivity from operating exclusively to the weavers' benefit, significantly augmenting their weekly earnings off the expanded number of looms operated by one worker, piece rates had to be adjusted downwards.

Averting Opposition

In view of the economic need for this twofold intensification of labour in conjunction with alterations to the long-established price lists to make investing in the new loom worthwhile, manufacturers warily anticipated fierce trade union opposition to any attempt at introducing the new machines. As the *Textile*

Recorder, a manufacturers' journal urging the need for technological innovation, opined in 1902, 'it is certain that, failing the willingness of the operatives, not only to acquiesce in, but also to aid in effecting a change in the present system of working a weaving shed, the adoption of looms of this type will be slow and halting'.[12]

In fact, the Northern Counties' Amalgamation of Weavers saw no reason to make a stand against the new loom. Their complacent attitude was largely induced by their conviction, buttressed by a visit to the USA from April to June 1902 in order to investigate conditions on the spot, that without any interference on their part the conditions in Lancashire cotton weaving themselves would prevent the new machine from becoming a viable option.[13] The Northrop, as the new loom came to be called after its inventor, bore all the marks of having been designed in the United States, where a better quality of yarn was used and looms were running more slowly.[14] Both contributed to minimizing machine downtime. Thus the Amalgamation's president expressed his organization's willingness to let developments take their course. Should the Northrop prove to be superior to the Lancashire loom in every respect, it would inevitably make its way into the county's weaving sheds. While not trying to impede the adoption of the new machine, he yet warned employers that operatives would make sure that its success was not secured at the expense of their wages.[15]

Despite these reassurances, manufacturers were at pains to dispel what fear union officials and the rank and file might harbour about the new loom. Thus the *Textile Mercury*, another manufacturers' journal,[16] played down the loom's innovative character by back-dating the true 'revolution' in weaving to the introduction of the powerloom. More to the point, the journal assured its readers that increasing global demand for cotton goods would enable the industry in Lancashire, grown more competitive thanks to the innovation, to absorb those weavers made redundant by the Northrop. Finally, and in total contradiction of its previous stand,[17] the journal played the trump card. It assured its readers that unemployment would in any case be averted by the reformation of the weaving workforce, reserving employment on the Northrops for male weavers, who would receive earnings sufficient to enable them to keep their wives at home.[18]

Married Women's Employment

If the new loom allegedly did not represent a revolution, the proposed manner of working it most certainly did. Put into place, it would amount to the eventual defeminization of the weaving workforce. This was presented as both an individual and a national advantage, in that the relegation of married women weavers to the home would significantly reduce infant mortality.[19] Coming as it did at a time of mounting national concern about population decline,[20] the scheme proposed in the article could be sure to meet with widespread approval. National fears aroused by contemporary levels of infant mortality were carefully interwoven with working-class men's status anxiety in the following issue of the *Textile Mercury*, which ran an article exposing Preston as the textile town with the highest death rate and attributing this to the 'near exclusive employment of women' in the local weaving sheds. Playing on male fears, the article depicted Preston men as unemployed in large numbers and dependent on the earnings of their wives, who in turn farmed their children out to unfit child-minders.[21]

In order to combat the high rate of infant mortality, the local council, opting for the remedy commonly adopted elsewhere,[22] had appointed two female inspectors who were to instruct working-class mothers on matters of infant hygiene. Without wishing to denigrate the course taken by the council, the journal

> look[ed] with much more hope ... to a coming change in the weaving industry – the introduction of the 'automatic loom' on an extensive scale ... By men becoming weavers and earning more money at the work than is possible at present, they will be able to take their proper place as the bread-winners of the family and keep their wives at home, which is their proper sphere. It has long been a reproach among the operatives in Lancashire that in Preston the natural duties of the sexes have been inverted, the men staying at home 'to mind the baby', while the women go to the mill to keep the family.[23]

By thus invoking the inversion of the gender division of labour and power with its adverse implications for masculinity, the *Textile Mercury* attempted to enlist male weavers' support for the introduction of the Northrop.

This was not the first time that Preston had been portrayed as epitomizing the pernicious effects of conditions in the industry on both infant welfare and male authority in the family. During the mass strike of 1878, when 100 000 North Lancashire operatives stayed out for two months in an abortive attempt to ward off a reduction in wages,[24] Thomas Banks, at that time president of the Preston weavers' association, was reported as saying at a solidarity meeting in Ashton:

> A great deal of misery at home and over-production in the mills was caused by weavers allowing their wives to go to the mill, and ... if it were at all possible ... [they should] keep the wives out of the mill. Let them suckle their infants at home, for a great deal of infant mortality was caused by the neglect of the mothers who had to attend their work at the mill and could not give their children the attention they required ... [because] the husbands could not earn enough money in the mill to keep their wives and children.[25]

This speech was highly reminiscent of the way in which, around 1840, J.R. Stephens, the Ashton-based Wesleyan minister and Chartist, had exhorted his male listeners to prevent their wives from going to the mill. While he had portrayed men's dependence on their wives' earnings as a contravention of God's will and hence an indictment of the factory system,[26] 40 years later, concern about the threat posed to male authority by wage-earning wives was passed off as solicitude for the well-being of their offspring.

Preston labour politicians' rhetoric, too, as Savage has shown,[27] revolved around this theme. They would denounce wives' employment in the local weaving sheds by presenting it as a result of male weavers' pay failing to amount to a family wage,[28] only to blame the absence of a bread-winner wage in a circular argument on the predominance of women in the industry's workforce.[29] J.T. Macpherson, Preston's Labour MP from 1906 to 1910, soon after his election even suggested that he might have to 'challenge' women mill workers, asserting that 'he made bold to say that wages and conditions would have been higher had the labour been confined to the [male] operatives'.[30] The ultimate indictment of large-scale factory employment of married women was implied in the latter's portrayal as the cause of women's neglect of their duties as housewives and mothers,[31] put forward by local labour activists in a bid to further their cause by inserting themselves in the continuing debate about the 'future of the race'.

Middle-class observers searching for the causes of infant mortality were prone to scapegoating mothers working away from home.[32] Their focus on female behaviour in breach of middle-class conceptions of femininity spared them the discomfort engendered by the recognition that their own unwillingness to improve conditions detrimental to people's well-being might lie at the root of the evil. Yet the causal link they believed to have established between mothers' factory work and infant mortality was refuted by contemporaries,[33] and more recently by Carol Dyhouse.[34] She has pointed out the lack of any clear link between levels of factory employment and infant mortality rates and the crucial difference made to the family's level of comfort by mothers' earnings, which enhanced infants' chances of surviving. With particular regard to Preston, Elizabeth Roberts has shown that, over the period 1901 to 1911, although the proportion of married women in employment rose (from 30.5 per cent to 35 per cent), infant mortality actually declined (from an average of 236 per 1000 live births for the five-year period 1896–1900 to 161 for 1906–10).[35]

Moreover, whilst infant mortality was undeniably high in Preston,[36] and, though declining, consistently above the average for England and Wales,[37] it was Burnley which topped the league of infant mortality rates.[38] Here the local economy was virtually monopolized by cotton weaving and the town had among the highest rate of married women's factory employment. The reasons for labour activists focusing concern on Preston[39] must therefore be sought elsewhere, and are more likely to be found in the conditions of the local labour market characterized by a specific gender division of labour.

According to Savage, in the first half of the nineteenth century men had found employment in mule spinning and engineering, while women had been working in weaving. The subsequent decline in mule spinning, combined with failures in engineering, placed male workers in a precarious position, while the steadily expanding weaving sector provided stable employment opportunities for women.[40] Savage has explained men's failure to enter weaving upon the contraction of the male labour market by pointing to tacklers' predilection for hiring female workers in order to safeguard their own position of authority on the shopfloor,[41] while omitting to consider the loss of status entailed by any shift to weaving from male occupations regarded as skilled and commanding corresponding wage rates.

While May Abraham, one of the first female factory inspectors, who investigated the employment of women in the cotton industry, found only rare instances of women being preferred over men,[42] the so-called 'boycotting' of male weavers did arouse a great deal of concern for its repercussions on the male headship of the family where, as at Preston, little alternative employment was available for men locally.[43] Thus an anonymous correspondent from Clitheroe, who was presumably male, vented his fear in the *Cotton Factory Times* in the following terms: 'where are the men to go? or what trade is there in the town for anybody? But to walk up and down the streets, and their wives and families working at the mill to keep them would be scandalous and outrageous'.[44]

Under these circumstances the panacea advocated was the exclusion of married women from factory work.[45] Yet in view of the dependence of cotton weaving households on the joint earnings of husband and wife, any adoption of this policy by employers without a concomitant rise in men's wages produced outcries of indignation.[46]

The Bread-winner Wage

As resentment of the need for wives' earnings to ensure family survival was not confined to the labour activists of Preston, employers could be certain that the prospect of a bread-winner wage would strike the right chord at least among union officials, if not their rank and file. Enmeshed as they were in the world of labour organizations with its strict code of masculinity, weavers' representatives smarted under the inability of their membership to maintain their families without recourse to the earnings of kin, usually their own wives. Thus, in 1893, the editor of the *Cotton Factory Times* asserted:

> Weaving is not a branch of the cotton industry suitable for men to follow, simply because the wages to be earned are not sufficient to enable married men to keep a home and bring up children as modern society requires. On an average, the earnings of a man weaver come under a pound a week, and any one with experience in domestic life will admit that such a sum is quite inadequate to meet the charges coming against a household.[47]

And D.J. Shackleton, the Amalgamation's president, deployed a similar argument in an organization drive. In 1909, he was reported as saying at a meeting at Shaw, near Oldham:

> He would be pleased to see their own trade in Lancashire being carried on without work in the mill being a mother's choice or a mother's necessity. The men ought to take their

proper places, and their women folk ought to demand their right to be kept out of the mill.[48]

It was presumably for reasons such as this that an old weaver stated in his recollections that 'most lads did not like weaving ... we thought it was a job more suitable for girls'.[49]

Upholding notions of masculinity and femininity that accorded well with non-working-class conceptions of gender helped to lend weight to the Amalgamation's efforts to have working conditions improved, not least through appropriate legislation. Thus, in 1892, David Wilkinson, appearing on the organization's behalf as a witness before the Royal Commission on Labour, asserted: 'I think the husband, the head of the family, ought to be able to keep his wife at home to look after her household duties, and that he ought to earn as much as would keep the family in a satisfactory condition.'[50] The representatives of the various local weaving unions, by contrast, confined themselves to impressing on the commissioners the economic need for married women's work,[51] obviously arguing from their familiarity, and primary concern, with the family economy of their rank and file at local level.

The difference of constituency between Amalgamation officials operating within all-male trade union circles at regional and even national level and local unionists more deeply involved in, and more immediately responsive to, the concerns of their members, had repercussions on these men's proclaimed attitudes to married women's employment. D.J. Shackleton, the Amalgamation's president, is a particularly telling case in point, because by virtue of his standing as a trade union official he was able to enter the realm of, first, local and, subsequently, national government.[52] In his various political offices he gained the respect of men across the class divide with whom he shared a notion of respectable masculinity. This rested centrally on men's ability to support their families without recourse to sources other than their own income.[53] Hence he had little compunction publicly to denounce married women's factory work and is known to have privately favoured a legal ban on married women's employment. Only his awareness that open support of such a measure would be tremendously unpopular in his constituency and would most likely cost him his parliamentary seat prevented him from putting his belief into practice.[54] Similarly, he was at best lukewarm on the issue of women's suffrage, despite the fact that a large part of his financial support came out of the pockets of voteless women in his cotton textile constituency of Clitheroe.[55]

Local union officials, by contrast, would have been very careful not to alienate their female rank and file by depicting them as deficient mothers. Women weavers' notion of good motherhood encompassed paid employment as a precondition for providing their children with the material resources enhancing their chances of survival. It is virtually impossible to gauge the effects of rhetoric portraying them as neglectful mothers on working women themselves.

Disenfranchised as they were, they had no chance to register a vote of protest. Yet the more politically aware among them failed to fall for reasoning which apportioned the major share of the blame to them.⁵⁶

The attraction of having automatic weaving made a male preserve and the improvements in men's status through the buttressing of male authority in both the workplace and the home that this entailed proved well-nigh irresistible. In contrast to powerloom weaving, which was considered semi-skilled on account of the large contingent of women among weavers, the new loom appeared to open up the long-term possibility of claiming weaving to be skilled work which, intricately bound up with masculinity as it was, would rightfully be the domain of men, whose masculinity stood to gain further from their ability to earn a family wage on which to support their wives and children without any recourse to a secondary income.⁵⁷ While male handloom weavers had responded to mechanization by holding out as long as possible against submission to factory discipline, male powerloom operatives appeared to be determined to turn their presence at this stage of technological development to their advantage by giving the new machine a masculine connotation on which could be based their claim to automatic weaving as a male preserve. Moreover, a gender division of labour based on the type of machine operated would enable male weavers on automatics to shroud their work in mystery, in very much the same way as did members of skilled trades, but which was denied them in powerloom weaving where men and women worked side by side on the same machines, producing the same types of cloth.

Employers, by contrast, ran a considerable risk by promising to tie the introduction of the new loom to payment of a family wage, thereby themselves providing workers with the yardstick by which to measure conditions around the Northrop. Unions would insist on the size of the machine assignment and the corresponding cuts in prices staying within limits that they deemed reasonable. These conditions were being thrashed out in the long-drawn-out struggle with that firm which pioneered the automatic loom in Lancashire.⁵⁸

Ashton Bros. at Hyde

The concern of Ashton Bros. at Hyde, east of Manchester, differed from the average cotton weaving enterprise in several ways, which suited it particularly to technological innovation on a large scale. Non-membership of the employers' association⁵⁹ removed any restriction upon the firm's wish to experiment with new technology and novel ways of organizing the labour process. The North and North East Lancashire Cotton Spinners' and Manufacturers' Association, like its counterparts in other industries, had been set up not least to control intra-trade competition on product price and for labour. The need to do so was particularly pressing in an industry like cotton weaving where, owing to limited product differentiation, competition was by price and where labour costs formed a high proportion of total costs. Yet Ashton Bros. was not alone in refusing to affiliate to the masters' association, following a course adopted by a number of the largest firms in the industry, which had neither the need nor the desire to have their independence curtailed.[60] The ability to act unfettered by restrictions imposed by the interests of other employers or the trade unions will emerge as the salient feature of company policy in the pages to follow.

Secondly, the firm specialized in the production of plain goods: drills for China and shirting and sheeting for the domestic market. Not only was the Northrop in the early stage of its development particularly suited for the making of this class of cloth,[61] but competition from automatically produced US cotton cloth was also keenest in the lower qualities of goods exported to China.[62] Moreover, since the early nineteenth century, the firm had been vertically integrated, producing textile goods from spinning through to finishing and marketing. Though quite exceptional by the standards of the north-east weaving district, combined firms had survived in the south-east of the county, where they controlled the trade at Glossop, Stalybridge, Ashton, Mossley and Hyde.[63]

Finally Ashton Bros. prided themselves on having consistently been in the vanguard of technological innovation.[64] In the early nineteenth century, Thomas Ashton was among the first factory owners to use steam instead of water power. The necessary coal came from the mill mine, with extra contingents arriving via the conveniently close Peak Forest Canal. The same Thomas Ashton provided facilities for manufacturing gas for lighting purposes and a foundry to have his own machinery made.[65] During the cotton famine, Ashton Bros. altered their machinery so as to enable it to deal with Indian cotton and jute and any other cheap fibre that could be procured and worked into a rough substitute for cotton cloth.[66]

Northrops at Ashton Bros.

Following this tradition in May 1902, Ashton Bros. had 500 Northrops installed in their Throstle Bank Mill, with the first of them going into operation on 24 September of that year.[67] Such costly re-equipment had been made possible by capital raised via the London and Manchester stock markets as well as accumulation of profits.[68]

It should be noted that these machines were allocated to 50 female weavers at the rate of 10 wide and 12 narrow looms per operative.[69] They used mule-spun cop weft, which required the cop to be skewered through with a metal prong,[70] filled their own batteries, from which shuttles were replenished, and wove coarse cloth.[71] The firm had been careful to sound out the union on this project. At a joint meeting, the Amalgamation's representatives had reiterated their organization's stand on the new loom by stating that they were 'aware that the day had gone by for opposing the introduction of new machinery, and that so long as [Ashton Bros.] made arrangements satisfactory to [their] own Northrop loom weavers [the

Amalgamation] would not interfere'.[72] This is why the Amalgamation closely monitored the conditions around the Northrop. When, in January 1903, the organization's executive paid a visit to Ashton Bros. to inspect the automatics in operation, they came away with their conviction fully upheld that in Lancashire the automatic was working under unsuitable conditions.[73]

Yet this complacency soon gave way to growing concern about the repercussions on the entire industry that Ashton Bros.' manner of proceeding was bound to have. The *Cotton Factory Times* considered that the firm aimed at a good weekly wage for their Northrop weavers, not, however, without increasing their output. Higher productivity lowered unit costs, thus rendering Ashton Bros.' cuts of cloth cheaper than those of their competitors. Such price competition conjured up the prospect of redundancy for those operatives employed on ordinary looms for standard rates, inducing the Amalgamation to change their attitude from complacency to concern.[74] Their anxiety was greatly added to by the excessive claims made by the loom's manufacturer about the Northrop's labour-saving potential, putting the possible size of the machine assignment at up to 40 looms per operative.[75] Ashton Bros.' weavers, too, deemed job security to be better ensured by the automatic than the ordinary looms.[76]

Given the significance of the issue, the Northern Counties' Federation of Textile Trades pledged to give the Hyde association its support.[77] This was the more welcome in view of the less than cooperative attitude displayed by Ashton Bros. towards the Amalgamation. The firm consistently preferred dealing directly with their workforce without the interference of 'outsiders', as they dubbed the representatives of the local union, and the Amalgamation in particular.[78] Thus union recognition was added to the list of grievances that was building up.

In a clear breach of negotiation etiquette, by which they clearly did not feel themselves to be bound, the firm had presented the terms on which the Northrops were to be operated directly to the 50 female weavers concerned, insisting on the decision being made immediately, thus precluding any consultation with union officials on the part of the workers. At a special shop meeting convened to consider the situation, the women complained about being pressurized by the firm in this manner and, revoking their initial consent, demanded to be given fewer looms and the higher rates pressed for by the Amalgamation.[79]

The firm consistently resisted trade union demands for both a discussion of wages and a restriction to be imposed on the Northrop assignment per weaver by arguing that the loom was still at an experimental stage, with the potential of machine and labour not yet fully tested.[80] In August 1903, in his capacity of vice-chairman of the company,[81] Henry Philips Greg brought the issue to the attention of a larger audience through an article in the *Manchester Guardian*, in which he justified the firm's conduct.[82] Greg himself hailed from the cotton dynasty owning Quarry Bank Mill at Styal. He had married into the Ashton family and was to rise to be chairman of the company from 1907 until 1936.[83] His experience of the Northrop at Ashton Bros. led him to encourage his cousin Robert Alexander to introduce the automatic at Styal in an attempt to save his family's ailing mill.[84] His quest for public support may have been sparked by the Northrop Loom Company, the maker of Northrops in Britain, and the *Textile Recorder* joining in the Amalgamation's assessment that the machine assignment was excessive in view of the conditions under which Ashton Bros.' weavers were working.[85]

Furthermore, the firm's intransigence clashed with the soft-pedalling approach advocated by the *Textile Mercury*. From the start, this journal had pleaded for the adoption of consensual procedures, proposing a conference of representatives of both sides to arrange matters on a temporary basis until modifications would be required by experience.[86] This appeal having remained unheeded, the journal called on the weavers to acknowledge the competition of those countries that had already adopted the automatic by arguing that 'it will be perfectly useless to settle the matter on any basis that shall not restore to this country the equality of the conditions we have had in the past for competing with all who have entered the field against us'. Having renewed its appeal for negotiation, it concluded: 'Let there be no attempt on either side to overreach the other, and then a peaceful industrial revolution will be effected, with a minimum of friction and loss and a maximum of peace and benefit to both sides.'[87]

The *Textile Recorder*, on the other hand, backed Ashton Bros.' unwillingness to make concessions to trade unions, which the journal believed to be the main hindrance to progress. Deeming the widespread diffusion of the Northrop to be inevitable, and acknowledging the rationality of the firm's argument from an employer's point of view, the journal pleaded for the discussion to be entered 'without preconceived ideas as to possibilities'.[88] The *Recorder*'s growing exasperation with alleged trade union inflexibility was expressed in the following strong terms:

> Every improvement a manufacturer may suggest which interferes with the methods customary with the operatives is looked at askance, and, in many cases, killed before it has had a fair chance to prove its worth. If Lancashire is to hold her high position as the greatest manufacturing district of the world, her operatives must be prepared to accept the new conditions which are being evolved. The world will not stand still, and methods and machinery which were modern twenty years ago, may not be fitted for the strenuous struggle of today.[89]

Yet Ashton Bros.' 50 female Northrop weavers were not prepared to let themselves be dictated to by their employer and, in May 1903, took the unanimous decision to give notice to strike. Only then did the firm agree personally to meet the Amalgamation representatives – all previous exchange having been by letter – and a compromise was worked out. Without any dissension this was accepted by the weavers as a temporary settlement for 12 months.[90] It was at this stage that Ashton Bros. for the first time asserted that their original intention had been to confine work on the new looms to men, believing that women were better off seeing to their homes and children. Only out of loyalty to their established workforce had they deviated from the original plan.[91] The timing of this revelation suggests that it implied a veiled threat: unless they acquiesced in the conditions offered by the firm, women Northrop weavers would be laid off.

Under the terms of the temporary settlement, the firm increased the rates of pay slightly, but, more importantly, this was a time-wage rather than a piece-rate, relieving Northrop weavers of some of the strain imposed on them by the machine assignment, which, much to the operatives' dissatisfaction, was left unaltered. However, strain was further reduced through the supply of better material, which was less likely to break and require mending. Moreover, one spare worker was employed per 100 looms to mend faulty places in the cloth and help fill the magazine from which shuttles were replenished, while a boy was taken on to keep the looms supplied with weft.[92]

When the 12-month trial period was up, the firm reverted from the standing wage to piece-rates, which the weavers only accepted 'under protest',[93] feeling that their working conditions had not changed for the better. They still had to operate more looms than they felt able to cope with and make do with inferior qualities of yarn, while their earnings failed to reflect the arduous nature of their job.[94] Moreover, the aspect of Ashton Bros.' Throstle Bank Mill in October 1904 drove home the impact of the new loom on the industry's workforce. Where previously 300 weavers had tended 700 ordinary looms, now 800 Northrops were operated by about 77 weavers. Given the size of the firm and the manufacturer's determination to make the new loom a success, the workers made redundant had been found employment either at the firm's other mills or as ancillary labour about the Northrop looms.[95]

The Strike of 1904

Exasperated, in October 1904 the female weavers together with the operatives in the preparatory departments at Throstle Bank Mill walked out, causing the workers in the mill's other departments to be locked out, while the overlookers, on being approached, refused to weave the deserted looms.[96] Their refusal may well have been connected with a strike of their own in October of the previous year. They, too, were dissatisfied with conditions around the Northrops, demanding a pay rise together with a reduction in the number of looms in the charge of each overlooker.[97]

At a popular concert in support of the Northrop weavers' strike, the audience were addressed by Ada Nield Chew from the Women's Trade Union League. After lauding the women weavers for their high degree of unionization, she pointed to the significance of the present strike as setting a precedent for the entire industry. Hence she called on the women to hold out against tyranny and injustice, in which endeavour they were able to count on their union's support.[98] This speech did less than justice to the fact that women as England's pioneer workers on the automatic loom had shown a great deal of courage and determination in their consistent refusal to be browbeaten by their employer. Throughout they had displayed a marked degree of awareness of their role as forerunners in shaping the conditions under which the Northrop was to be operated in England. Nor was Ada Nield Chew's assurance of union support made good by subsequent trade union conduct.

Given the local importance of the firm as one of the town's major employers – roughly one-half of the district's cotton operatives worked for Ashton Bros.[99] – the mayor felt the strike to be sufficiently serious for him to act as a mediator between both parties and managed to bring about a compromise within three days.[100] The speedy ending of the strike was surely helped by the fact that the dispute occurred during a boom period for cotton cloth.[101] While the wages offered by the firm were deemed entirely satisfactory, the number of looms per weaver remained a contentious issue.[102] As a result of the settlement arrived at, weavers who so desired were allowed to exchange a set of 12 for one of 10 looms,[103] to the detriment of their weekly earnings.

Undeterred by this dispute, Ashton Bros. pressed on with replacing ordinary with automatic looms, going a step further by introducing bobbin looms. These used weft produced on ring-spinning machines, which was more resistant to breakage than mule-spun yarn and required no skewering.[104] Work on these machines was confined to men at the rate of 20 looms each.[105] They wove cloth of medium fineness and had helpers to fill their magazines[106] as part of the firm's quest to maximize output from the new machines. It is not clear whether this manner of proceeding had been planned from the outset or whether, in order to prevent further disruption, the firm had picked up the idea of reserving work on Northrops for men from the *Textile Mercury*, which had first mooted the scheme in September 1902,[107] as noted above. The account produced by A.M. Fletcher, the company's managing director, of the introduction of the automatic would support the former view, though its retrospective character precludes any definitive answer.[108]

From then on the firm focused its efforts to increase productivity on the bobbin looms, tentatively expanding the machine assignment to 24 looms per weaver. When the trial period had expired, the male weavers unanimously decided to revert to 20.[109] As interviews with workers made to switch to Northrops in the inter-war period have shown, weavers strongly resented the feeling of competitiveness among the workforce engendered by the intensification of labour that the introduction of the automatic brought in its wake.[110] Additionally, they experienced the new technology as invalidating their knowledge and skill. The size of the machine assignment made it impossible for workers to know each loom well, and, denied the possibility of intervention, they suffered from being made to produce bad-quality cloth.[111] There is no reason to assume that their resentment was any more marked than that of their predecessors at the beginning of the century. Moreover, the deeply engrained habit of watching for broken threads, obviated by the warp-stop motion attached to the Northrop, died hard,[112] noticeably increasing the mental strain weavers on the automatic were labouring under.

At Hyde, dissatisfaction among weavers lingered on. Machine assignment and wages were at issue still, as was the speed at which looms were running.[113] In the union's view these conditions nullified the firm's intention to provide their male weavers with a family wage. According to William Pope, secretary of the Hyde weavers' association, in order for automatic looms to be accepted locally, fundamental improvements in working conditions were required, relieving the strain under which weavers were labouring. Pressure on operatives to increase output would need to be abolished, operatives would need to be supplied with better yarn, which was less likely to break, pay would have to be increased, the machine assignment reduced, and fining for faulty cloth done away with.[114] Less than two months later, Joseph Cross, general secretary of the Northern Counties' Amalgamation, reiterated that only the payment of a family wage could compensate for the exertion imposed on a weaver running 16 to 20 looms.[115]

In the firm's view, the introduction of the Northrops had been a resounding success. By October 1907, they claimed that 790 of these looms were running satisfactorily,[116] not least because of their ability to use bobbin weft as it came from the firm's own spinning department,[117] which obviated the need to change from cops to bobbins. According to the self-congratulatory lecture on the Northrop's introduction given by A.M. Fletcher to the Lancashire section of the British Association of Managers of Textile Works,[118] after initial difficulties the workpeople had become proud of being Northrop weavers. He smugly asserted that the firm had effected a revolution in the weaving trade with a stoppage of two and a half days and proceeded to extol the advantages of the new loom. The Northrops had enabled the firm to dispense with some of their married women workers. Earning 25 per cent more than before, the men employed on the new looms were able to maintain their wives at home. This was a development to be warmly welcomed, because married women's factory work caused a high rate of infant mortality. Overall, the Northrop made Britain more competitive.[119]

As Fletcher knew well, this favourable view was strongly contested by the Northrop weavers back at Hyde, who remained dissatisfied with conditions of work and pay. Their stubborn refusal to submit to the conditions imposed by management appeared to him as an indication of the machine-breaking attitude harboured by operatives and trade union officials alike. He alleged that 'when the workpeople and others who were prejudiced against any invention that was intended to do away with the old order of things heard that the looms were on the way to Hyde, they declared that they would never reach England, and that if they did they would be broken up and thrown in the cut'.

Coming to the defence of trade union officials, the *Cotton Factory Times* reiterated:

The underlying principles actuating their policy, as representatives and guardians of the workpeople's interest, have been a desire to bring about the transition as amicably as possible, consistent with the indisputable right of their clients to have a voice in saying what was a reasonable number of looms a weaver should run, and what should be considered a reasonable rate of remuneration.[120]

Fletcher may therefore have vented management's frustration with workers' obstinacy. The directors of the firm took what can be described as an enlightened paternalist attitude towards their employees.[121] Such paternalism was premised on the assumption that management knew best what was most conducive to workers' benefit.

The Strike of 1908

Meanwhile grumbling at being overworked and underpaid grew louder. Trade unions, too, watched developments at Hyde with mounting concern. Ashton Bros. were operating by far the largest number of Northrops in the country, and unions rightly feared that conditions there would set the standard for firms elsewhere.[122] Renewed attempts by the Amalgamation since the autumn of 1907 to induce the firm to discuss Northrop prices with them had failed, with Ashton Bros. still claiming the loom to be at an experimental stage.[123] Exasperated, the union balloted its members at all of Ashton Bros.' mills about strike action. Despite the small number of weavers immediately affected – 47 men altogether – the ballot was overwhelmingly in favour of a stoppage.[124] Thus Hyde lived up to its reputation of being among the most highly unionized districts of the Amalgamation of Weavers.[125] At Ashton Bros. more specifically, weavers and allied trades were unionized to the extent of 94 per cent.[126]

In what was presumably a last attempt to avert industrial action just prior to the strike being called, the firm had a circular printed, which was addressed to all its weavers. By the vastly superior conditions of work they had introduced on automatic as compared to conventional looms, the firm claimed to have 'hoped to accomplish what [they] had in view, namely that a married man could, on 25 Northrop looms, keep his wife at home'. This was reiterated in an interview with one of the local papers, in which a representative of the firm painted a picture of the Northrop as enabling 'a man to keep his wife at home, and ... secur[ing] that comfort which is impossible where both husband and wife go to the shed'. He further repeated that the firm had never dismissed any 'man' in consequence of introducing the new loom and, given the high wages to be earned, there was nothing to fear from the innovation.[127]

Family wage rhetoric on the part of manufacturers was quite novel and far from being the norm. At the same time as things were hotting up at Hyde, employers' journals took a firm stand in the current debate about the alleged evils of married women's employment, emphasizing that it was essential for the upkeep of their families.¹²⁸ Moreover, the removal of women from the textile mills would neither raise men's wages nor reduce employment. It would simply increase poverty.¹²⁹

Although employers keen to innovate consistently cloaked their wish to do so with their desire to relieve wives of the need to go to the shed, the change-over from ordinary to automatic looms, if pursued along those lines, was bound ultimately to put all women weavers, regardless of their marital status, out of work. Yet this prospect worried neither Ashton Bros. nor manufacturers in general.¹³⁰ In a spectacular display of insensitivity to, and ignorance of, conditions in England, Draper & Sons came down on Ashton Bros.' side by referring to two weavers in one of the southern states of the USA running 48 automatic looms each with the assistance of one child each. This statement prompted William Pope, the local union secretary, to respond angrily that 'we absolutely refuse to take an example from South America [*sic*]. The conditions existing in the Southern States are somewhat similar to those existing in Lancashire about 100 years ago, when the cotton industry was first introduced, and we have no desire to degenerate to these conditions.'¹³¹

Despite the strong show of support by the rank and file, the union remained conciliatory to the last, agreeing to post-date their members' notices so as to be able to meet the firm's representatives in a final attempt at negotiation. When this failed, too, the strike commenced in April 1908. As a result, Ashton Bros. locked out their workers in the non-weaving departments of their concern a few days later.¹³² A total of more than 2000 operatives were out of work, comprising 1200 strikers and about 800 who had been locked out.¹³³

The union initially faced considerable hostility locally, which extended even to the Trades Council.¹³⁴ To many outsiders not familiar with the intricacies of wage calculations in weaving, the difference between the rates paid by the firm and those demanded by the union appeared to be negligible. The difference was certainly not deemed large enough to warrant a strike, which hit the local economy hard, especially as there was a good deal of slack even at working mills, which further depressed disposable income.¹³⁵ Hence shopkeepers were among the most vociferous opponents of the strike. Moreover, Ashton Bros. enjoyed a reputation of being particularly good employers, having consistently treated their workforce reasonably.¹³⁶ The last strike of comparable scale, which had occurred 27 years previously, had collapsed within three weeks.¹³⁷

Thus, whilst in the throes of the Cotton Famine, Thomas Ashton, the grandfather of the Ashton involved in the company at the time of the 1908 dispute, had had Throstle Bank Mill built by the firm's own operatives to tide them over this period of severe unemployment. Considered a costly miscalculation by most contemporaries, the mill was known locally as 'Ashton's folly'.¹³⁸ Yet, when it finally opened in 1871, Throstle Bank Mill was able to take advantage of the shortage of cloth following a so-called 'Cotton Panic',¹³⁹ proving that Ashton's apparent philanthropy had been shot through with a large dose of shrewd business sense. Similarly, during the current dispute, the firm lived up to its reputation by financially assisting non-unionized workers, who were not entitled to any strike pay.[140] At the same time, this was a clever ploy, making the union out to be ruthlessly sacrificing the welfare of workers in a power play with employers.

It was the firm's alleged failure to fulfil its promise of paying a family wage[141] which helped the union win support. Thus, at an annual dinner of the Hyde Philanthropic Burial Society, one Councillor Fildes said:

> we cannot stand by and watch this great struggle going on without admiring the determination of the bread-winner struggling to establish what the firm itself say is to be a living wage for its workers on the Northrop looms. They (the firm) are anxious, they say, that every man who works upon those looms should be in receipt of a wage to keep his wife and children at home without any additional work.[142]

The use of family wage rhetoric both to plead with employers and to inspire solidarity among working people, as Sonya Rose has shown,[143] can be traced back at least to the big cotton strike of 1878.

Moreover, the goal of obtaining a family wage could be used to legitimate the struggle in trade union circles by presenting the weavers as fighting for what other trades had already achieved. At one strike meeting, William Pope accordingly took to task those members of the public who had criticized his union for bringing the workers out. These included trade unionists who were members of skilled trades, such as boilermakers, felt hatters, mechanics, fitters and turners. They had claimed that nobody who did not serve an apprenticeship like themselves deserved to be paid as much as the male weavers on Northrops. To this Pope replied that it cost as much to maintain the family of a weaver as that of a boilermaker.[144] In the last instance, as this line of argument shows, the dispute was aimed at bringing male weavers into the ranks of the skilled trades. The claim was made, not on the basis of any criterion related to work (the completion of an apprenticeship), but rather of gender: men's duty to maintain their families. Thus Pope's reply implied a challenge to the nature of skill on which the weavers' critics based their status. By placing it on the same level as that possessed by male Northrop weavers, Pope implicitly revealed skill as a social construct, while at the same time emphasizing its strong gender overtones. Ultimately, this argument runs, all work carried out by men is skilled by virtue of the gender of those performing it.

From among weavers elsewhere the dispute enjoyed considerable support. The strike occurred at a convenient moment for the firm, coming as it did while stocks were piled up high in the face of an oncoming depression,[145] yet the local union was backed by the Weavers' Amalgamation, whose coffers were sufficiently filled to guarantee strike pay for the duration of even a protracted struggle. Weavers' associations nearby also consistently voted grants in aid of the dispute.[146] Furthermore, regular collections at other mills were made to boost strike pay, and the workers' response showed that they clearly understood the significance of the struggle being waged, and that regardless of whether or not Northrops had already been introduced into their own districts.[147]

Weavers were left in no doubt about both the nature and the relevance of the issue at stake. At a public meeting, D.J. Shackleton, the Amalgamation's president, after praising the unity and firmness of the strikers, pressed home the significance of the issue in the following terms:

> the general introduction of the Northrop loom into the cotton industry would displace from one-third to one-sixth of the weavers affected, and that was a very serious business. They had to face it completely; and to see to it that it was possible for the man to earn such a wage as would enable him to keep his wife at home. (Loud applause.) It was something more than a Hyde question; it was a county question. They must not expect a man to keep his wife at home on 24s. or 25s. per week.'[148]

Quite clearly, Shackleton had not arrived at this assessment on the basis of sophisticated calculations. What sum of money amounted to a 'family wage' was culturally determined in ways similar to a 'fair price' or a 'fair wage'.

Precisely because attainment of a family wage for male weavers in conjunction with the phasing out of female weavers stood at the centre of the Amalgamation's struggle, the wages and working conditions of the women Northrop operatives at Throstle Bank Mill were not made an issue by the Amalgamation's representatives in their negotiations with the firm, much to the latter's amazement.[149] Ashton Bros. recognized that, although the women had their workload increased by the need to skewer through the cop weft they were made to use,[150] their wages were lower than those of their male counterparts, who were spared this extra operation and also worked a larger number of looms. They also produced finer cloth, which fetched higher rates.[151] Gender-specific allocation of product and machine design to the detriment of female weavers was apparently part of the firm's plan to dispense with women workers in future.

About half-way through the strike, Ashton Bros. decided to reopen their mills and invite their operatives back to work. Only about 14 weavers, all of them allegedly non-unionists, went in. Strikers' feelings ran high in the face of the 'knobsticks', who were harassed and verbally abused, with women very much to the fore.[152] In view of the hostile crowds, the number of weavers going in dwindled until after only two days the sheds were closed down again. As a result of the excitement caused by the 'scabs', one man, unconnected with the firm, and two female weavers on strike were summoned for assault and persistent following. The alleged physical attack by one of the women on a male 'knobstick' had occurred when the crowd shouted that he was working on her looms.[153] During the hearing before the magistrates, though denying the charges brought against her, she said in justification of her conduct: 'I didn't like the thought of anyone taking my work.'[154] This is a further instance of the proprietorial attitude weavers evinced towards their looms and the cloth they wove on them. This was based on the way in which they adjusted their machines to their specific needs, as spelt out in Chapter 3.

After 13 weeks' duration, the strike ended with a compromise being reached, thanks to the perseverance of two local clergymen, who had taken it upon themselves to bring about a resolution of the conflict, which even the intervention by the Board of Trade had failed to do.[155] Its attempt at conciliation indicates how seriously this strike was taken by the government, not only because of the numbers, but also, and perhaps primarily, because of the issue involved. State intervention in industrial relations had increased from about 1880 onward in order to prevent industrial unrest from, among other things, intensifying resistance to technical innovation.[156]

At Hyde the trade union negotiators, while winning an increase in pay, failed to have a fixed price list for work produced on Northrops adopted. Nor were they able to enforce any limitation on the size of the machine assignment per weaver, which was to be subject to agreement between employer and individual employee. Despite the settlement falling far short of the objectives formulated at the outset, local union officials presented the result of their protracted negotiations, in the course of which they had submitted to offensive behaviour on the part of the firm's representatives,[157] as being fully acceptable. This view was endorsed by the unanimous vote of their members,[158] though not necessarily by labour activists outside cotton weaving.[159] The prospect involved in the settlement of the Northrop making its way into the Lancashire weaving sheds led one of the local papers to quote a manufacturer who had tested the automatic in his own mills as hailing it in the following terms: 'If it should restore the woman to the home, abolish half-time, and bring an eight hours workging [*sic*] day for adults [*sic*] generations to come would bless and not curse its innovation.'[160]

The Northrop's Progress

The compromise which brought the strike of 1908 to a close appears to have encouraged Ashton Bros. to continue their policy of large-scale replacement of conventional with automatic looms. By 1913, they were operating about 3000 Northrops in their sheds.[161] Elsewhere in the county, the automatic failed to make significant headway, despite efforts to propagate the advantages of the machine.[162] The importance attached to this issue by the *Cotton Factory Times* is indicated by the fact that instances of automatic loom installation appeared under separate headings in bold print,[163] rather than in the column 'Voices from the Spindle and the Loom', where changes of equipment at individual mills were usually reported.

According to a survey carried out by the Northern Counties' Amalgamation in 1911 there were 5409 automatics in operation. The district of Hyde and Hadfield topped the list with 2666 machines, more than five times the number of looms in the district which came second. Of that total, 1800 were operated by Ashton Bros.

alone.[164] In 1914, Northrops made up 1 to 2 per cent of Lancashire's loom capacity, a proportion which was to rise to only 5 per cent by 1939.[165]

Reluctance to Innovate

The persistence of the mechanical loom in the face of its increasing replacement by the Northrop on the part of Lancashire's main competitors would appear to underpin the argument that the decline of the county's cotton industry after the First World War was caused by English industrialists' failure to invest in state-of-the-art technology.[166]

In a lively debate that has arisen around this issue[167] and has focused mainly on spinning, William Lazonick has attributed the failure to innovate primarily to cotton masters' reluctance to break through the rigid organizational structures of the industry. At the level of the labour process he has pointed to the persistence of subcontracting, which facilitated collusion between master and operative spinner over an intensification of labour on increasingly obsolete machinery at the expense of the subordinate piecers.[168] Bolin-Hort has subsequently applied the same argument to the weaving sector by highlighting the 'tenter-system', under which weavers' willingness and ability to take on a larger number of looms was assisted by a helper or 'tenter' being paid a fixed wage out of weavers' own earnings.[169]

As regards the industry as a whole, Lazonick has argued that vertical specialization, exacerbated by the concentration of spinning and weaving in different parts of the county, turned transport costs into a major issue. These were lower for mule-spun cops than for ring-spun bobbins, yarn from which had to be rewound for use in mechanical loom shuttles.[170] Finally, he has claimed, cotton industrialists relinquished managerial control, thereby facilitating the persistence of uncompetitive work practices.[171]

Lazonick has castigated British industrialists for having failed to live up to the Schumpeterian model of entrepreneurship, the salient characteristic of which is the ability to go beyond the constraints imposed by existing market conditions. He has developed his argument, which emphasizes endogenous factors, in refutation of Lars Sandberg, who has attributed the industry's decline mainly to the falling off of exports brought about by forces outside Lancashire's control. He has exonerated Lancashire industrialists, whom he credits with having acted in an economically rational manner:[172] they adopted new technology where it was appropriate, that is where the particular market circumstances and factor costs rendered new technology profitable. Sandberg's view has been supported by Saxonhouse and Wright, who have highlighted the unique ability of the spinning mule, deemed obsolete by Lazonick, to make maximum use of the wide variety of raw cotton available on the Liverpool spot market[173] as crucial to maintaining Lancashire's competitiveness.[174] Most recently, Leunig has identified two demand-side factors, the high amount of fine yarn produced in Lancashire and the county's sizeable export trade in yarn, as determining master spinners' continued preference for mules over rings.[175]

Lazonick's arguments have in turn been underpinned[176] by William Mass's study of automatic loom diffusion in Lancashire.[177] Mass, too, has emphasized the ossified organizational structures of the industry as the main impediment to innovation. Echoing a view expressed at the time of the 1908 Hyde dispute by the *Textile Mercury*,[178] in his account the unions are allocated a major share of the blame. He sees their inflexibility on the issue of piece rates as inducing manufacturers to adopt a specific cost-cutting strategy, which involved minimizing the number of looms per weaver, while maximizing the speed at which machines were running,[179] but which in the long run failed to yield profits as high as those to be derived from the newer technology. In addition, Mass has claimed, the large number of small runs of a great variety of weaves customarily dealt with by Lancashire manufacturers prohibited standardized operation and acted as a further impediment to adopting a loom which required less operative attention. Finally, as English manufacturers tried to meet international competition by minimizing both quality and quantity of cotton input per unit of yarn and cloth, yarn breakage and hence machine downtime were frequent, but less costly on the powerloom than on the far more expensive automatic.[180]

The cost advantage of the Lancashire loom over the acquisition and maintenance of extra parts on the automatic was perceived clearly by English manufacturers. On becoming available in Britain, the Northrop cost two and a half times as much as a plain loom of the same size.[181] Moreover, any speeding up of the Northrop required a corresponding redistribution of tasks between weavers and ancillary labour, thus adding to the wage bill.[182] Furthermore, at some mills, operating Northrops necessitated the use of humidifiers[183] to prevent the yarn from breaking, both making work unpleasant for the weavers and augmenting the necessary capital outlay.

Indeed, most manufacturers failed to see any competitive advantage of the new machine over the old one.[184] While some gave the Northrop a trial run prior to any change-over on a significant scale, which was by no means a foregone conclusion,[185] others were dissuaded by their overlookers, whom they consulted prior to any decision and who took a dim view of the productive capabilities of the new machine.[186] It was precisely in order to spare Lancashire manufacturers the need to invest in costly new machines that a number of improvements to be fitted to the conventional loom appeared on the market.[187]

Apart from blaming English manufacturers for failing to modernize, Mass has also criticized Draper & Sons for their organizational and technical incapability to adapt automatic loom technology for foreign customers. The Northrop had been designed to meet the specific conditions obtaining in US cotton weaving, which had developed on the basis of high-wage and high-throughput technology requiring a high quality of cotton to be used.[188] Moreover, the industry was beset by a scarcity of skilled labour, which was why US looms boasted a mechanism controlling the tension of the warp threads as the warp reduced in size and weight. This mechanism was less accurate than the manual adjustment of weights left to the English weaver's discretion,[189] thereby enabling the Lancashire loom to produce a wider range of cloths.[190] Moreover, being deprived of this way of bringing their judgment and experience into play further contributed to weavers' feeling of having their skill devalued.

Nor did Draper & Sons' marketing strategy succeed in winning English manufacturers over to their loom.[191] The firm took a major share in the British Northrop Loom Company established in Blackburn in 1902 and licensed to manufacture and sell the automatic in the European market.[192] It aimed particularly at Britain, but also the countries of the British Empire.[193] Henry Philips Greg of Ashton Bros. held a directorship with the loom company. This cross-directorship between equipment supplier and manufacturer, ensuring maximum support in any re-equipment venture, may have been another reason for Ashton Bros.' interest in experimenting with the new type of loom.[194] In 1904, the company took over Daisy Hill Mill at Rishton to prove to manufacturers that the Northrop could operate successfully under regular mill conditions,[195] a need the loom builder had recognized early on,[196] and which was achieved successfully, as even the *Cotton Factory Times* had to concede.[197]

Under the conditions characterizing the Lancashire cotton weaving industry at the beginning of the twentieth century, manufacturers had little reason to adopt the Northrop. After all, the industry appeared to be highly competitive and successful in the years leading up to the First World War, recording a considerable increase in labour productivity and rising to the height of its exporting power,[198] as noted in Chapter 2. Nor did manufacturers' failure to scrap their Lancashire looms at that stage inevitably lead to their loss of competitiveness in the inter-war period. Accounting for this development solely in terms of the type of production technology opted for assumes that there is 'one best way', rather than a multiplicity of, largely culturally determined, ways of achieving good results.

The myth of 'one best way' has recently been demolished by Mary Rose[199] in a comparative study of the British and US cotton industries, in which she has demonstrated how business attitudes were shaped by the historical, social, political and economic context that had evolved since the period of industrialization. This had occurred under markedly different conditions in either country. Britain was a colonial power and the first country to industrialize, while the USA was an ex-British colony and the first country of recent settlement to make the transition to factory-based production. Mary Rose has persuasively argued that the tendency to view the US model of business as a blueprint for international competitive advantage has often masked the exceptional nature of US economic change. Instead of blaming any institutional rigidities for preventing British businessmen from adopting the strategies of their US counterparts, she has attributed the different profiles of the industries by 1914 to entirely different competitive processes.

The story of Ashton Bros. is a case in point. The firm boasted all the features that both Lazonick and Mass hold to be prerequisites of a company's ability to innovate, such as vertical integration,[200] large runs of inferior products and readiness to tackle the reorganization of the labour process. Their attempt at the latter was unfettered by any affiliation to the employers' association. Nevertheless, as Toms has recently shown in an article taking issue with both Lazonick and Sandberg,[201] the company's performance was in no way superior to its competitors'. Furthermore, the firm's success in ultimately overcoming union resistance hinged on its adroit deployment of gender, throwing into relief the fact that the debate raging among economic historians is wide of the mark, owing to their assumption that the economy is an ungendered space.

In the long run, as a result of the upheavals in the cotton workforce caused by the First World War, work on the Northrops could not be sustained as a male preserve. By 1937, the proportion of men and women working on automatic looms was roughly equal. Both men and women were allocated either 12 or 16 looms, with men averaging 14 and women 13. Women earned less than men in all cases. This was the result of shift work being introduced in order to maximize output from automatic looms, something that had been unsuccessfully attempted as early as the beginning of the century.[202] Given the difficulty of obtaining an exemption for employing women on shift work, manufacturers tended to drive a harder bargain. Men, by contrast, were lured into shift work by attractive wages.[203]

Failure to tie the introduction of the Northrop to the defeminization of the weaving workforce did nothing to dissuade employers from adopting the same strategy of trying to head off male opposition to the implementation of the 'more looms system' in the late 1920s.[204] This time round, under conditions of a declining industry, with the decline seriously exacerbated by a severe global slump, women proved vulnerable to losing their employment, while maintaining their identity of skilled workers. The more looms system was designed to reduce unit labour costs by increasing the number of looms attended by each weaver. Although the wages of individual weavers increased as a result, total labour costs would fall because of the displacement of labour.[205]

The labour to be dispensed with was that of women weavers,[206] for under the more looms system fathers of families were to be given preference in employment and they would be paid a family wage. This proposal chimed well with the increasing hostility towards married women retaining their jobs under conditions of rising unemployment. While the union leadership appeared to be prepared to strike a deal with employers upon these terms, an overwhelming majority of the unions' rank and file were against the more looms system, as their 1931 ballot showed.[207] Clearly, women, who by that time predominated both among the weaving workforce and in weaving union membership,[208] were loath to lose their jobs in weaving and, along with their menfolk, concerned about the repercussions this would have on the family economy, already under threat on account of the increasing irregularity of employment, in the absence of alternative job openings.

During the slump they continued to see themselves as workers, though unemployed, rather than housewives.[209]

Suggestions that single women in the cotton district should seek work in domestic service,[210] that occupation universally disdained by women cotton workers, as shown in Chapter 3, met with a great deal of resistance both individually and collectively.[211] As a result, the government backed down and ceased trying to coerce unemployed single women into domestic service by threatening to deny them unemployment benefit.[212]

While the competitive market structure characteristic of the weaving branch of the cotton industry militated against any across-the-board introduction of the more looms system,[213] workers' militancy also played a crucial role. The strikes occasioned by resistance to wage cuts and the more looms system were second only to the General Strike in terms of militancy during the inter-war period. Both the militancy and the solidity of the strike wave, occurring as it did in an industry in decline, testify to the tenacity with which women weavers clung to their jobs as well as the persistent need for weaving families to have access to more than one income.

Conclusion

The course of events around the introduction of the Northrop demonstrates the relevance of gender to an understanding of the eventual outcome of the struggle. Yet both the significance of the events at Ashton Bros. for the composition of the weaving workforce and the crucial role played by gender have been ignored by historians of the cotton industry.[214] Throughout notions of gender held by the different parties involved came into conflict. The preference given to male weavers by Ashton Bros. for employment on the Northrop loom, though presented to the public as the firm's part in the national effort to beat down infant mortality, at the same time encouraged male workers to collude with their employer over the introduction of new technology in return for a boost to their masculinity. The firm's offer to make work on Northrops a male preserve appears to have been based on the reckoning that men's presumed physical ability to operate a larger machine contingent than women would be further enhanced by the opportunity of demonstrating in practice that only men were able to operate a great number of mechanically complex looms efficiently. Seen in this light, the concessions Ashton Bros. were prepared to make to their male weavers' gender sensibilities tie in with the firm's economic interest in raising profit margins through the use of new technology. As it turned out, the men concerned were not prepared to give unlimited priority to buttressing their masculinity over working conditions deemed reasonable. The employers' assumptions about working-class masculinity, geared as they were to their economic designs, involved extra exploitation based on superior physical strength. Male weavers' idea of masculinity, by contrast, appears to have been centred on the effective ability to resist such superexploitation. Though willing to work a larger machine contingent than women, they were not prepared to be stretched out indefinitely.

In the dispute, class-based notions of masculinity clashed with each other in a way that militated against cross-class male collusion over the Northrop loom. The need to ensure payment of a family wage was even more pressing in view of the implications for the family economy of the eventual denial of employment to women in weaving in a region where there was little alternative female employment available that was equally well paid.

Both the local weavers' union and the Northern Counties' Amalgamation were preoccupied with masculinity. It was precisely their eagerness to grasp the opportunity afforded by the introduction of new technology of bringing weaving into the realm of skilled trades that required them to take a firm stand on wages and working conditions, with good levels of both being hallmarks of skilled employment. However, closure of this particular kind of employment to women as a marker of skill appears to have taken precedence over wages and conditions and to have lain behind the conciliatory stand that the Amalgamation assumed towards the firm to the last and which laid them open to allegations of capitulation. This is also why they focused the struggle on male Northrop weavers alone. They were clearly not prepared to jeopardize their ultimate aim – confining work on the Northrop to men as the precondition for a family wage – by raising their demands to a level that might have induced the firm to reconsider their position on the gender composition of the weaving workforce. Their accession to employers' standards of wages and conditions shows them to have championed technological innovation, provided that this was implemented for the benefit of their male, and at the expense of their female, clientele.

Those women who had pioneered work on the automatic showed a great deal of courage and determination in standing up against what they considered unreasonable demands by their employer. Nor were they in the least willing to serve as the wedge driven between the firm's workforce and their union. They formed a large part of the united front put up by the weaving workforce against their employer, overwhelmingly voting in favour of strike action and supporting the dispute to the very last. Women were also at the forefront of the vociferous protests, verging on the violent, against those few weavers who resumed work on the firm's tentative reopening of their sheds. In the dispute they showed themselves to be self-identified workers as committed as their male counterparts to achieving acceptable working conditions and in the long run safeguarding employment in weaving by helping to impose limits on the productivity growth to be attained from Northrops. Like everyone else involved in the strike, they perceived the long-term implications of the large-scale introduction of the new machine. Their opposition to it fed not least on their desire to preserve their own jobs.

Trade union attempts at reconstructing gender relations in weaving manifestly failed in the long run. The reasons for this must be sought in the specific conditions of Lancashire cotton weaving, which circumscribed the action taken by both employers and trade unions.[215] Cost-cutting through the use of inferior qualities of yarn and running looms at higher speeds, in conjunction with lower wage levels and greater reliance on workers' skill in the adjustment of looms as compared to the USA, militated against the economic viability of a machine that had retained the birthmarks of its origin in that country. A high degree of unionization among the weaving workforce and elaborate procedures in place to defuse conflicts between capital and labour added further to Lancashire manufacturers' reluctance to invest in the costly new machine. Rather than run any incalculable risk, they banked on continued trade union support in their pursuit of cost-cutting methods that relied heavily on the cooperation of their competent workforce.

The significant degree of feminization of both the workforce and the trade union rank and file, which had played an important role in shaping the conditions in the weaving industry, acted to prevent any gains in male authority being achieved at female weavers' expense, because any attempt at reconstructing gender in the industry was ultimately restrained by trade union concern to safeguard jobs. Consequently, weaving unions emerge from the dispute over automatic looms as having acted in the interest of their female members by default. Complete defeminization of the workforce was only to be had at the price of concessions to employers' demands of an enormity impossible to reconcile with working-class masculinity and of the ultimate erosion of trade union power.

This account of the reasons for Lancashire manufacturers failing to adopt the automatic loom on a large scale, as against the course adopted by nearly all their competitors, has highlighted the deployment of gender. This formed the main strategy pursued by factory owners keen to adopt the new loom in their attempt to overcome anticipated resistance by the men among their weavers against the reorganization of the labour process deemed necessary to make the investment in costly new machinery profitable. The key role played by gender in accounting for the attitude displayed by Lancashire weavers, masters and workers alike, towards the automatic loom should caution against any simplistic view which uncritically equates more advanced technology with progress by paying scant regard to the social implications of the ways in which it is implemented.

Persistence was not confined to machinery which had been readily scrapped by Lancashire's competitors, but extended to gender relations as well. These continued to be at odds with the contemporary working-class ideal. In Lancashire cotton weaving masculinity did not revolve around the performance of work deemed skilled and the attendant ability to earn a family wage. Conversely, femininity was not characterized by domesticity. Rather it centred on paid work carried out away from home even after marriage and on a degree of competence in weaving that enabled women to bring home a pay packet matching, and potentially even exceeding, that of a male weaver. It was the specific way in which conditions in the industry were predicated upon gender that made for the resilience of these versions of working-class masculinity and femininity. This resilience emerged clearly when the attempt was made to use new technology to topple relations of gender that were characterized by an unusual lack of inequality. As it turned out, no inversion of gender relations in Lancashire cotton weaving could be had without a simultaneous erosion of the conditions of work and pay.

Notes

1 See Ellison (1968, p.35), Timmins (1996, p.45).
2 Powerloom development is an instance of the pattern of machine development identified by MacLeod. This involves an initial breakthrough being subsequently modified and complemented by further inventions to make the original design viable in the workplace; see MacLeod (1992, pp.290–91).
3 The beginning of modern powerloom weaving is given as 1822 by Ellison (1968, p.36), who attributes the corresponding loom design to Sharp and Roberts, and as 1830 by Townsend (1902, p.22,234), who credits Roberts alone, as does Timmins (1996, p.46).
4 See Timmins (1993, pp.17–24), reiterated in Timmins (1996, pp.47–8), emphasizing the slow and piecemeal adoption of the powerloom.
5 For details of these improvements, see Marsden (1895, pp.97, 177) and Bennett (1948, p.101). As noted in Chapter 3, in the 1830s looms had been running at 90 to 112 picks per minute, while by the 1880s speed had been increased to up to 400 picks per minute; see Ellison (1968, p.37).
6 See Ellison (1968, pp.36–7).
7 See Bolin-Hort (1989, pp.120–21).
8 See Aitken (1964, p.2).
9 See Mass (1989, p.896).
10 See Mass (1984, p.173).
11 Ibid.
12 *Textile Recorder*, 15.8.1902, p.97.
13 See *CFT*, 2.1.1903, p.4; 9.1.1903, p.5; 23.1.1903, p.8.
14 See *CFT*, 10.4.1903, p.4; see also Copeland (1909, p.147).
15 See *CFT*, 17.4.1903, p.1; 24.7.1903, p.1.
16 Its full title, which read *The Textile Mercury. A Representative Weekly Journal for Spinners, Manufacturers, Machinists, Bleachers, Colourists, and Merchants*, as well as its involvement in the debate about the Northrop, indicate that it had a much wider constituency than just the master spinners, as claimed by McIvor (1996, p.62).
17 For the journal's advocacy of women's employment in weaving and refutation of the claim that mothers' factory work was the cause of high infant mortality, see *Textile Mercury*, 19.1.1901, p. 41; 7.9.1901, p.163.
18 See *Textile Mercury*, 13.9.1902, p.197.
19 Ibid.
20 See Davin (1978).
21 See *Textile Mercury*, 27.9.1902, p.237.
22 See Davin (1978); for an extensive account of the infant and child welfare movement, see Dwork (1987).

23 *Textile Mercury*, 27.9.1902, p.237; see also a speech in a similar vein made by a local councillor who was also a member of the Preston weavers' association, *Preston Guardian*, 27.7.1907, p.12.
24 See Turner (1962, p.390).
25 *Standard* (Oldham), 11.5.1878, p.2, quoted in Rose (1992, p.175).
26 See Schwarzkopf (1991, p.50).
27 See Savage (1987).
28 See election speech by Luke Park, long-time leader of the local weavers, quoted in Savage (1987, p.152); see also speech by one of the Labour candidates standing for council election, *Lancashire Daily Post*, 30.10.1906, p.4.
29 For an editorial statement to the same effect, see *CFT*, 7.4.1893, p.1.
30 Quoted in Savage (1987, p.153). This view is shared by the historian Elizabeth Roberts; see Roberts (1982a, p.54; 1982b, p.151; 1986, pp.146–7).
31 See speech by J.T. Macpherson, quoted in Savage (1987, p.153); see also speech by one of the Labour candidates standing for council election, quoted in *Lancashire Daily Post*, 30.10.1906, p.4; see speech by a local councillor and member of the Preston weavers' association, *Preston Guardian*, 27.7.1907, p.12.
32 For an instance of this attitude see Sloan Chesser in *National Review*, 1909–10.
33 See, for example, *CFT*, 29.6.1906, p.7; *Manchester Guardian*, 22.2.1908, GTC, 23/2; see also the point-by-point refutation of Sloan Chesser's allegations in *National Review*, 1909–10; see also Szreter (1996, pp.244–5) for a Birmingham example.
34 See Dyhouse (1979); for Burnley and Nelson specifically, see Adams (1996).
35 See Roberts (1982b, p.157).
36 See Roberts (1986, p.90).
37 See Roberts (1982a, p.61).
38 Ibid., p.63. In 1913, the sweeping assertion by John Burns, President of the Local Government Board, that infant mortality was the result of mothers' employment engendered much resentment in Burnley. Against Burns was cited the report by the local Medical Officer of Health, which showed that the mortality of infants born to mill workers differed very little from that of infants of stay-at-home mothers. The officer attributed the high rate of infant mortality to Burnley's situation in a hollow and to the clayey subsoil, making for an unhealthy atmosphere; see *CFT*, 15.8.1913, p.5.
39 For an exception, see the testimony of Holmes of the Burnley weavers to the Royal Commission on Labour, *PP*, 1892, XXXV, p.190.
40 See Savage (1987, pp.67–9).
41 Ibid., p.79.
42 See Employment of Women, *PP*, 1893–4, XXXVII, Pt.I, p.664.
43 For instances of alleged boycotting of male weavers, see *CFT*, 17.7.1885, p.7; 30.3.1888, p.6; 6.4.1888, p.7; 27.4.1888, p.5; 18.5.1888, p.5; 13.7.1888, p.5; 12.1.1906, p.5; 16.11.1906, p.4; 4.12.1908, p.1.
44 *CFT*, 20.3.1885, p.5.
45 Ibid.; for an instance from Burnley, see *CFT*, 16.11.1906, p.4.
46 See, for example, *CFT*, 22.2.1889, p.4; 1.5.1891, p.5.
47 *CFT*, 7.4.1893, p.1.
48 *CFT*, 12.3.1909, p.7.
49 J. Rimmer, 'Early Recollections', *DDX*, 978, p.222.
50 *PP*, 1892, XXXV, p.190.

51 See, for example, the testimony by Holmes of the Burnley weavers (note 50, above), p.168; see also Birtwistle, ibid., pp.179–80; the only weaving official to deny this need was Booth of the Ashton weavers, ibid., p.168. This may be attributable to the fact that the bulk of the local cotton industry was spinning (see Jewkes, 1930, p 96), where the good wages paid to male spinners would enable most of them to dispense with the need to send their wives to the factory.

52 He had started work as a nine-year-old half-timer, and his commitment to trade unionism ensured his rising through the ranks from committee member of his local union to full-time secretary of a number of weavers' associations of increasing importance. He was successively appointed town magistrate, county magistrate and finally to Darwen Borough Bench. In 1902, he was elected Member of Parliament for Clitheroe, having gained the backing of the Labour Representation Committee. From 1906 until 1910, he was President of the Weavers' Amalgamation, resigning at the end of 1910 when he became senior labour advisor to the Home Secretary, Winston Churchill. He was knighted in 1917; see *Dictionary of Labour Biography*. For a full-scale biography of Shackleton, see Martin (2000).

53 McClelland has explored the implications of 'respectability' for male workers' access to citizenship; see McClelland (1996). The epitome of the 'respectable artisan' was the shipwright or the engineer rather than the weaver, making only more pressing the need for weavers' representatives publicly to endorse the elements of a masculinity unattainable by the majority of their male rank and file.

54 See *Blackburn Times*, 15.12.1908, p.3, and Martin (2000, p.177).

55 See Liddington (1984, pp.121ff).

56 For an example, see Selina Cooper, ibid., p.71.

57 For the evolution of the family wage and the emergence of the male bread-winner family among the working class, see Barrett and McIntosh (1980) and Seccombe (1986). For a highly empirical approach to the issue leading to the rejection of either capitalism or patriarchy as the sole cause for women's increasing economic dependence on men, see Horrell and Humphries (1997). For a critical assessment of the various approaches to this issue, see Creighton (1996).

58 For a dispute in many ways similar and arising out of the introduction of the Hattersley, a domestically produced automatic, into a mill near Todmorden, see *Textile Manufacturer*, 15.5.1903, pp.145–6; *CFT*, 5.2.1904, p.5; 19.2.1904, p.5; 26.2.1904, pp.1, 5; 11.3.1904, p.5; 5.1.1906, p.5; also Gibson (1948, p.74).

59 See *Textile Mercury*, 27.9.1902, p.236.

60 See McIvor (1988, pp.7–8).

61 See Mass (1984, p.235).

62 See *Textile Recorder*, 15.7.1901, p.65.

63 See Bowker (1983, p.7).

64 See *Making for a New Age*, p.16.

65 See Shortland, (n.d., p.36).

66 See *Hyde Reporter*, 29.10.1904, p.7.

67 See Fletcher, (n.d., p.20); also Gibson (1948, pp.70–2).

68 See Toms (1998, p.10).

69 See *CFT*, 6.3.1903, p.5.

70 See Mass (1984, p.237). The use of mule-spun weft on the first set of Northrops refutes Frankel's contention that the automatic loom always required ring-spun yarn; see Frankel (1955, p.313). This had only been true for the first generation of

Northrops. Subsequently, the machine was modified so as to enable mule cops to be transferred to the shuttle by means of skewers (see Copeland, 1909, p.146), presumably in order to induce English manufacturers, who preferred, or only had access to, mule weft, to change to automatics. Thus at Daisy Hill Mill, Rishton, the shed taken over by the British Northrop Loom Company as a showcase for the new machine, half of the 200 automatics installed worked with ring weft on bobbins, the other half operating with mule weft on cops; see *CFT*, 1.4.1904, p.8.

71   See *Hyde Reporter*, 28.3.1908, p.4.
72   *CFT*, 15.5.1903, p.5.
73   See *CFT*, 9.1.1903, p.1.
74   See *CFT*, 6.3.1903, p.5.
75   See Townsend (1902, pp.22, 324–5).
76   See Conference Report, Ashton Bros. and Weavers' Union, 23.3.1908, p.16.
77   See *CFT*, 10.4.1903, p.1.
78   See *CFT*, 13.3.1903, p.4; 17.4.1903, p.5.
79   See *CFT*, 6.3.1903, p.5.
80   See *CFT*, 15.5.1903, p.5; 21.8.1903, p.4; see also *Textile Recorder*, 15.5.1903, p.1.
81   See Fletcher, n.d., cover.
82   See *CFT*, 21.8.1903, p.4.
83   See Ashton Brothers, 1946, Introduction.
84   See Rose (1986a, p.97).
85   See *CFT*, 13.3.1903, p.4; 8.5.1903, p.7; see also *Textile Recorder*, 15.5.1903, p.1.
86   See *Textile Mercury*, 13.9.1902, p.197.
87   *Textile Mercury*, 27.9.1902, p.236.
88   *Textile Recorder*, 15.5.1903, p.1.
89   *Textile Recorder*, 15.3.1904, p.325.
90   See *CFT*, 15.5.1903, p.5.
91   Ibid.
92   See *CFT*, 22.5.1903, p.5.
93   See *CFT*, 17.6.1904, p.4.
94   See *CFT*, 5.8.1904, p.5; 19.8.1904, p.4; 23.9.1904, p.5; 7.10.1904, p.5; 21.10.1904, p.5; see also *Hyde Reporter*, 29.10.1904, p.7.
95   See *Hyde Reporter*, 29.10.1904, p.7.
96   See *Hyde Reporter*, 22.10.1904, p.4; see also *North Cheshire Herald*, 22.10.1904, p.5.
97   See *CFT*, 22.5.1903, p.5; for further instances of overlookers' dissatisfaction with conditions at Ashton Bros., see Hyde and District Overlookers: Minute Book, 8.4.1904; 6.5.1904; 13.5.1904; 3.6.1904; 1.7.1904; 10.1.1908; 6.3.1908; 3.4.1908; 26.6.1908; 24.7.1908; 21.8.1908; 18.9.1908; 16.10.1908.
98   See *North Cheshire Herald*, 29.10.1904, p.6.
99   See *Hyde Reporter*, 21.3.1908, p.7.
100 See *CFT*, 4.11.1904, pp.1 and 5; see also *Hyde Reporter*, 5.11.1904, p.4.
101 See *Hyde Reporter*, 29.10.1904, p.7.
102 See *North Cheshire Herald*, 5.11.1904, p.7.
103 See *CFT*, 4.11.1904, p.5.
104 See Toms (1996, p.81).
105 See *Hyde Reporter*, 21.3.1908, p.7.
106 See *Hyde Reporter*, 28.3.1908, p.4.

107 See *Textile Mercury*, 13.9.1902, p.197.
108 See Fletcher; unfortunately, the account is undated.
109 See *Hyde Reporter*, 28.3.1908, p.4.
110 See Bolton Oral History, no. 5, pp.7–8; see also North West Sound Archive, 5; for intensification of work, see Roberts (1981), respondent A1P, p.8.
111 See Ross (1991, pp.66ff); see also Lancashire Textile Project, respondent AF1, pp.14–15, albeit with regard to a more advanced type of automatic than the Northrop.
112 See Townsend (1902, p.22,324).
113 See, for example, *CFT*, 1.11.1907, p.1.
114 See *CFT*, 22.11.1907, p.1.
115 See *CFT*, 31.1.1908, p.8.
116 See lecture by A.M. Fletcher to the Lancashire section of the British Association of Managers of Textile Works, *CFT*, 11.10.1907, p.7.
117 See *CFT*, 10.4.1903, p.4.
118 Erroneously given as 'Textile Workers' in the *CFT*, 11.10.1907, p.1.
119 See *CFT*, 11.10.1907, p.7.
120 *CFT*, 11.10.1907, p.1.
121 See, for example, *Textile Manufacturer*, 15.5.1907, p.173.
122 See *Hyde Reporter*, 21.3.1908, p.7.
123 See *CFT*, 13.3.1908, p.5; see also *North Cheshire Herald*, 4.4.1908, p.6
124 See *Hyde Reporter*, 4.4.1908, p.6; for a slightly different ballot result, see *Hyde Reporter*, 4.7.1908, p.6.
125 See *North Cheshire Herald*, 4.7.1908, p.4.
126 See *North Cheshire Herald*, 4.4.1908, p.6.
127 *Hyde Reporter*, 4.4.1908, p.6.
128 See *Textile Mercury*, 29.2.1908, p.158. This argument could, however, be reconciled with the suggestion, made by the same journal in 1902, to pay male weavers a family wage; see note 18.
129 See *Textile Recorder*, 14.3.1908, p.335.
130 See, for example, *Textile Mercury*, 13.9.1902, p.197.
131 *Hyde Reporter*, 11.4.1908, p.4.
132 See *North Cheshire Herald*, 25.4.1908, p.7.
133 See *North Cheshire Herald*, 16.5.1908, p.5.
134 See *Hyde Reporter*, 11.4.1908, p.4.
135 See *CFT*, 8.5.1908, p.4.
136 For the continuation of this policy in the period beyond the First World War through attempts to create something like a corporate identity, see their *A.B.C. Magazine* and 'Introduction to the Mills', 1946, an information brochure handed out to all employees on joining the company.
137 See *Hyde Reporter*, 4.4.1908, p.6; 30.5.1908, p.4; see also *North Cheshire Herald*, 11.4.1908, p.5.
138 See Bann (1976, pp.27ff).
139 See Shortland (n.d., pp.34ff). Her chronology fails to tally with that of Bann, who gives 1869 as date of completion for Throstle Bank Mill; see Bann (1976, p.27). In this case the argument about extra profit to be made due to the shortage of cloth obviously would not apply. Conversely, Shortland fails to mention the allegedly philanthropic motivation behind the building scheme.
140 See *CFT*, 17.4.1908, p.4.

141 See, for example, *Hyde Reporter*, 11.4.1908, p.6.
142 *Hyde Reporter*, 18.4.1908, p.6.
143 See Rose (1992, pp.173ff).
144 See *North Cheshire Herald*, 23.5.1908, p.6.
145 See *Hyde Reporter*, 11.4.1908, p.4.
146 See, for example, South East Lancashire and Cheshire Weavers (Ashton District): Minute Book, 15.4.1908 and every week thereafter until the strike had ended; South East Lancashire and Cheshire Weavers (Stockport & District): Minute Book, 22.4.1908 and every week thereafter until the strike had ended.
147 See *CFT*, 1.5.1908, p.5; 8.5.1908, p.4; see also *North Cheshire Herald*, 23.5.1908, p.5; 18.7.1908, p.5.
148 *Hyde Reporter*, 20.6.1908, p.7.
149 See Conference Report Ashton Bros. and Weavers' Union, 23.3.1908, p.22.
150 For the difficulties involved in skewering mule cops, see Lancashire Textile Project, respondent AA3, p.16; respondent AC4, p.14.
151 See *Hyde Reporter*, 4.4.1908, p.6.
152 See *Hyde Reporter*, 20.6.1908, p.7; 11.7.1908, p.4; see also *North Cheshire Herald*, 11.7.1908, p.5.
153 See *Hyde Reporter*, 11.7.1908, p.4.
154 *North Cheshire Herald*, 11.7.1908, p.5.
155 See *Board of Trade Labour Gazette*, June 1908, p.165; July 1908, p.203. Given the futility of his efforts, it comes as no surprise that the Ashton strike fails to be mentioned in the year-by-year account of the disputes in the arbitration of which G.R. Askwith had been involved; see Askwith (1920). At the time of the strike, he was assistant secretary of the Railway Branch of the Board of Trade, later to become Chief Industrial Commissioner; see Fowler (1979–80, p.50).
156 See Davidson (1978, p.57).
157 See *Hyde Reporter*, 20.6.1908, p.7.
158 See *North Cheshire Herald*, 4.7.1908, p.4; see also *CFT*, 10.7.1908, p.5.
159 See the criticisms voiced by an 'avowed socialist', *North Cheshire Herald*, 11.7.1908, p.4, and by a member of the Amalgamated Society of Engineers, *Hyde Reporter*, 11.7.1908, p.4.
160 *Hyde Reporter*, 4.7.1908, p.6.
161 See *CFT*, 1.8.1913, p.6.
162 To this end, the *Textile Manufacturer* had run a 10-part series in 1907 explaining the mechanism of the Northrop in great detail; see 15.3.1907, pp.85–6; 15.4.1907, pp.125–6; 15.5.1907, pp.162–3; 15.6.1907, pp.194–5; 15.7.1907, pp.231–2; 15.8.1907, p.270; 15.9.1907, p.304; 15.10.1907, p.342; 15.11.1907, pp.374–5; 15.12.1907, pp.412–13.
163 See, for example, *CFT*, 10.2.1905, p.5; 27.10.1905, p.4; 24.11.1905, p.4; 7.6.1907, p.5.
164 See Amalgamated Weavers' Association: Northrop Weaving, *DDX*, 1274/14/4, pp.4, 7.
165 See Frankel (1955, p.313); also Lazonick (1981a, p.32).
166 For a survey of the debate about the decline of the British industry, see Edgerton (1996).
167 For a summary and assessment of this debate, see Marrison (1996, pp.253–64).
168 See Lazonick (1979; 1981b; 1981c; 1983).

169 See Bolin-Hort (1989, pp.119–21).
170 See Lazonick (1981a).
171 See Lazonick (1986); see also Cohen (1985).
172 See Sandberg (1969; 1974); see also Harley (1974), who has applied this argument to British industry in general. For a general critique of Sandbergs's neoclassical approach, see Coleman and MacLeod (1986, p.598). In a subsequent article, MacLeod has pointed out machine-makers' deference to Lancashire industrialists' preference for improvements of established machinery over investment in new technology (1992, p.303).
173 See Saxonhouse and Wright (1984).
174 For a summary and an elaboration of the debate between Lazonick and Mass and their opponents, see Mass and Lazonick (1990).
175 See Leunig 2001.
176 See Lazonick and Mass (1984), Mass and Lazonick (1990).
177 See Mass (1984).
178 See *Textile Mercury*, 28.3.1908, p.242; 20.6.1908, p.465.
179 See Mass (1984, pp.211, 219).
180 Ibid., pp.218ff; for a contemporary argument along these lines, see *Textile Recorder*, 15.7.1901, p.65.
181 See Toms (1996, p.92). This assessment was to be corroborated by an experiment carried out between 1931 and 1932 by the Lancashire Cotton Corporation, an amalgamation of spinning companies. This demonstrated that weaving costs on ordinary looms were substantially lower than on three types of automatic looms. The savings on labour costs achieved by automatic looms were more than offset by greater interest and depreciation charges; see Bowden and Higgins (1999, pp.26, 38).
182 See *Journal of the British Association of Managers of Textile Works*, 1913–14, pp.135, 141; see also *CFT*, 18.4.1913, p.4.
183 See, for example, Committee on Humidity and Ventilation, *PP*, 1909, XV, p.697.
184 See, for example, lecture by Ibzan Sagar to the Lancashire section of the British Association of Managers of Textile Works, *CFT*, 19.3.1909. p.4; see also an earlier observation to the same effect by a member of the Burnley Chamber of Commerce, *CFT*, 17.4.1903, p.5.
185 See, for example, *CFT*, 11.5.1906, p.4; 26.6.1906, p.5.
186 See Firth (1986, p.66).
187 See, for example, *CFT*, 22.5.1903, p.5; 29.4.1904, p.4; 20.12.1907, p.4.
188 See Mass (1989, pp.928–9).
189 For the adjustment of weights by the weavers themselves see, for example, Chew (1912, p.38).
190 See Mass (1984, pp.218ff).
191 See *Textile Recorder*, 15.7.1901, p.65; see also William Chase, *Five Generations of Loom Builders*, Hopedale, MA, 1950, p.15, quoted in Mass (1989, p.900); also ibid., p.928.
192 See *Textile Mercury*, 19.7.1902, p.42; see also Beattie (1992, p.147).
193 See Rothwell (1975, p.370).
194 See Toms (1998, p.13).
195 See *CFT*, 1.1.1904, p.6.
196 See *Textile Recorder*, 15.7.1901, p.65; see also William Chase, *Five Generations of Loom Builders*, Hopedale, MA, 1950, p.15, quoted in Mass (1989, p.900); also ibid., p.928.

197 See *CFT*, 1.4.1904, p.8.
198 See Marrison (1996, p.239).
199 See Rose (2000).
200 Interestingly, both Ashton Bros. and a similarly successful firm, Fielden Bros., were vertically integrated despite being family enterprises; for Fielden Bros., see Toms (1996).
201 See Toms (1998, p.13).
202 See *CFT*, 4.10.1907, p.4; 28.2.1908, p.5.
203 See Gray (1937, pp.35–8).
204 See Bruley (1993).
205 See Bowden and Higgins (1999).
206 This crucial fact receives no mention by Bowden and Higgins, who confine themselves to an exclusively economic analysis; see ibid.
207 See Fowler (1988, p.116); for a more detailed account, see Bruley (1993).
208 See Pope (2000).
209 See the example quoted in Bruley (1993, p.85).
210 See Fowler (1988, p.116).
211 See Bruley (1993, pp.96–7).
212 See Pope (2000, p.754).
213 See Bowden and Higgins (1999).
214 The only notable exception is Alan Fowler, who has carefully researched the strike of 1908 in order to exonerate the Northern Counties' Amalgamation from the allegation of being hostile to technical innovation. He manages to confine mention of the gender issue involved to half a sentence; see Fowler (1979–80).
215 The strength of a tradition that has become part of the regional working-class culture is demonstrated by Bolin-Hort with regard to the half-time system. This continued to enjoy huge support among spinners and weavers relying on juvenile assistants when the other trades comprised in the TUC had come to oppose it; see Bolin-Hort (1989, esp. pp.236–44).

Chapter 6

Weaving Fair and Weaving Free: England's Web of Destiny – Interweaving Shopfloor, Home and Street

'Weaving Fair And Weaving Free – England's Web of Destiny' read the motto on a banner woven and carried by weavers[1] who in 1908 had joined women from all over the country in London to demonstrate for their right to vote.[2] The ability to divert, to purposes of their own, labour, material and machinery intended for generating mill owners' profit derived from weavers' mastery of the labour process, enabling them, within limits, to manipulate conditions of work to their own ends.[3] They used their work-related skills to produce an item the object of which was to proclaim to the public at large the extent to which they saw themselves as determining how their country fared economically. Being employed in one of Britain's key industries, they regarded her economic destiny as hinging upon both the volume and the quality of the produce of their labour. Yet their participation in the big London rally at the same time demonstrates that they felt their crucial role for their country's economy to be at odds with the recognition denied them as citizens. Significantly, on that march, they adopted a stand, not only as disenfranchised women, but also, in a marked display of self-confidence, as female weavers claiming the recognition they felt was due to them in their double role of skilled workers and women.

True, representations of working women played an important role in the imagery deployed by the suffrage movement. While vigorously asserting women's contribution to the productive work of the world, suffragists also, as Lisa Tickner has argued, enforced the representation of working-class women as victims by focusing on the sweated and oppressed worker. Nor was the use made by middle-class suffrage artists of working women's oppression to further the progress of their own campaign free of an element of exploitation.[4] Furthermore, it was common practice for suffragists to march the streets behind occupational banners demonstrating women's ability successfully to operate outside the home. Yet most of these banners bore the emblems of careers that had newly opened up to middle-class women.[5] The outstanding feature of the weavers' banner was therefore its celebration of working women's pride in their contribution to the well-being of the country articulated by the women themselves.

Previous chapters have demonstrated the degree of skill and competence female Lancashire cotton weavers possessed,[6] as well as the centrality of waged work to their identity as women.[7] By 1900, many of them began to campaign actively for their rights as citizens. As becomes apparent via the weavers' banner, their political activism and their self-perception as workers were closely interrelated. This chapter will explore the linkages between work and politics, by arguing that female weavers' political involvement fed upon their specific experience of equality in the labour process. In order to do so it will be necessary to leave the sphere of paid employment, to which the consideration of weavers has hitherto been confined, and to follow them through the other activities their lives encompassed: family care, unionism and suffragism. Combining such varying activities involved reconciling the often contradictory pulls exerted by these different kinds of responsibility. Weavers' ability to integrate them all into their lives testifies to a high degree of motivation, ingenious coping strategies and a prioritizing of activities that was at odds with a conception of femininity to which domesticity was central.

Like the vast majority of working-class women, female weavers, once married, had to juggle their employment away from home and their household and childcare duties. The amount of time and energy spent on housework, pregnancies, births and the rearing of children crucially determine the extent to which full-time employment away from home can be reconciled with the family commitments of a wife and mother.

Elizabeth Roberts has attributed the reconciliation of the demands of paid employment with family care exclusively to the Victorian work ethic imbibed by her female working-class respondents from Lancashire. The belief that salvation lay through work, damnation lay through idleness appears to her to have actuated those female cotton workers who continued in the mill into old age and whose stamina was celebrated by the *Cotton Factory Times* in the following terms: 'The gospel of "work" seems so ingrained in [these veteran workers] that the prospect of a life of leisure has for them no charms.'[8] Yet by prioritizing the self-exploitative propensities of her interviewees, Elizabeth Roberts ignores the fact that their experience of the strength to cope could also be a source of self-confidence, militating against any self-image of women as the weaker sex. As one textile worker reasoned in an interview: 'I don't know really there's all this about us being the weaker sex, being looked after, its [sic] never happened to me, I reckon, what with my family and my job, I reckon I've worked as hard as any man, I really do.'[9]

Yet no-one can stretch their energies indefinitely, and female cotton workers adopted a number of strategies to cope with the exigencies of their lives. Redistributing domestic labour and limiting the number of children emerge as the most important coping strategies adopted by many cotton weavers.

Family Care

One way in which female weavers managed to combine full-time factory work with care for household and children consisted in delegating essential tasks for payment of cash. Thus they paid non-factory women for services, such as child minding and washing, as well as relying on ready-made meals and clothes. Hence the emergence of the fish-and-chip shop, which rapidly became commonplace in the Lancashire cotton district.[10] By the inter-war period, when new ways of cutting down the time spent on household chores became available, Lancashire weavers eagerly bought labour-saving consumer durables.[11] Similarly, where they wielded enough power locally by the sheer strength of numbers, as in Nelson, they successfully pressed for the provision of municipal services at optimum levels,[12] not least in order to lighten the burden of family care.

Despite the doubts expressed by contemporaries[13] and historians[14] alike about the economic rationality of working-class housewives' expenditure on domestic services, female weavers knew only too well the difference their wages made to family income. Yet there was more at stake than mere economic calculation. Delegating housework was also a matter of inclination, as shown by the following statement of a fictitious, yet typical, Lancashire weaver. When it is put to her that she would be better off staying at home, she replies indignantly:

> Stop at home! ... and live on a pound a week! The only expense which wouldn't be going on just the same would be the money for the children and for the washing. In a poor week I can more than double that at the factory, and what I get makes all the difference between having summat decent to eat and wear and going short ... [If she were to stay at home] that means nursing other folks' childer, and washing other folks' clothes – besides doing all your own. I know what that sort of life is. My mother did it, and the house was always messed up wi' babbies and wet clothes. I'd rather go to t'factory by half![15]

Delegation of household chores for cash was subject to the variations in weavers' income, and never complete. Like other working-class women, cotton weavers relied on the help of their children, predominantly their daughters,[16] but significantly also on their husbands' assistance. In this respect female weavers' husbands differed markedly from the majority of their working-class contemporaries. Interviews conducted by Diana Gittins, Miriam Glucksmann and Elizabeth Roberts reveal that men's help varied in extent and regularity[17] and involved cleaning windows, carrying coal, lighting and tending open fires, stoking the boiler for washing days[18] and making beds.[19] Apart from household chores with a possible masculine connotation, quite a few took over part[20] or all of the cooking,[21] some helped with the family washing[22] or shared in caring for children,[23] occasionally even taking over the particularly onerous task of getting up at night to bottle-feed the baby.[24]

Men's participation in housework was so much accepted and taken for granted that it passed into regional folklore. 'Mary Anne' was the nickname[25] for men who could actually be seen doing housework, without however suffering any damage to their masculinity.[26] 'Mary Anne night' was the particular evening in the week when men would customarily do jobs about the house. Then 'you'd see the men doing the windows, you'd say he were a Mary Anne ... you see? It's a right Mary Anne, doing t'windows, outside and shaking the mats ... But ... they'd a right to do when the wife were out running four loom.'[27] Women themselves shared in the community belief[28] that weaving wives not only deserved, but were actually entitled, to be helped by their husbands, not least because the latter, too, benefited from the extra income generated by their wives' factory labour.[29] This belief may well be seen as the feminine variety of a respectable life style that women weavers laid claim to on the basis of their earnings derived from the skill with which they performed their job.

Men's willingness to share in the housework and the extent of their assistance were shaped, though not determined,[30] by their wives' employment away from home.[31] While some ceased doing household jobs when their wives abandoned mill work,[32] others carried on regardless.[33]

The following example of a weaver, who was married to a clothlooker, demonstrates that domestic labour was allocated in amount and kind not by gender but by availability. The clothlooker husband worked in a mill nearer the family home than his wife's. As she was unable to go home during the midday-break, he used to put the dinner in the oven, get the children up and see them off to school, come home again at dinner-time, see that the children had dinner, wash up, see them off to school again, and on his way home in the evening he would call at the butcher's for meat, which he cooked at night for the following day. He was apparently particularly well loved by his children for the butter toffee and other sweets he made for them.[34]

Diana Gittins has found that, in marriages with both spouses employed as weavers, couples shared household duties to an extent that she has qualified as 'evenly and equally'.[35] True, those of her interviewees who were weavers had all been born between 1894 and 1908[36] and were therefore unlikely to have married before the end of the First World War. Nevertheless, their descriptions of married life reveal the embeddedness of domestic cooperation in community values and traditions of long standing.[37] This comes also across in the way in which those of Miriam Glucksmann's interviewees who were weavers mention husbands' help as a matter of course.[38] Nor did they complain of husbands getting a better deal or lament the unfairness of doing a 'double shift'. Overall, Glucksmann found little evidence of any gender hostility over domestic labour and little suggestion that men made hard lives even harder.[39]

Her comparative study of working-class women's condition in Barrow, Lancaster and Preston, the only town in her sample with a sizeable cotton industry, has led Elizabeth Roberts to conclude that 'patterns of women's employment cannot be ignored in the study of role-relationships within marriage'.[40] She thus echoes Thompson who, in his oral history study of the Edwardian period, has concluded that husband and wife quite commonly shared household work where an unusually high proportion of women were engaged in waged labour away from home, as in the textile districts and the Potteries. Conversely, he believes that the most rigid separation of roles occurred in regions dominated by heavy industry, such as mining, where men's work was entirely segregated and physically exhausting. Those tended also to be areas with few employment opportunities for women, who were therefore expected to devote themselves full-time to servicing their menfolk.[41] Accordingly, the importance attached by women to housework varied with their own involvement in waged work.

As Miriam Glucksmann has discovered, female weavers' memories revolved around, and were temporally anchored in, their paid work in the mill, while family events, and housewifery in particular, faded into the background.[42] When recounting their lives they used historical events as an external time grid to locate temporally the events of their own lives. In their case, personal changes and life transitions occurred against a largely unchanging backdrop of paid employment which spanned their whole lives.[43] Clara Collet, investigating women's employment in the mid-1890s, had also observed that, especially in the cotton industry, women regarded industrial employment not merely as a means of gaining a livelihood for a period prior to marriage, but as their occupation in life far more than domestic management. Accordingly, they were ambitious to be good workers.[44] This is further borne out by those female weavers who carried on working in the mill into old age.[45] One such weaver was reported as being 'quite proud of the fact that she brought up her family without leaving the mill'. What is more, this woman had had four children, yet proudly remarked that she 'never served a notice with one of them'.[46]

By attributing men's willingness to help in the home to the need to assist wives in full-time employment to survive at all,[47] Elizabeth Roberts underplays the shift in the distribution of power that underlies such domestic cooperation. Weavers' husbands relinquished a number of mainstays of male dominance apart from taking over tasks commonly seen as feminine. They usually tipped up their wages,[48] leaving their wives to manage the couple's pooled earnings.[49]

Although the custom of tipping up wages was not confined to the weaving districts of Lancashire, the practice contrasted sharply with the reticence over financial affairs that dominated relations between working-class husbands and wives elsewhere.[50] The absence of such reticence in female weavers' families was intimately connected to weavers' family wage economy and the small differential in the contributions made to it by husband and wife. Although wives, as elsewhere, were left in charge of managing the family exchequer, they did so by right and not by concession on the husbands' part. In conjunction with the openly acknowledged absence of a male bread-winner wage and the concomitant need for wives to earn an income, these conditions militated against both any sharp gender division of familial roles with the husband as provider and the wife as the home-manager and the marital tension, frequently erupting in violence, resulting from either partner's failure to live up to the respective ideal.[51] As a result, male violence was not condoned by the norms of the weaving community.[52] Moreover, weaving couples shared not only the responsibilities of supporting a family as well as domestic chores, but also leisure pursuits.[53] This became perhaps most obvious in the mass exodus of entire families from the cotton district to the seaside resort of Blackpool in the summer.

Miriam Glucksmann has attributed any coexistence between a gender division in paid work and in domestic labour to the particular nature and degree of segregation characteristic of the local labour market. Local cultures of work, gender relations and household arrangements, she has argued, affected both expectations and practices.[54] The picture that emerges of female weavers' families, and of weaving couples in particular, is one of a degree of overlap in the experience of husbands and wives, which was more pronounced than among other working-class couples.[55] Owing to their 'identical relations to the occupational system',[56] actually doing identical work, these men and women knew the ins and outs of each other's jobs, which precluded any denigration of female labour and also the shrouding of male jobs in any kind of mystery. Couples may even have been employed at the same mill, as demonstrated in Chapter 3, or may at least have met through being co-workers.[57] The similarity of work experience was underpinned by the negligible or non-existent difference in the amount of wages each of them brought home. Coupled with the indispensability of the wife's earnings to family income, this enabled female weavers to be sparing of services for husbands, who in turn were unable to enforce such services, because they could lay no claim to being chief earners.[58]

Acknowledgment of their wives' workload and relevant contribution to the family's well-being induced husbands to share in at least part of the double burden their wives had to shoulder and generally to treat them with some degree of consideration and respect. The lack of segregation by gender typical of the weaving shed equally characterized home life and leisure pursuits. This significant degree of overlap has led Diana Gittins to characterize marriages with both spouses employed in weaving as joint-role relationships.[59] This has been echoed by Miriam Glucksmann, who has pointed to women weavers' greater gender equality in employment and in the home as mutually self-reinforcing and to the emergence of a picture of a more 'companionate' marriage of partners.[60] Conversely, Elizabeth Roberts's rejection of Diana Gittins's conclusion, namely that working wives failed to exert any more power and influence in their families than their non-working counterparts,[61] is not only at variance with her emphasis elsewhere on the relevance of women's employment to role relationships within marriage,[62] but also fails to tally with some of the evidence her own interviews have generated.

Fertility Control

A most important way of making family needs compatible with full-time employment, while also preserving women's physical well-being, consisted in limiting the number of children. Significantly, this also involved a major shift in weavers' masculinity away from the centrality of the capacity to inseminate. The fact that Lancashire cotton operatives, and weavers in particular, were in the van of the British working class in controlling their fertility was at least suspected as early as 1832,[63] and has long been accepted by historians.[64] At the beginning of the twentieth century, in 14 out of 28 districts in the county, the birth rate was only just over half of what it had been between 1851 and 1876.[65] Lancashire cotton operatives thus refuted in practice the prevailing 'diffusionist' explanation of fertility decline, which assumes that the limitation of family size was first practised by the upper social strata, seen as the pioneers of modernization, and only gradually trickled down to the lower reaches of society.[66]

Recently Szreter has persuasively argued that, among the working class, at least, the decline of fertility was achieved in most cases by spacing births rather than stopping,[67] that is, the deliberate cessation of childbirth prior to menopause. Spacing of births without any resort to contraceptives, which were difficult to procure, expensive as well as morally tainted,[68] obviously required a considerable degree of self-control. Such behaviour, as Szreter has argued, was embedded in a culture of working-class respectability of which, since at least the beginning of the nineteenth century, self-control, including sexual restraint, had become one of the hallmarks.[69] The 'culture of abstinence'[70] characterizing the fertility regime of cotton workers did not preclude recourse to abortion as a last resort when attempts at abstinence had failed.[71] Abortion, though illegal since 1803, was an accepted part of working-class life,[72] and female cotton operatives had been known to resort to it since the early nineteenth century.[73] Moreover, the *Cotton Factory Times* catered for its female readership's specific needs by regularly carrying thinly veiled advertisements for abortifacients.

Fertility control, as Szreter has asserted, aimed at maintaining, defending or enhancing a specific standard of living.[74] It was therefore subject to changes in the relative costs and benefits of childrearing,[75] on which labour market negotiations between workers, employers and the state all had a bearing. Yet, far from being determined by economic conditions alone, the relative costs and benefits of childrearing, Szreter maintains, are culturally variable, hinging as they do on potential parents' perception.[76]

In the cotton weaving industry the abundance of female and juvenile labour, the deployment of which was controlled and hence institutionalized by the early Factory Acts, outlined in Chapter 2, made for a negligible gender differential in wages, while juvenile earnings, as a result of protective legislation, were significantly lower than those of either parent. It therefore made most sense economically for couples to arrange their childbearing so as to maximize both spouses' ability to earn or at least not to have so many children so quickly that the wife was forced to abandon factory work before the first child reached teenage earning capacity. This tendency was reinforced by subsequent factory legislation restricting child labour even further.[77]

Underpinning the conclusions reached by Gittins,[78] Szreter has emphasized 'the way in which gendered working practices in different industries could strongly influence the general pattern of associations and quality of communications between the sexes and therefore between spouses, something of great importance in determining the capacity of spouses to negotiate birth control together'.[79] Joint decision making in sexual matters, according to Szreter, was embedded in the rather more egalitarian gender relations among couples who shared in mutually agreed family survival strategies. Central to these was both partners' engagement in paid work away from home which generated roughly the same amount of income for each.[80]

Conditions conducive to such joint decision making prevailed in the weaving towns, where large numbers of men and women worked side by side in the local mills. Thus evolved communities with specific norms, beliefs and practices shaping people's reproductive behaviour,[81] the transmission of which was greatly facilitated by the congregation in the weaving sheds of numerous women and men, who discussed sexual matters in gender-homogeneous groups.[82] The mill was appreciated as a source of information not available elsewhere. Two weavers interviewed by Elizabeth Roberts stated that they learnt about 'the facts of life' at the mill, where they mixed with girls older, and presumably more sexually experienced, than themselves. While one of them maintained that 'you grew up more at work than anywhere',[83] the other one emphasized that sex was talked about jokingly,[84] which would also imply a certain degree of openness.[85] It is not at all clear how, in the face of these statements, Elizabeth Roberts can conclude that 'There is no evidence that women discussed sexual topics in the mill.'[86]

Yet at the same time there was a high degree of localism even in a seemingly homogeneous region like the cotton district.[87] Localism may account for Preston, which had an exceptionally high fertility rate in spite of large-scale employment of married women in the cotton mills.[88] Savage has shown that the majority of the married female cotton workers had husbands in well-paid jobs in cotton or metal production. In these families there was a marked discrepancy in income between husband and wife, and spouse relations were less egalitarian.[89] At least equally relevant may have been the sizeable Anglo-Catholic community[90] with a peculiar fertility regime of its own that Preston boasted in contrast to other Lancashire weaving towns.

As Chapter 3 has shown, female cotton weavers derived a considerable degree of personal satisfaction from their ability to carry out a skilled job over and above their awareness of making a vital contribution to family income. The chapter has also demonstrated their delight in female companionship at work. Taken together, these factors accounted for women's desire to stay on at work after marriage, making them averse to letting the demands made by a large family interfere with their jobs. If married weavers' continuation at the mill is accounted for in terms of the combined impact of economic need and personal inclination, then husbands' concurrence with their wives' desires appears even more significant in indicating a decisive shift in the gender distribution of power among weaving couples.

Furthermore, in the few cases where it is possible to explore fertility control at the individual level, the potential for shifts in the notions of femininity and masculinity become apparent. Contact with contemporary socialist or feminist movements, or both, facilitated such shifts to a certain degree, as well as reinforcing couples' decisions to limit the number of their offspring. As a result, couples actually 'stopped' reproducing once their ideal family size of one child only had been attained.[91]

Selina Cooper is a case in point. Her prominence in the suffrage movement, coupled with unusual closeness to her daughter, enabled a biography to be written of her.[92] She was a winder in the cotton boom town of Nelson and met her future husband, a weaver, through their mutual involvement in the local branch of the Social Democratic Federation, a socialist organization with Marxist leanings founded in 1884.[93] On the basis of their shared interests and similar outlook on life, they decided to get married. By this time Selina was 32 and Robert four years her junior, thereby presenting a true case of late age at marriage. Selina's first child, who, not at all unusually by the standards of the weaving community,[94] had been conceived prior to marriage, died at only four months old. Three years later she had a daughter, who survived into adulthood. Selina never became pregnant again.

The Coopers thus exemplify a range of strategies in shaping the size of their family. There is late age at marriage followed by the spacing of children and finally stopping altogether once the second child has proved sufficiently resilient to survive. Indications are that the Coopers practised birth control. They possessed a well-worn copy of *The Law of Population*, a birth control pamphlet originally published in 1877 by Annie Besant, a secularist and freethinker moving in socialist circles. The pamphlet assessed the value of various contraceptive devices and came complete with the addresses of suppliers and prices charged.[95]

Selina Cooper's case exemplifies three distinct, but mutually reinforcing, influences. Firstly, both she and her husband worked in a weaving shed and shared in the fertility regime characteristic of the weaving community. Secondly, they were both involved in the Socialist Revival, a term denoting the springing up of a whole range of bigger or smaller, long- or short-lived socialist organizations in the Britain of the 1880s. One such was the Social Democratic Federation that the Coopers had joined prior to switching their allegiance to the socialist Independent Labour Party formed in 1893,[96] and which they found more congenial. Some varieties of late nineteenth-century socialism, at least, legitimized birth control as a temporary yet acceptable expedient for combating poverty.[97] And some socialist organizations, as becomes apparent via Annie Besant's pamphlet, to some extent helped spread birth control knowledge among members and sympathizers.[98]

The Women's Co-operative Guild, which Selina Cooper also belonged to, was particularly important in this respect. Formed in 1883 in order to give the wives of cooperators an interest in the movement, in the period prior to the First World War it evolved into a progressive and autonomous section of the working-class movement with a sharp awareness of the specific ways in which sexual and class oppression fused in the lives of working-class wives.[99] The North West, which had been the heartland of the Cooperative movement ever since the first shop was opened at Rochdale in 1844, also proved the strongest area of support for the Guild.[100] Many a cotton operative thrived in the atmosphere of support and encouragement offered by this organization.[101] True to its commitment to improving the condition of working-class wives, the Guild took a positive stand on birth control, until after the First World War it increasingly dovetailed its campaigns with the concerns of the Labour Party.[102] Under Guild auspices there were also women-only lectures given, including those in some Lancashire towns, at which sexual matters were explained and birth control devices sold.[103]

The influence exerted by her immersion in the weaving community, coupled with her involvement in the Socialist Revival, enabled Selina Cooper to give her life a distinctly different shape from that of her mother, who had had to cope with eight children as well as the serial unfaithfulness of her husband, on whose financial support she yet depended. Hence Selina's resolve to preserve her economic independence regardless of marriage and against the kind of drudgery her mother had had to bear.

The important influence of both childhood experiences and involvement in the socialist movement becomes equally clear via Selina Cooper's contemporaries Hannah Mitchell[104] and Ada Nield Chew,[105] neither of whom was a weaver, but both of whom took up their residence in the cotton district of Lancashire. They further shared with Selina Cooper their active involvement in socialist and feminist movements. Both were later to trace the seeds of their feminism to their childhood experience of blatant gender discrimination when each of them was regularly relied upon by her mother for help with household chores, while their brothers were allowed to play. Moreover, the birth of Hannah Mitchell's only son proved to be exceedingly protracted and painful, so that she resolved not to undergo such torture ever again.[106] Each of these women had only one child, and the cooperation of the husband, which was openly acknowledged by Hannah Mitchell,[107] can be presumed in the other two cases. As the mother of an only child, each of these women was able to engage in political activity full-time. Their political activism stood out in degree, though not in kind, from that of the majority of female Lancashire cotton weavers.

Unionism

Power relations in the family apart, once at work in a factory environment cotton weavers were willy-nilly forced to take their stand in the field of tension generated by the conflicting interests of capital and labour. This caused men and women to join their local trade associations in large numbers. For many, starting work in the mill and enrolling in the union were one and the same thing. It was not unusual for mothers or other female kin smoothing girls' entry into the factory to ensure that passage from pupil to mill worker was authenticated by membership of the appropriate union.[108] In the cotton industry as a whole, 75 per cent of the female operatives were organized, while among women weavers the proportion was nearer 80 per cent.[109]

Union membership proved to be an ambivalent experience for women. The large proportion of females among cotton weavers was seen as a liability rather than an asset by the invariably male union officials, who deemed women and young girls to be difficult to organize[110] and to pose a threat to the standard of wages and conditions achieved by decades of trade union struggle. Men, by contrast, were thought to be much better qualified to defend the interests of labour,[111] since they were believed to be imposed upon less easily by mill owners. Thus an official of the Weavers' Association of Hyde and Hadfield districts was reported as saying: 'Women ought to be connected with trade unions, because no one was more liable to oppression ... He defied anyone to contradict his statement that where only females were employed the most tyranny was practised, because the employers took it for granted that the women would stand anything.'[112] Interestingly, by the beginning of the twentieth century, the same district counted among the best unionized of the entire Amalgamation, as shown in the preceding chapter.

Conversely, the increasing unionization of women in any one locality was used as a warning to employers against presuming that women workers could easily be tyrannized. According to the secretary of Oldham Weavers' Association:

> they had as sensible women in their trades union as men. What surprised him was that employers put down women generally as fools. It was the fault of the weavers that they were looked upon in that manner, and because they did not take that interest in the trades union that they ought. He could assure them that the women of this country were getting more sensible every day.[113]

Female sensibility, in union officials' opinion, hinged upon their degree of involvement in the union. If women failed to see sense, pressure was brought to bear. Thus, at a particular shed in Oldham district, male weavers threatened to abandon their custom of helping their female co-workers to carry cloth from the looms to the warehouse unless the latter joined the union.[114]

Complaints about female lethargy in matters of conditions and pay were refuted in practice by women realizing for themselves the need to organize and take matters into their own hands.[115] Nor did they necessarily lack in commitment. Thus one woman stated, 'It was a matter of principle to be in the union. To fight the bosses, you see. I don't remember anything from benefits'[116] – as if to say that she was never interested in the friendly society side of the union.

In those localities where weaving was nearly exclusively female, while male employment was concentrated in other branches of the cotton industry, men appeared to be the main obstacles to the unionization of women. Not even staunch unionists could be relied upon to ensure that their female kinfolk were organized. Thus spinners, carders and tacklers, all of whom belonged to the best paid sections of the cotton workforce, were called upon to let their wives and daughter join the union.[117] Oldham, the outstanding centre of the spinning industry, for this very reason was a black spot regarding the unionization of the local women weavers.[118] Spinners' conception of themselves as bread-winners appeared to them to obviate the need for their womenfolk to safeguard their own interests as waged workers. According to one correspondent of the *Cotton Factory Times*, 'when asked, by canvassers for the Weavers' Association, to enter their wives their reply is invariably that they can keep them if anything happens'.[119] Despite their eagerness to organize women workers the weavers' associations in such localities deferred to patriarchal authority by not approaching the women directly but going through the male heads of household instead. Thus male unionists at Ashton were castigated in the following way: 'No man ... can be consistent in his unionism if he does not extend precept and principle to those relatives over whom he has influence and control.'[120] Where such beliefs and practices had taken hold of the local union hierarchy, the organization of women workers suffered.[121] Only if men failed in their supposed duty to help organize the women were the latter urged to act autonomously.[122]

Whether they were called upon to induce their female kinfolk to enrol in the union or to discontinue preventing them to do so, men consistently figured as actors in trade union rhetoric, while women were depicted as the passive victims of their male kinfolk's designs. Nor did union membership make any difference, because enrolling women workers was seen by officials as taking over control from husbands or fathers. It was precisely this transfer of male authority from kin to non-kin that was resented by those men preventing their wives and daughters from joining the union. As far as the women were concerned, male hegemony remained essentially the same, no matter whether it was located in the family or in the labour organization.

Yet when their opponents seized upon male dominance to denounce trade union activities, the *Cotton Factory Times* was quick to repudiate them. Thus, when some 'middle-class people' complained that strikes in the cardroom and the weaving shed had been solely instigated by union secretaries, who 'had the women and girls in "leading strings", and that the latter could not reason out the merits of a dispute like men', the paper's commentator made the following rejoinder: 'The idea that the weaver and tenter do not understand their own grievances is not an uncommon one among a certain class; but the initiated will smile at the absurdity of the idea.' What started off as apparent praise of women's own ability to assess conditions at work swiftly turned into the reassurance of middle-class opponents that male trade unionists kept a close check on women. No strike, they were assured, could be called without the consent of either the local committee or the Amalgamation's Executive, both exclusively male.[123] Clearly, this emphasis on male dominance was aimed at enhancing trade unions' respectability in the eyes of their opponents.

On occasion, the recalcitrance of female workers had to be acknowledged. In 1886, one Albert Simpson, a spinner, manufacturer and merchant at Preston, had appeared as a witness before the Commission on the Depression of Trade and Industry. He had taken the opportunity to complain about disputes, from which trade was suffering badly. As a solution he proposed that the settling of disputes be left to heads of families who, he believed, behaved more responsibly. When asked by the commissioners how he would deal with it if the women and children employed in the industry preferred not to leave the settling of disputes to heads of families, he replied: 'Then it would have to go on as it is',[124] thereby implying a significant degree of influence on the part of juvenile and female labour.

By contrast, weaving mothers were called upon in the following terms to ensure that their sons enrolled in the appropriate union for their trade:

> [A union official] ... thought it was every mother's duty whenever she sent a boy to earn his livelihood – it ought to be her first duty – to see his name was enrolled as a member of the association connected with the trade at which he was employed. He hoped that mothers would see that that part of their duty was carried out, and if they did so they might depend upon it that any unjust treatment administered to a boy or girl coming to the knowledge of the officials of the association would soon be looked into.[125]

This speech openly acknowledged the literally patriarchal role assumed by the unions, whose promise to act *in loco parentis*, as it were, aimed at easing parental misgivings at having to let their offspring pass beyond the reach of both their authority and their protection.

In all union matters men were to take the lead, while women were to let themselves be led.[126] According to one official, 'It was often said that women were careless about the prices paid, but he always contended it was not a woman's work to bother with prices. It was the men who ought to look after them and then he believed the women would assist them all in their power.'[127] Nor did union officials believe that women could be trusted with responsible jobs, such as taking temperature readings[128] to determine whether or not humidity in the shed was kept within the legally prescribed limits.

Union officials concurred with one another in complaining about the lethargy of female workers, maintaining that women would go to union meetings only if they had a particular grievance, but were indifferent otherwise.[129] Female attendance at meetings varied. Instances of total absence[130] contrasted with women's numerical predominance in a reflection of the local gender composition of their trade, as was the case at Bolton.[131] Apart from shouting critical comments on suggestions made,[132] active participation appears to have been confined to seconding motions.[133] Although this testifies to women's readiness and ability to speak up as well as a degree of familiarity with formal procedure, all that seconding a motion involved was a simple statement to this effect without any need to argue a case or make a lengthy speech. The gender division of labour operating at these meetings appears to have involved men putting and women seconding motions,[134] in a fair reflection of union belief that men should lead and women be led.[135]

In contrast to officials' allegations, women were by no means lagging behind men when it came to taking strike action. The *Reports on Strikes and Lock-Outs* compiled by the Chief Labour Correspondent of the Board of Trade on an annual basis from 1889 onwards[136] are full of strikes involving, or even instigated by, women. Women struck work for numerous reasons. The following list is anything but exhaustive: the intended discharge of all male weavers at their mill, overbearing superiors, fines, the dismissal of weavers for being trade unionists, driving, bad material given out, a charge for assistance given in carrying beams to looms. True, not all of these disputes were successful,[137] but they nevertheless testify to women's unwillingness to tolerate conditions of work deemed unsatisfactory. Moreover, and not always to their advantage, women weavers staged walk-outs whenever their patience was exhausted, in total disregard of the elaborate procedures to be observed in any attempt to have grievances put right. In such cases they might prove reluctant to act on union officials' advice.[138] Nor were women lagging behind when operatives formed deputations to lay their complaints before their bosses.[139]

Female militancy came to the fore when tension over strike breaking erupted, turning with a vengeance against strike breakers, or 'knobsticks', as they were called locally. Female strikers regularly found themselves summonsed for alleged assault.[140] On such occasions, when the livelihood of entire communities was under threat, women weavers' militancy can be seen as an attempt to preserve the community's integrity as well as their own jobs. The latter was particularly apparent in the examples cited in the preceding chapter in connection with the automatic loom strike at Hyde.

Furthermore, this militancy formed part of the cultural heritage women emigrant weavers took with them to the textile mills of New England. As Mary Blewett has shown,[141] female weavers infused their memories of Lancashire popular radicalism into strike action, in which they took a leading part as agitators. Their militancy stood in marked contrast to the staid and responsible behaviour which immigrant male textile operatives had imported from Lancashire. There it had stood them in good stead in their dealings with employers and had also functioned, as Sonya Rose has argued,[142] as a potent device for marking themselves off from the unruly others, who included many women. US factory owners, by contrast, read this type of behaviour as a sign, not of respectability, but of deference, disparaging the fighting force of their male workers.

Finally, Sam Fitton, the highly popular cartoonist and writer, whose work formed a regular feature of the *Cotton Factory Times* between 1907 and 1917,[143] created Sally Butter'orth, a strong-minded and strong talking woman who gave a female view on the issues of the day. In depicting her as willing and fully capable to stand up for herself, if need be by resorting to violence,[144] he may have paid tribute to the strength of women cotton operatives.

Bastions of Male Power

The gender division of labour and power was most blatant in the union hierarchy. Trade union officials were almost exclusively male, while women predominated among the rank and file. Ashton weavers' union may be cited as one of the most salient examples of male dominance. Here the local union was made up overwhelmingly of women weavers. In 1896, the union had 6500 members, of whom 325 were men; in 1906, there were 240 men out of a membership of 4500; and in the period from 1907 to 1909 total membership was in excess of 5000, no more than 64 of whom were male. Yet not until 1919 were women appointed as collectors and union representatives.[145]

Although as early as 1888 a lone voice had advocated the need for female committee members in order to promote unionization among women,[146] female officials were by and large confined to those localities where weaving was exclusively or overwhelmingly female, because the local labour market offered men more attractive employment than the weaving shed. The literally patriarchal attitude underlying the male exclusiveness of union committees was made perfectly clear by D.J. Shackleton when appearing as a witness before the Truck Committee in his capacity of Amalgamation president. Called upon to explain the internal make-up of the Amalgamation's local associations, he explained that 'These committees are composed exclusively of persons now working inside cotton mills as weavers. They are almost all of them fathers of families having their families working in the mills, and they represent therefore in the most direct way possible the operatives employed.'[147]

In the absence of large numbers of male weavers able to represent their female colleagues 'in the most direct way possible', women stood a chance. Thus Oldham weavers boasted a female president, at least in 1896 and 1897,[148] as did Wigan, where the president continued in her office even after marriage[149] and where, by 1914, the entire committee as well as all the collectors were women.[150] In Oldham, there were usually about four women on the committee of 15 or 16.[151] One of these was Nellie Devine, who has figured in Chapter 4 as a witness before the Truck Committee. At Stockport, where weaving was 98 per cent female, in 1914 there were seven women on the committee, four of whom were married, and the union boasted 14 women collectors. In view of such opportunities to become involved in union management, it comes as no surprise that women should have been reported as taking an interest in the union and attending meetings in large numbers.[152]

Where weaving was mixed, women officials remained few and far between. In 1897, there were women on the committee of the weavers' union at Glossop,[153] and in 1911 the *Blackburn Weekly Telegraph* hailed 'a new and interesting departure in connection with the management of Blackburn and District Weavers' ... Association' with the election of two women, one married, one single, to the committee. Their election was the result of pressure by winders and warpers for direct representation. Both were exclusively female trades and commonly organized alongside weavers. The large number of female weavers, by contrast, carried on being represented by men.[154]

Likewise in Bolton, where, as noted in Chapter 2, weaving was divided between men making counterpanes on broad looms and women working on narrow looms, the latter had managed to have a seat on the committee reserved for one of their number from at least 1903 onwards.[155] Previously, union business had been the exclusive affair of the male counterpane weavers. They appear to have promoted union involvement among the female narrow-loom weavers[156] so as to safeguard themselves against female competition.

Female representation on the committee was only on sufferance, as is revealed by a closer look at the way in which female weavers made use of their new-won right. Not every woman felt comfortable representing the interests of her group of weavers, and at least one of those elected failed to take up her seat.[157] This increased the burden shouldered by those sufficiently self-confident not to be deterred. One particularly committed woman served at least four terms of office, two of which were consecutive, though the second was not completed, and there was a three months' break between the third and fourth terms. During the fourth term she was delegated, along with the association's president, to attend a regional meeting of unions. One woman was also among the delegates sent to participate in the Federation meeting of weavers and tacklers in 1906.[158] Furthermore, in 1906, one female committee member was to represent the association at the annual conference of the Trades Union Congress (TUC), but only because the man nominated originally was unable to obtain leave of absence. This was quite in accordance with general practice. Between 1901 and 1906, weavers' unions sent six women to the annual TUC conferences, and in 1910 and 1912 one each, both of whom were from Oldham. Over the same period more than 125 male weavers attended.[159]

At Preston, where 73.5 per cent of the weaving union membership was female,[160] until the 1890s the local union had organized only about a quarter of the industry's workforce, representing mainly the interests of male weavers. Initially, the union had tried to erect craft barriers around weaving. Having failed, it embarked upon a recruiting drive deliberately aimed at women in order to ensure that they received full rates and were not given preference over men.[161] As women figured only as pawns in men's union strategy, the first woman was nominated for the committee only prior to the First World War. Yet the men flatly refused to have her.[162] Only after 1918 did the union become more open to women.[163]

Although this is a particularly blatant example, women were generally not made welcome.[164] Thomas Birtwistle, secretary of the Northern Counties' Amalgamation, maintained in 1889:

> Females take no part in the management, although we do not prohibit them from doing so; on the contrary, we have on several occasions endeavoured to induce them to do so, but have failed. Yet it must be remembered that men in dealing with their women members are at present at a great disadvantage: one of the most capable and experienced of men unionists in the kingdom, after addressing a large meeting of women, turned round to me and said: 'It is very strange, somehow: say what we will we cannot get at these women.' He forgot that the women had been for so long treated as a class apart, and as an inferior class, that they naturally distrusted the good intentions of men whom they had been led to regard as rivals.[165]

This is the nearest any cotton union official ever came to revealing any insight into male dominance in the unions impeding the organization of women. As late as 1913, David Shackleton, erstwhile president of the Amalgamation, showed no such insight, blaming women's apathy for the absence of female officials. This is particularly ironic, since he himself, who had only joined the local union upon getting married, involved himself in running the union at his wife's prompting. Her commitment to unionization was put to a severe test when David found himself blacklisted on account of his labour activism. Concerned about the depressing effects the futile search for work was having on her husband, she persuaded him to give up job hunting, turning herself into the sole earner for a period of 17 weeks.[166] Convinced that only single women would have the time and energy to take up office, Shackleton maintained that until recently 'girls' had not wanted to do committee work after returning home from the mill and had been reluctant to run the risk of victimization for becoming involved in union management.[167] Yet avoiding the risk of victimization appears to have been subject not so much to gender as to the importance of a particular individual's earnings to family income.[168] In a striking display of gender blindness, the secretary of Burnley Weavers' Association attributed women's lack of interest in union management to their work and interests being identical with men's so that they were happy to let the latter run the union.[169]

Acting as a union representative or contact within her own mill[170] or taking a seat on the committee of their local union was as far as women's active involvement in union management was allowed to go.[171] The element of 'blocked mobility' that Joanna Bornat has found in the General Union of Textile Workers organizing Yorkshire woollen weavers[172] applied in Lancashire cotton weavers' unions, too. Any post wielding responsibility and authority was beyond their reach. This was particularly true of the secretaryship, which carried a great deal of influence on the local committee. Moreover, the secretary represented his association on the Amalgamation's executive. Though not explicitly barred from this post, women were clearly given the impression of being unfit. When they failed to be discouraged, they were actively blocked, as the following particularly well-documented example demonstrates.

Alice Foley, having worked in a Bolton weaving mill for seven years, was taken on by her local union as a sick visitor. Under the 1911 National Health Insurance Act, trade unions could qualify to administer the Act's regulations and appoint sick visitors to assess the claims of sick or injured union members. During the First World War, Bolton weavers' union was governed by an all-male committee composed mainly of counterpane weavers, who were antagonistic to the idea of women being anything more than paying members. When, in January 1917, the assistant secretary of her local union resigned, presumably to join the Forces, the executive decided to leave the post vacant for the time being and took on Alice Foley as a 'temporary clerk' instead. For a long time her presence in the union office, she felt, was tolerated rather than accepted.[173] Basically, she was doing the assistant secretary's job without commensurate pay or recognition.

By January 1918, the pressures of work were such that the union decided to advertise the post of assistant secretary. Of the eight applicants shortlisted, three were women, including Alice Foley. They had to sit the examination customary for full-time union officials.[174] This was usually conducted by the secretary of some District Weavers' Association, who was generally also a member of the Central Committee of the Weavers' Amalgamation, and aimed to assess candidates' knowledge of the regulations governing the weaving trade. Candidates would have had to work out weaving prices for a number of cloths in accordance with the Uniform List, they might have had to answer a question relating to winders, who were always organized alongside weavers, or a question as to what they would do if required to deal with a matter of dispute between a union and an employer.[175] At Bolton one man gave up during the examination and did not submit his papers. Of the remaining five, one obtained 72 per cent and the next nearest 38 per cent. Evidence suggests that Alice Foley came out top. Yet the union decided against appointing an assistant secretary and to keep the position open for two members currently in the army.[176]

In 1918, Alice Foley applied to the union to be allowed to attend various meetings and conferences to which the association had been invited to send representatives. Although the secretary himself was unable to go, the union preferred to remain unrepresented rather than send a woman. At the end of 1919, the post of assistant secretary was re-advertised, with the proviso that men only need apply. Not until 1942 did Alice Foley become assistant secretary of her union under the sobriquet of Woman Officer.[177]

Elsewhere women unionists profited from large-scale army recruitment during the First World War. At Nelson this enabled women for the first time to become active in the affairs of their Association. Yet no woman was actually elected to the committee until after the war,[178] and this despite the fact that at Nelson 100 per cent trade union membership had been achieved by 1911.[179]

The Benefits of Union Membership

The various ways in which male unionists displayed their domination of the organization casts a different light on women's apathy, so vociferously deplored by union officials. Women confined themselves to using their trade organization to have specific grievances alleviated, because this meant tangible benefits in monetary terms and was sure to receive male backing. By contrast, any attempt to become involved in union management not only increased the burden women had to shoulder anyway, but also required stamina and self-confidence in facing up to men who were anything but keen on, or even openly hostile to, women breaking into their ranks.

Female weavers were in and out of their local union offices,[180] asking for their weekly pay to be checked, lodging complaints about abusive tacklers, fines[181] or unfair dismissal,[182] and experiencing the satisfaction of having their complaints looked into and, where possible, put right. Thus the secretary of Burnley Weavers' Association informed a mother and union member of an impending visit by two union officials wanting to investigate her daughter's complaint about the conduct of a certain tackler. Three days later, a letter was sent inviting the two women to a meeting. Another week later, the two of them were requested to come to the union office. The daughter's complaint was laid before the local Manufacturers' Association, whose committee received a deputation of weavers and heard the girl repeat her allegations as well as evidence by her mother and another weaver. The tackler was heard, too. As a result of the hearing the committee resolved that, while there had not been sufficient evidence of the tackler's alleged misconduct to justify a recommendation for 'extreme measures', presumably dismissal, he was believed to have acted somewhat imprudently and was to be reprimanded by his employer.[183]

Recognizing the effort involved in repeating her allegations in front of a committee composed of men and employers exclusively, union officials sent the girl a letter in appreciation of her conduct. While somewhat exaggerating the outcome of the proceedings, they wrote to

> tender you their hearty thanks for the splendid manner in which you fought your case yesterday, and also to your mother for being such an admirable witness and the Committee think that the capital manner Bob Clegg [the tackler] was punished, we shall hear less in the future of overlookers molesting young girls than has been the case in the past.

Moreover, the girl was promised compensation for work lost through attending meetings. A further letter mentioned that the incriminated tackler was prosecuted by the union, presumably his own.[184]

The situation in Burnley was highly unusual by Lancashire standards because of the temporary existence of two rival unions. The town was one of the strongholds of the Social Democratic Federation, which was anxious to win over the local Weavers' Union. The local branch had a membership of about 400 and more than 1000 sympathizers.[185] Amid growing dissatisfaction of the rank and file with union officialdom in 1896, the New Textile Operatives' Society (Weavers' Department) was established under SDF auspices. Over the years the influence of this socialist-inspired section increased, and control of the union passed into their hands.[186]

Despite the rhetoric indulged in by Lancashire weavers' officials about alleged female apathy, trade unionists elsewhere looked with envy upon the degree of female unionization achieved in the cotton industry.[187] The Women's Trade Union League, which had evolved from the Women's Protective and Provident League in 1891 and was intended to promote unionization among women workers, was intimately familiar with the difficulties involved in setting up and sustaining female unions. In many ways, the cotton industry represented the goal the organization was aiming at. WTUL organizers consistently pointed to the cotton district as demonstrating the benefits unionization brought in its wake.[188] One such eulogy read:

> There is not a more impressive sight in the labour world than such a crowd as that which assembles for a Lancashire demonstration, and the long train of women and girls each wearing the badge of their union remains for ever in the spectator's mind as the most graphic object lesson in Women's Trade Unionism.[189]

Such praise notwithstanding,[190] the WTUL realized that even among the female cotton operatives there was room for improvement and from the 1890s it dispatched some of its organizers to the cotton district.[191]

Ada Nield Chew, who from personal experience[192] was particularly sensitive to the issue of equal pay for equal work, consistently warned women weavers against undercutting male wages.[193] By contrast, Mary Macarthur, the WTUL secretary, tried to raise women's sights by describing the beautiful things in life, such as comfortable houses, nice clothes, the best possible education for their children and an annual seaside holiday of at least three weeks' duration, to which they were entitled, but which they had as yet failed to attain.[194]

Yet it was Annie Marland who appears to have been particularly popular and therefore in greatest demand among the cotton unions.[195] The reasons for her popularity are not difficult to see. Prior to becoming a WTUL organizer, in which capacity she has already figured in Chapter 4, she had been a cardroom worker in a cotton mill at Mossley, near Manchester, for 18 years.[196] The authenticity of her work experience was appreciated by her female audiences, rendering them highly receptive to her message. Moreover, she was critical of the male domination of trade unions. While emphasizing the necessity of women taking a more prominent part in the labour movement, she put the onus on the unions by calling on them to encourage women in the work of improving the world and to stimulate them to strengthen their unions.[197] To this end they needed to educate their women members. Female operatives should not be kept in ignorance of factory legislation and should be taught to calculate their own wages rather than leaving this for union officials to do.[198] Her message was clearly aimed at encouraging and empowering women.

Relations between weaving unions and the WTUL had become cordial[199] following the shift in League policy from the emphasis on organizing women workers separately, seen as a temporary but necessary expedient, to the search for cooperation with men's unions. In 1889, the League changed its constitution so as to enable mixed-gender unions to affiliate for a small annual payment per woman member in return for the services of a female organizer.[200] The Northern Counties' Amalgamation had been advocating mixed-gender unions all along. What was being paraded as the most effective way of organizing workers[201] at the same time made sure that a close check was kept on women.

Encouraging Female Autonomy

Cotton weaving unions were the sites on which male weavers played out their dominance. As Joanna Bornat has observed, trade unionism is not only concerned with protecting and defending workers against employer action. Unions also play an important part in providing explanations for and perpetuating social relations between members of the working class.[202] Pervasive male dominance was not conducive to female self-determination. This required a more encouraging and anti-hierarchical atmosphere to flourish, as was the case in Manchester. On 1 February 1895, the Manchester and Salford Women's Trades Council was formed as an offshoot of the male council. It aimed at promoting the unionization of women and was set up in the manner of a philanthropic society, boasting a large number of middle-class men and women on its committee. Sarah Welsh, later to become Sarah Dickenson, a working-class woman, was appointed organizing secretary and was to remain the leader of the Women's Council until it merged with its male counterpart in 1918. In 1900, she was joined as co-secretary[203] by Eva Gore-Booth, who hailed from the Anglo-Irish gentry.[204] During the 25 years of its existence, the Women's Trades Council was instrumental in setting up more than 40 unions or branches of unions.[205]

Sarah Dickenson, who had probably been a weaver,[206] was highly sensitive to, and equally critical of, the gender discrimination at work in weaving unions, pointing to the exclusively male leadership,[207] male representation of women on Trades Councils,[208] and to women's concerns being generally passed over in the interest of men.[209] Against this background, Manchester and Salford Women's Trades Council attempted to achieve what others had tried in vain before, namely to organize the local female cotton weavers. The Council felt that the total lack of organization in such an important cotton centre as Manchester presented far more than merely a local disadvantage, tending to depress wage rates in the industry all over the county. Their efforts met with success, because they adapted their organization drive to the particular needs of their clientele. They arranged for female speakers, such as Annie Marland and Sarah Dickenson, both with personal experience of work in the cotton industry, to address the workers, they canvassed, held shed meetings and made house-to-house calls to get the women drawn in.[210] This way of agitating took account of the difficulties encountered by women lacking the male support characteristic of weaving centres in fitting union involvement in with full-time employment away from home and care for family needs.[211] Overall, the Council's efforts were geared towards improving women's unionization in conjunction with female self-determination. Presumably at the Council's instigation, in the early 1900s Manchester Technical School set up classes instructing weavers to calculate their wages.[212]

The Council's efforts were not in vain. In April 1902, Salford and District Powerloom Weavers' Union was formed, which was women-only in composition, including officials.[213] By 1904, it boasted a full-time paid secretary.[214] This association flourished and by its very existence encouraged the formation of further branches,[215] as well as leading to improved conditions of work.[216] True, this exclusively female union was subject to fluctuations of membership.[217] When looms stood idle, the women found it even more difficult to make ends meet, and in hard times union dues appeared to be the most easily dispensable item in the budget. Yet this was not tantamount to any lack of commitment because, as soon as trade picked up, the women rejoined.[218]

In 1903, far from displaying any separatist tendencies, the association for the first time debated the question of affiliation with the Northern Counties' Amalgamation, but decided to hold the matter over until it would be able to afford the requisite fee.[219] Relations became acrimonious when, in 1908, Nellie Keenan, the long-standing treasurer, described her own union as being able – and, one might add, forced on account of its members' meagre pay – to continue on lower subscriptions than those unions affiliated to the Amalgamation, because unlike the latter it refrained from embarking on expensive political campaigns. Such campaigns, she was reminded by both an Amalgamation offical and an equally piqued correspondent of the *Cotton Factory Times*, had helped secure factory legislation that benefited all workers in the cotton industry, including the members of her union.[220] Yet political campaigns paid for out of trade union funds extended to ensuring labour representation in Parliament, something sure to remind Nellie Keenan and women of her ilk of their own disenfranchisement. Implied in her statement was a critique of the Amalgamation's pursuit of gender-exclusive goals.

Such criticism was bound only to harden the Amalgamation's resolve not to make any concessions to the financial weakness of the Salford weavers. The Amalgamation had learnt from bitter experience to set great store by union coffers filled to the brink in the event of industrial disputes. Yet setting a high affiliation fee at the same time discriminated against newly organized weavers who stood in particular need of Amalgamation backing in order successfully to press for list prices to be paid in their locality as a precondition for higher subscriptions.

On being approached again about affiliation two years later, the Powerloom Weavers claimed the right to continue to appoint a woman secretary and thus to have a female representative on the Amalgamation executive. Whilst willing to leave the women to organize their own affairs, the Amalgamation was not prepared to have its own masculine image tarnished. It sent a male organizer to Manchester to set up a male-officered rival organization in 1908 or 1909, thereby considerably weakening unionization among the local weavers.[221] In 1910, Manchester and Salford Trades Council became involved in the affiliation issue. After three months of deliberation, the council executive recommended that the society affiliate to the Amalgamation, yet their recommendation was voted down by the union members concerned,[222] who were apparently quite unwilling to let any male-dominated organization interfere in their own affairs.

By January 1911, the gender antagonism underlying the rivalry between women-only unions and the Amalgamation became explicit. When some unspecified trouble occurred at one of the large firms in the Manchester district, both the Amalgamation and the Manchester and Salford Association of Patent Cop Winders, Bobbin and Hank Winders, Gassers, Doublers and Reelers tried to organize the workers concerned. The women's union issued a circular announcing an organization meeting, calling on the workers in terms that foregrounded gender solidarity:

> Fellow Women Workers – Don't be patronised to-day by the men who refused to organise you when there was no society in existence to look after your interests. Fellow Women Workers – Show to these men that you have the administrative and organising abilities to manage your own affairs and also to look after your own interests. Fellow Women Workers – Join the above named trades union, which has withstood the misrepresentation for so many years of these would-be friends of yours. Sisters – Don't be misled by specious promises, but turn up at the above meeting on Tuesday next, and join with your sisters, who have worked side by side with you, who understand your wants and aspirations, and, above all, understand every detail of your occupation, and who have been successful in removing innumerable grievances that your sisters in other factories have suffered from.[223]

This circular elicited the following resentful comment from the *Cotton Factory Times*'s correspondent, who was clearly irked by the stress laid on gender solidarity:

> Thus are we reminded once again that nought but man is vile, whilst woman – lovely woman – is the only friend and sister of the winders and reelers in Ancoats, and that the business of organising these 'sisters' is peculiarly that of Mesdames Dickenson, Keenan, Grundy & Co. As an example of exaggerated and extreme femininity, the Women's Social and Political Union are not to be mentioned in the same breath as these interesting members of the sex. And as an effort at inculcating the principle that (as the leaflet concludes) unity is strength, it is in its ill-concealed malignity surely a unique document.[224]

It was the links between the women's unions and the suffrage movement, to be further explored below, which provoked the particular ire of the *Cotton Factory Times*. In December 1912, the paper was pleased to report that non-unionist winders at a mill whose workers were organized by the women's union specifically asked to be enrolled in the Amalgamation's organization, because they wanted 'to join a proper one, and not a suffragette union'. In its comment the paper cast doubt on the women's union's officials' personal experience of mill work and depreciated their effectiveness as trade unionists, only to extol the virtues of the Amalgamation in the following terms:

> There are many indications that the women workers in the Manchester mills are becoming more and more alive to the advantages of being part and parcel of an Amalgamation officered by men of experience and tact, who can use all the resources of their powerful organisation in protecting the rights of one member or ten thousand.[225]

Despite this competition and the Amalgamation's determination to organize the women's unions out of existence[226] the original Powerloom Weavers' Association held out at least until 1920,[227] because, among other things, its female officials successfully wrung concessions from employers. According to the union secretary, 'The men secretaries ridiculed the idea of women interviewing employers, but in practice it has worked out all right.'[228] The amazing tenacity of the organization in the face of open male-inspired competition must also be attributed to members' wish to preserve female self-determination in union matters.

Linking Unionism and Suffragism

Manchester and Salford Women's Trades Council played a key role in encouraging women's self-determination in union affairs. Even more importantly, the organization's historic significance lies in its role of linking up the campaign for the unionization of women with the movement for female suffrage.[229] Since its inception in the mid-nineteenth century, the women's movement had included the suffrage in its demands for the improvement of women's condition. Over the second half of the nineteenth century some progress had been made. The rights of married women had been enhanced, particularly through the Married Women's Property Acts of 1876 and 1882 and the Infant Custody Act of 1886.[230] Women had also gained access to institutions of higher education[231] and ever larger sections of the labour market. The advances made in the areas of women's legal rights, their education and employment opportunities showed up only more sharply the lack of any progress concerning female citizenship. Hence the women's movement's increasing focus on the demand for the franchise.

Moreover, the gains made by the end of the nineteenth century, while addressing the specific needs of middle-class women, were of far less significance to the lives of working-class women. Their perceived needs had begun to be taken care of by organizations largely composed of middle-class women pervaded by the desire to help their needy sisters.[232] This desire fed upon the perception of all women sharing the condition of subordinate gender group, while often failing to acknowledge the impact of class on working-class women's lives.[233] The Women's Protective and Provident League, from which the Women's Trade Union League had evolved, had been set up in this mould, as had Manchester and Salford Women's Trades Council, as already pointed out.

By tapping the large pool of support represented by the highly unionized women cotton operatives, the council contributed to widening the social base of the suffrage movement in a significant manner,[234] as well as paving the way for the ultimate winning of labour movement support for women's suffrage as a necessary precondition of success. Linking up the two campaigns also signified a definite break with the non-political, philanthropic stance of the council. As it turned out, such breaking of the organizational mould was not countenanced by the majority on the committee.

In 1904, when a motion calling upon the council to support women's suffrage was narrowly defeated on account of the non-political stand taken by the middle-class members of the committee, Sarah Dickenson and Eva Gore-Booth withdrew, taking the majority of women unionists with them. The breakaway group formed the Manchester and Salford Women's Trades and Labour Council,[235] which was bound by its constitution to campaign for the unionization and the enfranchisement of women workers in tandem.[236]

Eva Gore-Booth, for one, had come to realize that women workers' disadvantaged position in the labour market, their restriction to ill-paid jobs carried out under deplorable conditions, was the result of their lack of both organization and citizenship. She argued that

> the working woman's position is, indeed, a forlorn and difficult one. She has no social or political influence to back her. Her Trade Union stands or falls by its power of negotiating; it cannot hope to have the weight with employers that the men's Unions have, for instead of being a strong Association of Voters, bound together by common interests in trade and politics, and able by numbers to change the issue of elections, and force its politics on the House of Commons, it is merely a band of workers carrying on an almost hopeless struggle to improve conditions of work and wages forced on them by arbitrary authority. A vote in itself is a small thing, but the aggregate vote of a great union is a very different matter.

Yet the cotton unions, though among the biggest in the country, were to a large extent disenfranchised on account of the majority of their members being female.[237]

Women workers' position was exacerbated by the growing realization among male unionists of the need for direct political representation. To this end, the Labour Representation Committee, the forerunner of the Labour Party, was formed in 1900. When the cotton unions balloted their members about sponsoring a labour candidate for Parliament, the outcome hinged on the female majority among the rank and file to vote in favour, which they did.[238] This helped to heighten the awareness among female cotton operatives of their own disadvantaged position. As Selina Cooper, the cotton winder from Nelson, explained:

> I carefully watched the proceedings and policy pursued by such great unions as the Miners, Cotton Spinners and Engineers, who all pressed for State interference with the object of improving their industrial conditions. I was compelled to recognise the power of Parliament – a power that can and ought to be utilised for the public good. Those well-organised industries had the ballot-box as a lever to raise their standard of life, but the women workers, however well they combined, had no such lever to help them in their demand for the redressing of their grievances.[239]

Insight into female cotton operatives' lack of power to exert any influence on industrial issues in the political sphere was gaining ground, a disempowerment which was exacerbated by the government's increasing willingness to intervene in economic matters. As a result, large numbers of women cotton workers became involved in the campaign for women's suffrage, the fullest account of which has been produced by Jill Liddington and Jill Norris.[240]

Some of the women cotton workers had come into contact with the suffrage campaign through membership of the Independent Labour Party,[241] which until their breaking away in 1907 counted the Pankhursts in its ranks. In 1903, they had founded the Women's Social and Political Union, which from 1905 onwards was to resort to increasingly violent tactics in its struggle for the suffrage. In the Independent Labour Party, support for women's franchise, though far from general, was not confined to Keir Hardie, the party leader. A striking display of male solidarity with a party comrade and militant suffragette occurred in Preston. This local weaver had been sent to prison for insisting on seeing the MP for the town. On returning to her job in the mill, she found herself ostracized by her co-workers, who thoroughly disapproved of her militancy. Presumably through her acquaintance with a tackler and fellow-member of the Independent Labour Party, she managed to obtain work at another mill. What is more, this tackler put her on four looms to ensure good weekly wages for her.[242]

Benenson has identified three stages that cotton workers' suffrage campaign went through: 'self-discovery', the linkage of economic and political claims, and the formulation of a programme.[243] From 1894 to 1899, middle- and working-class organizers held factory meetings and assemblies in Manchester to agitate for female suffrage among the cotton operatives. Secondly, in 1901 and 1902, Parliament was presented with petitions praying for female suffrage which had been signed by female textile workers only. The Lancashire petition bore the signatures of 29 359 women, while the follow-up one was signed by 37 441 female textile workers in Cheshire and Yorkshire.[244] Members of the Women's Co-operative Guild had assisted in the collection of signatures,[245] concurring as they did with the hope thereby to improve women's industrial condition.[246]

The petitions reiterated that lack of the vote placed women at a disadvantage both at home and in the workplace by stating that

> in the opinion of your petitioners the continued denial of the franchise to women is unjust and inexpedient. In the home, their position is lowered by such an exclusion from the responsibilities of national life. In the factory, their unrepresented condition places the regulation of their work in the hands of men who are often their rivals as well as their fellow workers.[247]

These women's suffrage rhetoric was shot through with a sense of gender rivalry derived from the recognition that their near equality with men in the labour process was nullified by the male exclusiveness of citizenship.

In 1903, finally, the Lancashire and Cheshire Women Textile and Other Workers' Representation Committee was formed to lobby trade unions and the nascent Labour Party for support of female suffrage.[248] It also gave working women a suffrage organization of their own, independent of the middle class-dominated North of England Society.[249] The rather cumbersome name had been chosen both for precision and in allusion to the Labour Representation Committee. The committee's manifesto rehearsed the familiar argument for women workers' need for the vote:

> Fellow workers – During the last few years the need of real political power for the defence of the workers has been felt by every section of the Labour world. Among the men the growing sense of the importance of this question has resulted in the formation of the Labour Representation Committee ... Meanwhile the position of the unenfranchised working women, who are by their voteless condition shut out from all political influence, is becoming daily more precarious. They cannot hope to hold their own in industrial matters, where their interests may clash with those of their enfranchised fellow-workers or employers. The one all-absorbing and vital political question for labouring women is to force an entrance into the ranks of responsible citizens.

They had therefore decided to sponsor their own parliamentary candidates pledged to the enfranchisement of women. The manifesto concluded on a self-confidently optimistic note by asserting: 'What Lancashire and Cheshire Women think to-day England will do to-morrow.'[250]

The precedence given to political over industrial emancipation caused the *Cotton Factory Times*, which otherwise faithfully reported the activities of the Committee, growing concern about such display of female autonomy. The paper consistently emphasized that unionization must precede enfranchisement[251] and advised the suffragists, even at international level, to model their movement on trade unionism:

> The leaders of the women's movement will do well to study the means whereby working men have secured their present position in the industrial and political world, and in so far as they copy the same trade union methods will they succeed in lifting their sex to a more equitable status.[252]

True, the working-class suffragists did take some of their cues from trade unions in that they brought up women's suffrage at TUC conferences in order to try and exert pressure on union-funded MPs to support female franchise. Frustrated by the futility of these attempts, they sponsored their own parliamentary candidates.[253] Yet the *Cotton Factory Times*'s advice smacks of the patronizing belief that men know best and women are well-advised to follow their example.

Cotton suffragists' determination to sponsor their own parliamentary candidates committed to female suffrage had been hardened by their experience of the 1902 by-election at Clitheroe, a constituency including also the weaving strongholds of Nelson and Colne. David Shackleton, who won that traditionally Liberal seat for Labour on that occasion, was financially supported out of a fund into which the voteless women cotton workers of his constituency were also made to pay. This gave them the lever to get Shackleton to pledge himself to support women's suffrage, a pledge he was to prove quite dilatory about.[254] Only in 1910 did he introduce a private member's bill for women's suffrage, which had been drafted by the Conciliation Committee,[255] a non-partisan body made up of all pro-suffrage MPs.

The fusion achieved by the Textile Workers' Representation Committee of suffragism and female trade unionism becomes apparent not least from the composition of the organization's committee, which comprised, among others, Eva Gore-Booth, co-secretary of Manchester and Salford Women's Trades Council; Sarah Reddish, erstwhile winder and reeler and president of Bolton Women's Co-operative Guild;[256] Clara Staton, committee member of Bolton Weavers' Association;[257] Selina Cooper, trade unionist and founder of Nelson and Colne Suffrage Committee; Helen Fairhurst, president of Wigan Weavers' Association;[258] Sarah Dickenson, co-secretary of Manchester and Salford Women's Trades Council; and Nellie Keenan, treasurer of Salford Powerloom Weavers' Union.[259]

Although the suffragists were able to bring the weaving unions with their large number of women members behind the demand for the franchise,[260] achieving the same at the annual TUC conferences, dominated as they were by the powerful and exclusively male unions of the miners, spinners[261] and engineers, proved far more difficult. Despite a resolution passed by Burnley Weavers' Association instructing their committee to bring the matter before the TUC conference in 1903,[262] the proceedings led Julia Varley, a suffragist woollen weaver from Yorkshire, who had represented her union at the congress, to note sceptically:

Altogether I think that the women of the labour world could have done almost as well if they had had the congress under their management, and I hope that they will begin to realize that they must keep the 'superior sex' toeing the line regarding the questions that deal with the needs of women. I think that we must take a leaf from the book of the men and begin lobbying our own Parliament of labour, and I trust that before next congress the working women of England will have risen in their might and have a scheme ready for the canvassing of our own Cabinet, viz., the Parliamentary Committee of the Trades Union Congress.[263]

Born into a family with a long tradition of involvement in radical politics,[264] she saw quite clearly that male labour activists rather than female inertia or lack of experience were the real stumbling-blocks in women's path to the vote. Yet winning the support of the labour movement, which finally occurred in 1913,[265] was crucial for achieving the vote. At that year's annual conference, the Labour Party, while reiterating its support for adult, that is universal, suffrage, the line consistently taken by the TUC, at the same time decided to oppose any bill that did not include the franchise for women.

The Politicization of Women Weavers

Trade unionism played an important role in stimulating cotton weavers' involvement in the suffrage campaign in two ways. On the one hand, it taught them the strength of numbers, while on the other it heightened their awareness of gender inequality through its display of male hegemony.[266] While facilitating the agitation among women workers in large numbers, trade unions themselves, and the TUC in particular, represented some of the battlefields on which women cotton operatives had to wage their struggle for the recognition of their demands.

Selina Cooper, for instance, though a staunch unionist, was anything but uncritical of the male dominance operating within unions,[267] as was one E. Evans, a weaver at Chorley. She corresponded with Barbara Hutchins, a member of the Fabian Women's Group, who was compiling data on female industrial employment. This weaver was herself collecting data on wages in cotton weaving as well as being engaged on some unspecified work to do with 'women'. Though not neglecting her housework, she resented its interfering with her other interests. By December 1913, she was busy reading *Women and Economics* by Charlotte Perkins Gilman, the US feminist, whose book was to become a feminist classic. By May 1914, she had applied for a scholarship for an Oxford summer school,[268] presumably run by Ruskin College, set up for the benefit of active trade unionists.

Despite their critique of male hegemony in the labour organizations, the cotton suffragists' campaign was inspired by their allegiance to both class and gender. Around 1900, the majority demand for the enfranchisement of women on the same terms as men – that is, subject to a property qualification – clashed with the call of the labour movement for adult suffrage. By proposing womanhood suffrage, that is the right to vote for every woman over the age of 21,[269] cotton suffragists tried to promote the concerns of women as a gender group without alienating those who saw the suffrage issue primarily as one of class in a period when a considerable section of the male population remained barred from citizen rights.[270] This did not preclude women like Eva Gore-Booth, Esther Roper, Sarah Reddish, Sarah Dickenson and Nellie Keenan, most of whom were working-class themselves, from welcoming any measure bringing women nearer the right to vote.[271] They gave priority to breaking through the gender barrier of citizenship as an important first step towards universal suffrage, which, true to their democratic beliefs, they endorsed as the ultimate goal.[272] Unlike the adult suffragists they were not convinced that giving the vote to women on the same terms as men would necessarily benefit non-working-class women only. According to a house-to-house canvass conducted at Nelson by the local suffrage committee, even under the limited franchise, 95 per cent of the women included would be working-class.[273] Whatever the validity of this survey, it managed to convince at least some members of the Women's Co-operative Guild[274] and the *Cotton Factory Times* alike.[275]

Cotton workers' suffrage activism stood in the long tradition of Lancashire women's involvement in radicalism stretching back at least to the Reform Movement of the early nineteenth century. By the 1880s, the Socialist Revival, which received a particularly enthusiastic response in the North West,[276] reinvigorated Lancashire women's politicization, while also helping to point it in a new direction. The socialist ideas that were being aired in the Revival revolved around the quest for freedom and equality in social relations. Despite the far from unequivocal stand on women's rights adopted by both the Independent Labour Party[277] and the Social Democratic Federation,[278] the Socialist Revival did create an atmosphere in which it was possible for women both to reflect upon and to speak out about the problematic of gender.

In the period up to and including Chartism, the plebeian women of Lancashire had taken political action primarily as mothers of families and members of the community, whose way of life had come under threat. Their stance had been one of radical wife- and motherhood.[279] By contrast, the cotton operatives who fought for the suffrage did so as female waged labourers conscious of themselves as workers and female individuals in their own right.

The valorization of their own experience and aspirations comes across not only in their involvement in the suffrage campaign, but also, and perhaps even more strikingly, in the writing of full or partial accounts of their lives by some of the leading activists.[280] Suffragism marks a turning-point in the history of working-class women, enabling them as it did to emerge as the agents of their own history, breaking their prolonged silence.[281] These women clearly felt that they had a message, that is something meaningful and relevant, to convey to the public at large and to women in particular.

Female cotton operatives' campaigning for their rights in the public domain was further facilitated by the absence in their communities of the ideal of female domesticity. As generations of Lancashire women, married as well as single, had been leaving their homes on a daily basis to go to the factory in open breach of the precepts of domesticity, by the closing decades of the nineteenth century they thought nothing of taking to the streets in order to voice their demands.

The absence of the female domestic ideal can be traced back at least to the Cotton Famine in the early 1860s. During that period of mass unemployment women cotton workers became the target of a philanthropic onslaught aimed at teaching them 'feminine' domestic skills and weaning them off factory employment. Philanthropists tried to achieve this by tying relief for unemployed, female cotton workers deemed to be sufficiently needy to the condition that they attend sewing schools set up for the purpose. Yet weavers', winders' and throstle-spinners' attendance at these schools was disproportionately of the shortest duration, because they were able quickly to move on to new jobs or leave the school. This behaviour was interpreted by Clare Evans as implying 'a greater degree of security and control over their life courses'.[282] True, a large number of these women found employment as domestic servants, something usually scorned by factory women, as demonstrated in Chapter 3, until they were able to return to their previous jobs in the cotton mills. Their willingness to transfer their labour power for the duration of the famine to a less remunerative sector of the labour market was seen by Clare Evans as an indication that 'these women had a far greater sense of themselves as *workers* and were as willing as the men to transfer their labour power to seek remunerative work'.[283] The absence of the ideology of domesticity among women cotton operatives persisted well into the twentieth century.[284]

Working-class suffragism remained by and large confined to cotton workers. Its only other base was in the East End of London, where Sylvia Pankhurst led the East London Federation of Suffragettes.[285] Among the cotton suffragists, the weavers formed the largest and most enthusiastic group.[286] The higher pay and better organization that they enjoyed by comparison with other women workers, including those in the other departments of the cotton industry, have variously been cited as conducive to their politicization.[287] Donning their traditional clogs and shawl, they might stand out from the fashionably dressed women working in shops and offices, yet they felt superior to them because of their higher wages.[288] Moreover, and even more importantly, women weavers' gender position in the labour process differed from that of other female cotton workers in that they alone performed identical work with men for equal piece rates.

Female cardroom hands, by contrast, were paid less than the male workers in the cardroom, the strippers and grinders, who supervised them and were deemed more skilled.[289] Ring-spinners, who were as exclusively female as the mule-spinners were exclusively male, formed the most downtrodden group of women operatives in the cotton industry and also worked under male supervision. They failed to respond to the suffrage campaign.[290] Conversely, the winders, also women only, formed a fairly select group in the weaving shed, though being paid less than weavers. They supplied suffrage activists, such as Sarah Reddish or Selina Cooper, out of proportion to their number.[291] Here the close companionship of women at work, who remained undisturbed by any male intrusion, appears to have been particularly conducive to female bonding as the seed-bed of feminist awareness.

Women weavers' experience of the labour process thus emerges as both a precondition and the salient motive of their involvement in the suffrage campaign. Their self-image as skilled workers holding their own with men in the labour process and with their earnings making a vital contribution to family income gave them the self-confidence to take action on their own behalf. They also had the resources required to articulate their demands, something they had learnt either in their unions or in the socialist organizations many of the activists were members of. This is why, contrary to Benenson's assertion of the decisive importance of interaction with middle-class women,[292] they did not need to rely on any external support to voice their critique of women's condition. This was recognized by Eva Gore-Booth, who, drawing on her personal experience of collaboration with them, celebrated Lancashire's women weavers in the following terms. In Lancashire, there

> has grown up a race of proud, upright, and self-reliant women, able to think and laugh and dream, with souls greater than their circumstances ... We are all greatly dependent for our self-esteem on the world's valuation of our services, and it may be that the economic self-respect and independence that spring from a consciousness of the recognised value of the workers' skill are at the root of the broad sense of life's powers and possibilities, characteristic of the labouring women of the North.[293]

Moreover, given that women weavers enjoyed more leisure than those women workers subject to lives of incessant toil, they were able to engage with issues beyond the confines of their immediate concerns:

> she reads, and not by any means only her daily paper, and as she is above all a woman of strong convictions with a talent for forcible expression, she sometimes does a bit of journalism in the evening for the local paper, and is often a good public speaker and well known in her club or guild.[294]

Having learnt to stand up to male trade unionists or socialists who were unfriendly, if not openly hostile, to women's issues, women weavers had no need to submit to the lead of their social betters. Yet they were happy to collaborate as equals with women who, though of different class origin, shared with them the disadvantaged position of their gender group.

Conclusion

The uncommon degree of equality between men and women weavers in the labour process sharpened the latter's sensitivity to the multifaceted forms of female degradation. Being men's equals with regard to skill and competence at work, they had yet to submit to factory legislation which they opposed,[295] because it denied them agency by construing them as standing in need of particular protection, as argued in Chapter 2. In addition, the male officialdom of their trade unions, which they joined in large numbers, did their utmost to portray them as both inferior workers and deficient unionists. In the family their quest for equality was limited by their legally prescribed dependency on their husbands, mitigated though it was by the importance of their wages to family comfort. In the political sphere, finally, lacking the franchise, they were unable to make any impact on the framing of the laws that had important bearings on their lives.

Working-class suffragists perceived the franchise as the central lever in their efforts to ameliorate their condition. It would allow them, they believed, to bypass their trade unions by enabling them to press for legislation benefiting women in the workplace; it would enable them to go over the heads of their husbands in urging for the legal rights of women; it would generally empower them to campaign for laws addressing the specific concerns of women in their double capacity of wives and mothers as well as workers. Given the male exclusiveness of citizenship, it was tempting to succumb to the lure of the suffrage as the panacea curing the social ills that beset women's lives. This belief was shared, both contemporaneously and historically, by all social groups suffering from this exclusion. It was endorsed by non-working-class suffragists, by those men who had failed to be enfranchised by the 1884 Reform Act, and it had been equally prevalent among the Chartists. The founding of the Labour Representation Committee, by signalling the labour movement's determination to press for independent parliamentary representation, cast in even sharper relief working-class women's lack of rights as a result of their disenfranchisement. Around 1900 when the women's movement had come to focus almost exclusively on the vote as the way to challenge the separation of spheres,[296] the labour movement was beginning to free itself from the political tutelage of Liberalism, and the achievement of universal male suffrage became a distinct possibility, it should come as no surprise that female cotton workers' quest for equality should have led them to support the suffrage movement.

Yet their political activism was more than merely a function of the historical juncture at which it occurred. It was shaped and given direction by the specific intermingling of equality and inequality in women weavers' lives. Near gender equality in the labour process allowed them to perceive their inequality elsewhere as socially constructed, that is as the result of the exercise of arbitrary male power, and hence as changeable. The suffrage was not only an important lever for bettering women's condition, it also held a particular appeal for them, addressing them as it did as individuals in their own right, with interests and desires that were different from, if not openly clashing with, those of the men with whom they associated, their fathers, husbands or co-workers. While women wished to achieve gender equality, men were loath to relinquish their privileges.

Women weavers' political activism, arising as it did from the specific intermingling of equality and inequality in their lives, does not present the paradox puzzling Benenson,[297] who apparently expects resistance to oppression to be most likely among the most downtrodden sections of society. Moreover, by identifying a clash between gender equality in the workplace and patriarchal subjugation in the home and the labour organizations,[298] he ignores the extent to which power relations in the family were shaped by women weavers' position in the labour process.

This connection has meanwhile also been acknowledged for the mid-nineteenth century by Carol Morgan, who has reneged on her earlier denial of any element of patriarchy in either the workplace or the labour organizations, a denial based solely on women's increasing involvement in waged work, that is powerloom weaving.[299] Meanwhile she has taken on board the existence of male dominance and come round to perceiving cotton weavers as agents shaping their roles in both the workplace and the home.[300]

Women weavers' quest for the improvement of their condition became manifest in militant activity in the workplace, in the way they shaped relations in the family as well as in their political struggle for the franchise. Laying claim to being rightful members of the working class shows them to have espoused a concept of class that was clearly gendered and opposed to any attempt to sideline them in struggles around class issues. At the same time, their notion of femininity involved the rejection of the centrality of domesticity in favour of competence in the workplace, militancy in work-related struggles, irrespective of union backing, and determination in political campaigns. This version of femininity evolved in conjunction with a notion of masculinity that did not revolve exclusively around waged work and sexual prowess. It did not preclude housework and childcare or acknowledgment of the burden shouldered by wives and active consideration of their concerns. This renegotiation of gender occurred at the workplace, where it was anchored in the specific organization of the labour process in cotton weaving, whence it radiated to the other sites on which gender is constructed.

Notes

1 The author gave Haslemere as the place whence these weavers hailed; see Brooks (1926, p.216). As there is only one place of this name in Britain, Haslemere in Surrey, which was not known for its weaving trade, this is most likely a misprint, and the actual place may be Haslingden, one of the little weaving villages in Rossendale. For another suffrage banner presumably embroidered by female cotton workers from Nelson in the home of one of their number, see Tickner (1987, p.255).

2   See Brooks (1926, p.216). The occasion was probably the march sponsored by the National Union of Women's Suffrage Societies which involved 10 000 women walking from the Embankment to Albert Hall on 13 June 1908; see Rosen (1974, p.104).
3   For weavers diverting material provided by management usually to private rather than political uses of their own, including the practice of weaving out what was left on the beam when a cut was finished and the tackler was not looking, see Roberts (1981), respondent H8P, pp.7, 23–4; respondent O1P, p.26; respondent T4P, p.14.
4   See Tickner (1987, pp.180–81).
5   See ibid., pp.67–8.
6   See Chapter 3.
7   See Chapter 4.
8   *CFT*, 7.2.1913, p. 5; see also *CFT*, 18.4.1913, p.5.
9   Kenny (1994), case 5, p.5.
10 For the history of the fish-and-chip shop, see Walton (1992). For the proliferation of fish-and-chip shops in Preston, where in 1892 there was one shop to 1530 people, while by 1936 the ratio had increased to one to 345, see Roberts (1982b, p.162).
11 See Glucksmann (1995, p.280).
12 See Mark-Lawson (1988).
13 See, for example, *National Review*, 1909–10, p.686.
14 See, for example, Roberts (1982a, pp.49–52).
15 Chew (1912, p.44); see also Glucksmann (1995, p.281).
16 See Glucksmann (2000, p.85).
17 See Glucksmann (1995, pp.283–4); see also Roberts (1981), Gittins (1982).
18 For the commonplace presence of the set-pan, or boiler, for washing clothes in Lancashire cotton operatives' homes, see Chew (1912, pp.35–6).
19 See Blackburn (1980, p.48); see also Roberts (1981), respondent B2P, p.3, for a husband doing a wide variety of cleaning jobs.
20 See Mr & Mrs H., Tape 664, MSU TLSL; see also Roberts (1981), respondent A3P, p.9; respondent D1P, p.11; also Lancashire Textile Project, respondent AK3, side I, p.18.
21 See Roberts (1981), respondent A1P, p.3.
22 Ibid., respondent H8P, p.30; respondent B2P, p.23, for a man's willingness to do at least some of the washing, which was never put to the test, though.
23 See ibid., respondent B9P, p.6; see also Bruley (1993, p.95), for an inter-war husband looking after his two small daughters, while his wife served a prison sentence for her involvement in the unemployed movement.
24 See Middlebrook (1983, ch.3, p.2).
25 Unfortunately, it has been impossible to determine the precise connotation of this nickname. The choice of a female name would suggest that it was meant to express the feminization of husbands doing domestic chores. The overtone of effeminacy is clearly apparent in the meanings 'weakly coward', given in *The Slang Thesaurus*, 'effeminate actor', given in the *Dictionary of Slang and Unconventional English* and 'effeminate male homosexual', given in the *Cassell Dictionary of Slang*. However, the selection of this particular name invites speculation. It might possibly allude to 'Marianne', the female figure representing the French Revolution, in acknowledgment of the liberating impact on wives of husbands sharing in housework. After all, according to the *Dictionary of Slang and Unconventional English*, between about 1865 and 1890, 'Mary Ann' denoted a female destroyer of

recalcitrant labour sweaters, though this use of the word was confined mainly to Sheffield. More innocuously, 'Mary Ann' is listed as a type-name for a housemaid or charwoman, giving rise to 'maryanning' as denoting 'cleaning, sweeping, polishing'; see *Dictionary of Slang and Unconventional English*.

26   In Salford, by contrast, male participation in housework was confined to 'kindlier' husbands and occurred on condition that it was strictly indoors and thus invisible to neighbours; see Roberts (1977, pp.53–4).
27   Lancashire Textile Project, respondent AD4, p.9; see also Bruley (1993, p.85).
28   See Roberts (1981), respondent A1P, p.53.
29   Ibid., p.52.
30   See Glucksmann (1995, p.283), reiterated in Glucksmann (2000, p.67).
31   Moreover, in Preston, at least, some women felt uneasy about the shift in gender responsibilities that such sharing of tasks involved; see, for example, Roberts (1981), respondent H8P, p.30.
32   See Roberts (1981), respondent G1P, p.9; respondent M2P, p.128.
33   See Roberts (1981), respondent H8P, p.30; see also Middlebrook (1983, ch.11, p.73). Interestingly, despite his strong reservations against married women's employment away from home, even David Shackleton took over the housework during a prolonged period of unemployment that he suffered on account of being blacklisted for his union involvement. During that period the couple subsisted solely on his wife's earnings; see Martin (2000, p.13).
34   See Mr & Mrs H., Tape 664, MSU TLSL.
35   Gittins (1982, p.130).
36   See ibid., p.205.
37   See Glucksmann (2000, p.75).
38   See Glucksmann (1995).
39   See Glucksmann (2000, p.64).
40   Roberts (1982b, p.153), reiterated in Roberts (1986, p.124).
41   See Thompson (1975, pp.78–80).
42   See Glucksmann (1995, pp.281–2), reiterated in Glucksmann (2000, p.55). For similar findings relating to Scottish women in a variety of occupations, see Stephenson and Brown (1990).
43   See Glucksmann (2000, pp.120–21).
44   See Report by Miss Collet, *PP*, 1894, LXXXI, Pt. II, p.881.
45   See, for example, *CFT*, 7.2.1913, p.5; 29.8.1913, p.1.
46   *CFT*, 7.2.1913, p.5.
47   See Roberts (1982b, p.152), reiterated in Roberts (1986, p.118).
48   See Chew (1912, p.39); see also Roberts (1981), respondent C1P, p.69; also Glucksmann (1995, p.281).
49   See Roberts (1981), respondent A1P, p.53; see also Roberts (1986, p.110).
50   See Ayers and Lambertz (1987, p.196), who have found this pattern of behaviour to prevail in dockland Liverpool in the inter-war period.
51   For contrasting studies of working-class London between 1870 and 1918, and dockland Liverpool in the inter-war period, where such marital tension bred violence, see Ross (1993, esp. pp.84–6) and Ayers and Lambertz (1987).
52   See Mark-Lawson (1987, pp.3, 8–9), who has found this attitude to prevail in the typical weaving town of Nelson. Blackburn, by contrast and for reasons entirely unclear, apparently had a reputation for wife beating; see Trodd (1978, p.277).

53 See Gittins (1982, p.130). For Blackburn's textile community engaging in leisure pursuits segregated by gender, see Trodd (1978, pp.276–7). For female visits to the pub as a matter of course, see Roberts (1982a, pp.58–9); for Nelson, see Hill (1997, p.50). This would indicate that the notion of femininity being incompatible with drinking in public, propagated by the temperance movement, had failed to take hold in the weaving communities on any large scale.
54 See Glucksmann (2000, p.75).
55 For a contrasting study of working-class London, see Ross (1993, esp. pp.78–84).
56 Gittins (1982, pp.130–31); for an illustration of this through the depiction of a weaving couple working in the same mill, see Chew (1912).
57 See, for example, Blackburn (1954, p.29).
58 See Mark-Lawson (1987, p.320); see also Glucksmann (1995, p.283), reiterated in Glucksmann (2000, p.65).
59 See Gittins (1982, p.129).
60 See Glucksmann (2000, pp.64–5).
61 See Roberts (1982b, p.153), reiterated in Roberts (1986, p.118).
62 See note 40 above.
63 See McLaren (1977, p.70).
64 For the most recent statement, see Szreter (1996, p.317); for earlier statements, see, for example, Elderton (1914), Innes (1938).
65 See Elderton (1914, p.23).
66 See, for example, Innes (1938).
67 See Szreter (1996, p.432). For the conflicting view that the fertility decline was the result of 'stopping', see, for example, Seccombe (1990, p.153).
68 See Szreter (1996, p.435).
69 See Taylor (1983, pp. 76–7).
70 See Szreter (1996, p.439); see also Roberts (1986, p.84), for the esteem in which were held men who 'indulged themselves' least and for the equation of sexual abstinence in marriage with 'behaving oneself'; for the desirability of abstinence, expressed as exhortations to husbands to exercise greater self-control, see the collection of letters from members of the Women's Co-operative Guild, ed. Llewelyn Davies, 1978.
71 See Szreter (1996, p.439). This assessment of abortion as a last resort contrasts with McLaren, who has elevated working-class women's recourse to abortion to a display of their power to control their fertility in a self-determined way; see McLaren (1977).
72 See Knight (1977, p.57).
73 See Gittins (1982, p.150).
74 See Szreter (1996, p.434).
75 For an earlier formulation of this economic argument, see Elderton (1914, p.233).
76 See Szreter (1996, pp.464, 483).
77 See ibid., pp.490–91; for a local study confirming this pattern, see Lichfield (1978). On the basis of the Registrar General's Reports for 1901 to 1910, Elizabeth Roberts has compiled the following table indicating the number of live births per 1000 married women (five-year averages) in textile towns; see Roberts (1986, p.101):

Place	1901–5	1906–10
Blackburn	197	189
Bury	177	174
Rochdale	176	169
Bolton	227	208
Preston	233	212
Burnley	193	185

Detailed local research and complex computations would be required to arrive at the average number of children had by women weavers.

78 See Gittins (1982, pp.147–8).
79 Szreter (1996, p.496).
80 Ibid., p.508.
81 See ibid., p.546.
82 For the segregation of the weaving workforce along gender lines during meal-breaks, see H. & B.D., Tape 701, MSU TLSL; see also Blackburn (1954, p.15).
83 Roberts (1981), respondent A1P, p.28.
84 Ibid., respondent H7P, p.24.
85 This is further corroborated by the shock felt at least by some about the way in which sexual matters were talked about. Thus Margaret McCarthy, an ex-weaver, wrote in her autobiography: 'I entered into the world of the cotton factory and into a shocked understanding of human sexual relations at one and the same time' (McCarthy, 1953, pp.45–6).
86 Roberts (1982b, p.155), reiterated in Roberts (1986, p.102).
87 See Szreter (1996, p.553).
88 In 1911, Preston's fertility rate was even above the national average; see ibid., p.512.
89 See Savage (1988, p.211).
90 See Savage (1987, pp.110, *passim*). Elizabeth Roberts, however, doubts the impact of the Anglo-Catholic community on the local fertility rate; see Roberts (1986, pp.86–8).
91 By the inter-war period, cotton workers' families with only one child or none at all were becoming less and less unusual even in a place like Preston; see Roberts (1981), respondent H8P, p.36.
92 See Liddington (1984).
93 For the history of the Social Democratic Federation, see Crick (1994).
94 For further examples, see Roberts (1981), respondent T5P, p.17; respondent T4P, p.46.
95 See Liddington (1984, p.73).
96 For the history of the Independent Labour Party, see Howell (1983).
97 See, for example, Mitchell (1968, p.89).
98 See, for example, McLaren (1978, p.226) for a birth control tract being recommended in the socialist *Clarion*. Even among the SDF, noted for its highly equivocal stand on women's issues, birth control was suggested at least by one member as a means to free women to participate in socialist politics; see Hunt (1996, p.193).
99 See Scott (1997; 1998a); for a more detailed treatment of the organization, see Scott (1998b).
100 See Scott (1988, p.20).

101 For another Nelson woman, a weaver, thriving on the encouragement and solidarity experienced within the ranks of the Guild, see Smith (1933). For the organization's emphasis on agency rather than victimization, generating self-confidence among its members, including vis-à-vis male cooperators, see Scott (1997).
102 See, for example, Margaret Llewelyn Davies's Introduction to *Maternity: Letters from Working Women* (1978, pp.13–15; see also references to birth control in some of the letters included. For the change of the Guild's attitude to birth control in the inter-war period, see Scott (1998b).
103 See McLaren (1978, p.226).
104 See Mitchell (1968).
105 See Chew (1982).
106 See Mitchell (1968, p.102).
107 See ibid.
108 See, for example, A.H., Tape 646, MSU TLSL; see also Liddington and Norris (1985, p.96). Allen Gee, General Secretary of the General Union of Weavers and Textile Workers, which organized the Yorkshire woollen weavers, considered that in Lancashire women were socialized into unionists, as it were, having their first contact with trade unions as half-timers, at which stage their subscriptions were paid by the parents; see *Women's Trade Union Review*, Jan. 1900, p.6, *WTUL Papers*.
109 See Drake (1984, p.119).
110 See, for example, *CFT*, 11.12.1885, p.1; see also *Webb Collection*, XLVII, p.231.
111 See, for example *CFT*, 23.1.1885, p.5.
112 *CFT*, 17.5.1889, p.5.
113 *CFT*, 1.11.1889, p.6.
114 See *CFT*, 1.8.1890, p.4.
115 See, for example, *CFT*, 16.10.1891, p.5; 1.5.1903, p.6.
116 See A.H., Tape 646, MSU TLSL.
117 See, for example, *CFT*, 7.6.1889, p.4; 20.9.1889, p.5; 6.12.1889, p.5.
118 See, for example, *CFT*, 31.1.1890, p.4; 21.2.1890, p.4; 13.5.1904, p.5; 4.1.1907, p.1.
119 See *Women's Union Journal*, 15.11.1890, p.86, *WTUL Papers*.
120 See *CFT*, 15.7.1904, p.1.
121 This has been argued with regard to Preston by Savage (1981, pp.29–30).
122 See, for example, *CFT*, 28.3.1890, p.5.
123 See *CFT*, 7.10.1904, p.1.
124 *PP*, 1886, XXI, p.199.
125 *CFT*, 23.10.1891, p.6.
126 For an example of a female union member operating within this framework, see *CFT*, 20.2.1891, p.5.
127 *CFT*, 16.5.1890, p.7.
128 See Committee on Humidity and Ventilation, *PP*, 1909, XV, p.721.
129 See *Webb Collection*, XLVII, pp.231–2, 247–8, 252.
130 See, for example, *CFT*, 6.7.1888, p.4.
131 See, for example, *CFT*, 4.7.1890, p.5.
132 See, for example, *CFT*, 1.8.1890, p.8.
133 See, for example, *CFT*, 20.3.1885, p.6; 30.11.1888, p.6.
134 See, for example, *CFT*, 15.2.1889, p.7.
135 For a rare example of a woman seconding a motion by actually making a speech, see

CFT, 30.1.1891, p.7; and for women taking part in the debate at meetings, see, for example, CFT, 16.10.1891, p.5.
136 For the origins and evolution of strike statistics, see Creigh (1982).
137 See Report on Strikes and Lock-Outs 1889–1898. In 1898 appeared the last report to break strikers down by gender.
138 See, for example, CFT, 11.6.1886, p.5.
139 See, for example, CFT, 20.1.1888, p.5.
140 See, for example, CFT, 18.12.1885, p.5; 27.1.1888, p.6; 31.8.1888, p.6; 18.9.1891, p.7.
141 See Blewett (1990; 1993).
142 See Rose (1993).
143 See Fowler and Wyke (1995, p.12).
144 See the extracts quoted in ibid., pp.94–5.
145 See Bowker (1983, pp.15, 42).
146 See CFT, 12.10.1888, p.5.
147 Report of Truck Committee, PP, 1908, Cd.4443, lix, p.391.
148 See CFT, 11.12.1896, p.8; 15.1.1897, p.8.
149 See CFT, 13.3.1903, p.5.
150 See Webb Collection, XLVII, p.226.
151 See Liddington and Norris (1985, p.98).
152 See Webb Collection, XLVII, p.224.
153 See CFT, 5.2.1897, p.1.
154 See Blackburn Weekly Telegraph, 16.9.1911, p.13. This marked the reversal of a decision taken by the union in the early 1900s to admit no woman to the committee, after one of their female members had been arrested as a result of suffragette militancy; see Trodd (1978, p.279).
155 According to the account produced on the occasion of the union's centenary, two women were coopted onto the organizing committee when it decided to accept women powerloom weavers in July 1880. Female involvement in running the union appears to have been fairly erratic at that stage; see Bolton Weavers, 1965, p.9.
156 See Foley (1973, p.64).
157 See Bolton & District Weavers: Minute Book, committee meetings, 23.10. 1905; 9.1.1906.
158 See ibid., committee meeting, 15.6.1903; 8.2.1904; quarterly meeting, 11.10.1904; 9.1.1906; committee meeting, 23.7.1906; 17.12.1906.
159 See White (1978, p.233); Soldon (1978, p.56); for a comment on the number of women present at the 1905 annual TUC conference, see CFT, 26.5.1905, p.1.
160 See Savage (1981, p.29).
161 See Savage (1987, p.82).
162 See Roberts (1981), respondent C1P, p.13. According to an official union source, she was actually elected: see Webb Collection, XLVII, p.263. The memory lapse of Elizabeth Roberts's interviewee may well have reflected general union hostility to women striving for office.
163 See Savage (1982, p.50).
164 See letter, E. Evans to B. Hutchins, 20.12.1913, p.275, Webb Collection, XLVII.
165 Fortnightly Review, vol. 45, Jan.–June 1889, p.8, WTUL Papers.
166 See Martin (2000, p.13).

167 See *Webb Collection*, XLVII, p.218; for similar views expressed by the assistant secretary of Nelson Weavers' Union, see ibid., pp. 234–5.
168 See, for example, ibid., p.236, for a Nelson weaver who decided against standing for the local committee, because she had a mother dependent on her.
169 See ibid., p.252.
170 See Foulger (1992–3, p.115).
171 Drake's contention – see Drake (1984, p.121) – that the job of collecting union dues was kept exclusively male must be modified for those towns where weaving was almost exclusively female, as in Oldham, reported above.
172 See Bornat (1988).
173 See Foley (1973, p.82).
174 See Whitehead (1987, pp.18–20).
175 See Blackburn (1954, pp.45–6). For the type of questions set, see also Fowler (1999), who attributes the lack of politically able weaving union officials in the inter-war period to the method of their selection. This favoured the able calculator, though not necessarily people of broad political vision.
176 See Whitehead (1987, p.3).
177 See ibid.
178 See Fowler and Fowler (1984, p.21).
179 See Mark-Lawson (1987, p.241). For an earlier example of women actually ensuring union survival at Accrington by taking over during an unspecified emergency, see *CFT*, 11.9.1908, p.4.
180 See Bulletin of the Bureau of Labor, no. 83, July 1909, p.10, *WTUL Papers*.
181 See, for example, Roberts (1981), respondent A1P, p.50.
182 See, for example, *CFT*, 19.9.1890, p.5.
183 See Burnley Manufacturers' Association: Minute Book, 1894–1906, Committee meeting, 1.1.1896.
184 See Burnley & District Textile Workers' Union: Letters 1885–99, letters 491, 498, 540, 541; for another complaint made by a weaver about an overlooker's conduct, see ibid., letter 177.
185 See Liddington (1984, p.42).
186 See Bennett (1951, p.129). Unfortunately, he fails to quantify the support enjoyed by the SDF-inspired section.
187 For the *CFT* conceding success, see, for example, 1.7.1904, p.1; 26.10.1904, p.1.
188 See, for example, *CFT*, 11.11.1904, p.6; 3.11.1905, p.8.
189 *Women's Trades Union Review*, Jan. 1902, p.3, *WTUL Papers*.
190 Despite his belief in women's apathy, quoted above, even D.J. Shackleton was harnessed to WTUL efforts to improve the unionization of women elsewhere; see *CFT*, 14.9.1906, p.4. This was presumably due to his capacity as treasurer of the WTUL, whose only male official he was; see Martin (2000, p.63).
191 See Soldon (1978, p.38); for Preston Weavers' Association hiring the services of a WTUL organizer, see *CFT*, 23.9.1904, p.6; see also *CFT*, 30.9.1904, p.4, for the weavers' union of Radcliffe approaching Mrs Fairhurst, President of Wigan Weavers' Association, for an organization drive.
192 She had worked as a tailoress at a factory where women were paid less than men for equal work; see Chew (1982).
193 See, for example, *CFT*, 27.11.1903, p.1; 18.3.1904, p.5.
194 See *CFT*, 3.11.1905, p.8.

195 See *Women's Trades Union Review*, July 1901, p.27, *WTUL Papers*.
196 For Annie Marland's career, see *Daily Chronicle*, 29.5.1891, p.6; see also *The New Weekly*, 2.2.1895, p.3; *CFT*, 10.7.1903, p.8.
197 See *CFT*, 5.2.1897, p.1.
198 See *CFT*, 8.11.1895, p.4.
199 See, for example, Burnley District Textile Workers' Union: Letters 1885–99, letter 791, for an invitation of Lady Dilke, the WTUL president, to open the association's new offices.
200 See Boone (1942, pp.26–8); see also *CFT*, 18.3.1904, p.5.
201 See *Women's Trades Union Review*, Jan. 1900, p.11, *WTUL Papers*, quoted also in *CFT*, 5.1.1900, p. 8; see also *Woman in Industry*, 1908, p.xii.
202 See Bornat (1988, p.97).
203 See Frow and Frow (1976, p.42).
204 For the life of Eva Gore-Booth, see Lewis (1988).
205 See Bather (1956, p.98).
206 See Liddington and Norris (1985, p.290).
207 For an equally incisive critique of the male domination of weavers' unions, see letter, E. Evans to B. Hutchins, 20.12.1913, *Webb Collection*, XLVII, p.275.
208 As a result, women might see no point in sending a representative. For a long-standing female Trades Council representative failing to be re-elected owing to women's non-appearance at union meetings, see Bulletin of the Bureau of Labor, no. 83, July 1909, p.10, *WTUL Papers*.
209 See *Webb Collection*, XLVII, pp.47, 49.
210 See M&SWTC, 4th annual report, 1898, p.16; 8th annual report, 1903, p.5.
211 For married women at Bolton, where spinning predominated, growing restless at union meetings on account of impatient husbands awaiting a delayed dinner, see Foley (1973, p.64).
212 See M&SWTC, 9th annual report, 1903, p.7.
213 See ibid., p.11.
214 See M&SWTC, 10th annual report, 1904, p.12.
215 See South East Lancashire and Cheshire Weavers (Manchester & Salford): Minute Book, 21.9.1908.
216 See M&SWTC, 9th annual report, 1903, p.5.
217 The union started off with a membership of 700, which fell to 320 in 1904, reaching a peak of 1107 in 1907; see White (1978, p.53).
218 See M&SWTC, 9th annual report, 1903, p.8; for a contrasting example of women leaving the union for good as a result of dwindling strike pay on account of the low subscriptions paid in, see Roberts (1981), respondent H8P, p.24.
219 See M&SWTC, 9th annual report, 1903, p.13.
220 See *CFT*, 17.7.1908, p.4; 24.7.1908, p.4; 31.7.1908, p.8; 7.8.1908, p.4.
221 See Frow and Frow (1976, pp.49–50); *CFT*, 2.8.1912, p.1; see also the misrepresentation of events given by the male organizer in an interview, *CFT*, 7.1.1910, p.5. For the persistence of the trade union movement's refusal to acknowledge the need to abolish discrimination on the grounds of gender in its own ranks, see Trades Union General Council Organization of Women, 1931.
222 See *CFT*, 13.12.1912, p.4.
223 *CFT*, 27.1.1911, p.1.
224 Ibid.

225 *CFT*, 20.12.1912, p.5.
226 See *CFT*, 13.12.1912, p.4.
227 See Drake (1984, p.119).
228 *Webb Collection*, XLVII, p.258.
229 Ellen DuBois has attributed the politicization of British working women to their having organizations of their own, correctly citing the Women's Trade Union League and the Women's Co-operative Guild, but also, incorrectly, the textile unions as examples. The significance of the Manchester Women's Trades Council eludes her account; see DuBois (1991, pp.35–6).
230 See Holcombe (1983); see also Shanley (1989).
231 See Fletcher (1980).
232 Isabella Ford, a Quaker, socialist and feminist, for one, was highly critical of any outside attempts to improve working women's condition and emphasized the need for self-help by asserting: 'Only one thing is necessary for us all to remember, *viz.* that the industrial woman must work out her freedom for herself. We cannot, we have no right to, do it for her. We cannot possibly know her needs as well as she herself can' (Ford, 1900, p.183).
233 For the resulting tensions between organizers and their clientele, see, for example, Feurer (1988); see also Mappen (1985; 1988).
234 For the predominantly middle-class composition of the women's movement, see Park (1988) and Banks (1986), who yet draws attention to an increasing minority of working-class women from about the 1890s.
235 See M&SWTC, 10th annual report, 1904, p.14.
236 See clipping from *Manchester Guardian*, GTC, 604/9.
237 See Gore-Booth, *Women Workers*, p.6.
238 See Gore-Booth (1907, p.54).
239 *The Queen*, 17.4.1909, quoted in Liddington (1984, p.101).
240 See Liddington and Norris (1985).
241 See, for example, Roberts (1981), respondent C1P, p.13.
242 See ibid., respondent C1P, pp.13, 16, 20; see also Hesketh (1992, p.44).
243 See Benenson (1991, p.93).
244 See ibid., p.85.
245 See Scott (1988, p.80).
246 See *CFT*, 5.5.1905, p.1.
247 Quoted in Liddington and Norris (1985, p.145).
248 See Benenson (1991, p.85). For the lobbying of weavers' unions, see, for example, Bolton & District Weavers: Minute Book, quarterly meeting, 14.4.1903; see also *CFT*, 24.7.1903, p.8; 25.9.1903, p.7; 22.4.1904, p.6.
249 See Liddington and Norris (1985, p.27).
250 Quoted in Gore-Booth (1907).
251 See *CFT*, 30.10.1903, p.7.
252 *CFT*, 10.6.1904, p.1.
253 See Gore-Booth (1907, pp.64–5).
254 See Liddington and Norris (1985, pp.155–9); see also Martin (2000, p.43), who on this as well as on other occasions proves to be highly insensitive to issues of gender.
255 See Liddington and Norris (1985, p.246); see also Martin (2000, p.100).
256 See Liddington and Norris (1985, p.291).
257 See Bolton & District Weavers: Minute Book, 1904–6, quarterly meeting, 10.4.1906.

258 See *CFT*, 13.3.1903, p.5.
259 See M&SWTC, 8th annual report, 1902, p.11; 9th annual report, 1903, p.13. According to the committee's self-description, Nellie Keenan was the union's secretary: see Committee, p.4, Women's Suffrage Collection, M 50.
260 See, for example, Bolton & District Weavers: Minute Book, quarterly meeting, 14.4.1903; *CFT*, 24.7.1903, p.8; 25.9.1903, p.7; 22.4.1904, p.6.
261 In 1913, the president of Bolton Spinners' Union was one of the four delegates to the TUC conference to vote against a resolution endorsing women's enfranchisement; see White (1982, p.218). Men's lukewarm attitude at this conference with regard to any attempts at improving working women's conditions led the *Textile Mercury*, an employers' journal, to dub the TUC 'a man-"bossed" institution'; see *Textile Mercury*, 13.9.1913, GTC, 26/117.
262 See Gore-Booth (1907, p.52).
263 *CFT*, 18.9.1903, p.1.
264 See Bornat (1988, pp.218–19).
265 For the rapprochement between the National Union of Women's Suffrage Societies and the TUC, see Holton (1988, pp.98, *passim*).
266 For a rather more favourable assessment of weavers' unions in fostering women's suffrage activism, see Liddington (1977, p.31) and Liddington and Norris (1985, pp.95, *passim*).
267 For further examples of women politicized through their experience in the workplace, see Liddington and Norris (1985, p.125).
268 See letter, E. Evans to B. Hutchins, 23.11.1913, pp.273–4; 20.12.1913, p.277; 5.5.1914, p.278, *Webb Collection*, XLVII.
269 See Liddington and Norris (1985, p.182).
270 See Blewett (1965).
271 See, for example, *CFT*, 16.12.1904, p.8.
272 For democratic suffragists, see Holton (1988).
273 See Liddington (1984, p.144).
274 See, for example, *CFT*, 5.5.1905, p.1.
275 See *CFT*, 27.1.1905, p.1.
276 See Paul (1988, pp.30–31).
277 See Hannam (1992).
278 See Hunt (1996).
279 For Chartism, see Schwarzkopf (1991, esp. ch.4) and Clark (1997, esp. chs 12 and 13); for a conflicting assessment of Chartist women's stance, see de Larrabeiti (1998).
280 See Mitchell (1968) and Chew (1982). Selina Cooper failed to produce an autobiography, feeling inhibited about writing because of her deficient education. The spoken rather than the written word was her preferred medium, and by all accounts she was a highly effective speaker with a message to convey.
281 For working-class autobiographies and 'the silence of women', see Vincent (1982, pp.8–9). The autobiography of ex-mill worker Annie Kenney (1924) is a counter-example. Cast in the 'religious revelation' mode, it denies, rather than affirming, female agency.
282 Evans (1990, p.261).
283 Ibid., p.263.
284 See Gittins (1982, p.185); see also Glucksmann (1995, p.281).

285 For an account of this group, see Pankhurst (1988), esp. Books VIII and IX.
286 See Bryan (1977, p.34); see also Liddington and Norris (1985, p.93).
287 See Paul (1988, pp.30–31); see also Frost (1988, p.29).
288 See *Daily Dispatch*, 27.11.1912, GTC 5/67.
289 See Liddington and Norris (1985, pp.85–6).
290 It should therefore come as no surprise that the suffrage movement at Oldham, that epitome of a spinning town, was very upper-middle-class in composition; see T.J. Berry (1986), 'The Female Suffrage Movement in South Lancashire with Particular Reference to Oldham, 1890–1914', unpublished MA dissertation, Huddersfield Polytechnic, quoted in Leneman (1998, p.46).
291 See Liddington and Norris (1985, pp.92–3).
292 See Benenson (1993, p.628).
293 Eva Gore-Booth, 'Women Workers in the Cotton Industry', in *The Guardian*, quoted in *Textile Mercury*, 16.1.1904, p.45.
294 Ibid.
295 See Liddington and Norris (1985, p.240).
296 For the fundamental challenge posed by the British women's movement to the separation of spheres and women's confinement to domesticity, of which the right to political participation was but one element, see Kent (1987).
297 See Benenson (1993, p.614).
298 See ibid., p.613.
299 See Morgan (1992, pp.26, 29, 41).
300 See Morgan (1996, p.38), reiterated in Morgan (2001, esp. chs 2 and 3).

Chapter 7

Gender Unpicked: Conclusion

This study has set out to make a contribution to both gender and labour history by going beyond the concerns that have for long been dominant in either historical subdiscipline. By focusing on the labour process, it has foregrounded a site for the construction of gender that has received scant attention in gender history hitherto. Conversely, by demonstrating the centrality of paid work to the identity of women cotton weavers, it has demolished the tenet, long held in labour history,[1] that male workers' identity is forged at work, while women's is formed at home. This study has depicted female cotton weavers in Lancashire as taking pride in their skilled trade and challenging their subordination under the factory regime by reappropriating production time as well as space; it has portrayed them as members of their unions who, though virtually barred from office, stood up for their rights and dignity at the workplace actively, even militantly, with or without union backing; it has outlined the manifold ways in which they fitted their family commitments around their paid employment; it has shown them actively refashioning the gender division of domestic labour,[2] giving it a more equitable direction; finally it has outlined their commitment to the cause of women's suffrage.

Displaying all the hallmarks of disciplined political activity geared towards a long-term goal, this kind of political activism stood in marked contrast to the spontaneous outbursts of discontent by so-called 'primitive rebels'. These two ideal types, as it were, of political activism have been frequently gendered, although their implications for gender have rarely been explored.[3] Disciplined action has been presented as the domain of sober, respectable men who possessed a clear idea of their social and economic situation, while the angry outbursts of rebellion, the riot, or the charivari, have been seen as forms of activity particularly suited to women, who allegedly lacked the time and dedication required for consistent commitment to a particular cause.

In demonstrating the inaccuracy of the way in which these types of political activism have been gendered, this study not only echoes previous findings,[4] but has also adduced further evidence demonstrating that a dichotomous conception of the public and the private is often inappropriate. In this particular case, it fails to capture the multiple ways in which work and family meshed in female weavers' lives. Through its focus on the labour process, this study has shown the shopfloor to be far from forming a 'family-free' zone. For many weavers, co-workers and kin partly overlapped, and the women among them bonded, not only as workers battling to earn a living under adverse conditions, but also in their familial capacities of daughters, wives or mothers.

Most of the works investigating female workers' activism have focused on women whose subordination to male control in the home is reproduced in the workplace, the superposition of male dominance in both spheres adding to the significance of the numerous instances of women's insubordination. Female cotton weavers, by contrast, were positioned differently. By highlighting the gender equality characteristic of the labour process in cotton weaving, this study's claim goes beyond the assertion that women are the agents of their own history.

To be sure, women weavers have been consistently portrayed here as agents, as constructing a version of femininity that embraced pride in performing a skilled job, the active defence of both their own right to paid employment and the well-being of their communities as well as the struggle for citizenship, which they saw as the central lever for improving their condition. In sum this portrayal underscores women weavers' experience of gender equality in the labour process as enabling them to challenge gender as a power relation in a fundamental way. Their experience of equality in the labour process both sensitized them to their inequality in other spheres of society and empowered them to take action against it by demonstrating inequality to be constructed rather than naturally given or divinely ordained.

The central argument of this study thus makes a statement about the linkage between women weavers' perception of their position in the labour process and their political activism. In the research on gender, the labour process has received scant attention, having been regarded, quite unlike the home and the family, as accidental to the formation of women's gender identity. Yet placed at the centre of an investigation into the construction of gender, the labour process emerges not merely as another site in which gender is being formed, but as potentially crucial to this formation. This is not to accord primacy to the economic sphere of paid employment in the social construction of gender. The point is rather that gender need not be constructed identically in all spheres of society.

This assumption has, however, informed a great deal of feminist historiography. On the basis of her investigation of Courtauld's silk mills in Essex, Judy Lown, for one, has claimed rather sweepingly that industrialization had 'common implications ... for women's relationship to paid employment across different regional locations and economic sectors ... Notions of masculinity and femininity were directly connected to ideals of the patriarchal family which in turn were intrinsically harnessed to a hierarchical ordering of economic positions'.[5]

This observation, while applying to conditions at Courtauld's, is singularly inappropriate in relation to the women cotton weavers of Lancashire. Their example demonstrates how the friction produced by varieties of gender failing to be fully coterminous with each other can act as a catalyst for change. Women weavers' equality in the labour process clashed with the foreclosing of promotion both at work and in the union; their pride in their jobs and their commitment to trade unionism were denied by union officials harping on the fickleness of a female rank and file; their commitment to their jobs was ignored by employers who, in league with male weavers, challenged women's right to paid employment. Women weavers inferred from the multiplicity of ways in which their equality in the labour process was negated that the contestation of gender was not confined to the sphere of paid employment. This enabled them to recognize their exclusion from citizenship as a denial of gender equality in another sphere. Possession of the franchise, they hoped, would empower them more effectively to renegotiate gender, giving it a more equitable direction in politics as well as in the family, in paid employment as well as in their unions.

This study therefore urges the need to trace other examples of gender inequality being challenged in fundamental ways to the friction generated by varieties of gender coexisting, but not necessarily fully corresponding with one another. Such friction may occur between gender as constructed in paid employment and in the home, in charitable work and in politics, in religious devotion and in the church hierarchy, in theories of social equality and in political practice. It is the very volatility of gender as a construction, its fluidity and malleability, which renders it amenable to buttressing other relations of subordination and dominance. Yet at the same time this non-fixity, the result of a continuing process of negotiating, of challenging and reaffirming, of contesting and reproducing, opens up the possibility of reconstructing gender as a rather more egalitarian relation.

What needs to be emphasized throughout is the possibilities and potentials inherent in the non-fixity of gender as a construct. There is no determinism implied in the central argument of this study. The clashing of relations of equality and inequality in the lives of female cotton weavers bore the potential for, yet did not necessarily entail, political activism. Though forming by far the largest contingent of working-class women among suffrage activists, women weavers did not join the suffrage campaign in a body, and the intensity of their commitment varied, both over time and between individuals.

Furthermore a brief look beyond the boundaries of Lancashire suffices to show that the gender equality characterizing the organization of the labour process in cotton weaving in this region was the inevitable outcome neither of economic rationality nor of technological requirements, but was itself a construction.[6] It was the volatile result of the way in which the conflicting interests of employers and workers, both male and female, intermingled. In the continual renegotiation of this conflict, concerns of class meshed with those of gender. In the heartland of cotton weaving, however, conditions remained relatively stable during the period under consideration. When economic conditions deteriorated markedly in the global crisis of the late 1920s, women cotton weavers tenaciously maintained their identity as skilled workers, albeit laid off.

Any understanding of gender as a relational category prohibits the consideration of femininity in isolation. The version adopted by Lancashire female weavers was constructed in tandem with, if not in opposition to, a corresponding notion of masculinity. In the cotton communities of Lancashire, to be a good woman involved competence at skilled work as a precondition for wages forming a substantial part of the income of a family whose size and needs were fitted around the requirements of paid employment. Moreover, this version of femininity proclaimed allegiance to the working class through union membership and active participation in strike action. Nor did it preclude political activism. What emerges is in fact the centrality of competence at paid work to women weavers' identity, a centrality affirmed in a particularly dramatic fashion by those young female weavers whose vitality was sapped by their failure to achieve the status of skilled worker, on which rested both the ability to defy male dominance in the family and a woman's reputation in the community, leading them to commit suicide.

To be a good man, by contrast, encompassed competence at one's job and the ability to earn reasonable wages, readiness to help with household chores, even childcare, and renunciation of a large number of children as proof of one's virility. This version of masculinity might include holding office in one's union or party, possibly with a view to embarking on a political career that would place the stamp of public approval on this version of working-class male respectability. Alternatively, by thus stepping out into the public sphere, men might use their political involvement to affirm a version of masculinity denied them within the weaving community.

Of overriding importance is the embeddedness of these notions of gender in the expectations and practices of entire communities.[7] In the weaving communities of north-east Lancashire the large-scale factory employment of women, including wives and mothers, and the significant contribution they made to the income of families unable to subsist on a male wage alone, along with the repercussions this had on relations of gender, formed a way of life that was as difficult for the individual to deviate from as it was distinguished from the expectations and practices characteristic of working-class communities elsewhere.

Weavers' versions of masculinity and femininity had a long pedigree, as Anna Clark's work has shown.[8] In her investigation of the ways in which the emerging working class was being gendered, she has consistently emphasized the differences between gender relations among artisans, who enforced their dominance powerfully and often violently, and those among the textile workers of domestic industry, where male dominance was toned down by the need for husband and wife to cooperate in order jointly to produce the family income.

In addition, these versions of masculinity and femininity, which were endorsed by entire communities, demonstrate the partial collapse of demarcation and opposition as central modes of constructing gender. The overlap between some components of gender identity, which formed part of both femininity and masculinity, coming close to jeopardizing the sameness taboo, had a differential impact on men and women, empowering the latter, but rankling with the former. Unable effectively to mark themselves off from women at work, men held on to the unions as the sphere in which to assert their masculinity, making sure that their organizations projected an image of unimpaired virility. This was, moreover, a precondition for achieving recognition in the world of labour. What emerges is the reversal of the way in which gender on the shopfloor, in the home and in trade unions is frequently assumed to be linked. Rather than domestic gender relations being reproduced in the workplace and the unions, the latter strove particularly hard to remove the taint they felt was placed on them by insufficient gender demarcation at work and in the home.

In doing so they selectively drew upon elements of gender notions current in other sections of society. Thus they emphasized women's frailty and fickleness, which allegedly made them less productive workers and less committed unionists, while carefully avoiding allusion to women's 'nimble fingers', which in weaving counted as an asset, but, though undoubtedly a quality required by skilled male weavers, too, was difficult to incorporate into a notion of virile masculinity.

Furthermore, although labour rhetoric was steeped in the idea of the family wage and the male bread-winner family, weaving unionists were careful to avoid such language when dealing with the local rank and file, among whom women predominated in many localities. They knew only too well that such talk would have the women up in arms. Though at times acutely sensing in their fatigued bodies the effects of combining paid employment with domestic labour, women weavers emphasized the benefits, rather than the costs, of continuing in paid employment well after marriage. They were unwilling to forgo either the independence their wages bestowed on them or the satisfaction derived from performing a skilled job. Added to this was the attraction held out by the possibility of socializing with other women at work, a source of strength not to be belittled. No wonder female weavers should have a marked predilection for mill work over domestic drudgery. Family wage rhetoric was not even sure to win unequivocal male support at grassroots level, for the weaving family crucially depended upon the joint income of husband and wife. Unless male weavers' wages were raised to a level adequate to family needs, the notion of the male bread-winner failed to gain purchase in the weaving communities of Lancashire.

Trade union officials displayed remarkable adeptness at fine-tuning their messages to specific audiences and purposes. It was no contradiction for one and the same individual to deploy the need for weavers' wives to earn an income to win their middle-class betters' sympathy for their degraded manhood, and on another occasion to dispel the doubts cast on the skilled nature of weaving by the large numbers of women employed in the industry by lauding women's competence at work. Yet, whatever message they aimed to convey, what mattered most was the fact that they had access to the political realm as an arena in which to enact and reaffirm their masculinity.

The lack of support for the ideal of the family wage in the cotton districts of Lancashire extended to the spinning towns, which boasted a high level of female factory employment in spite of the good wages earned by male spinners. The high female employment rate throughout the entire cotton district bears witness to the degree to which notions of gender that did not revolve around men as providers and women as home-makers had taken root in the working-class culture peculiar to this region.

True, the elusiveness of the family wage was far from being confined to the Lancashire cotton weaving industry, yet the absence of a male bread-winner wage in many instances only hardened adherence to the ideal.[9] While it is well-nigh impossible to determine differences in the degree to which the ideal of the male bread-winner family had taken root in various Western countries, Britain stands out for the broad consensus achieved at a comparatively early stage between the labour movement, certain sections of the state and many middle-class feminists, all of whom saw the family wage as a desirable goal and designed social legislation around it, from its inception to the setting up of the welfare state. Though not necessarily endorsing women's, especially mothers', right to paid labour, the welfare policies implemented by Germany[10] and the United States[11] were less unequivocally premised upon the man as the provider of the family. In France, the state refused altogether to see its role in determining appropriate gender roles, leaving these to be negotiated by individual men and women.[12]

As an interactive process, the construction of gender is by definition not confined to one group alone. The process involves various groups of actors operating in alliance with, or in opposition to, one another, thereby demonstrating the way in which gender is fractured by class. Thus women weavers were able to ally themselves with middle-class suffragists in their struggle to include citizenship in their version of femininity. By contrast, some manufacturers sought to build an alliance with trade unionists and their male workforce in an attempt to link the introduction of new technology to a reconstruction of gender. The offer to implement the new machines in a way that would have buttressed masculinity and disempowered femininity was intended to buy off male workers' resistance. Had this attempt been successful, Lancashire cotton weavers' femininity would have been purged of the right to paid employment, while masculinity would have been enhanced by payment of a family wage. Though cleverly latching on to one of the main grievances of male weavers, the attempt failed on account of the degree to which employers let their gender solidarity be constrained by economic rationality.

The extent to which male dominance was structured into weaving unions makes the degree of unionization among women weavers all the more astonishing. In contrast to their achievements in the home, in the unions women were unable to translate their numerical preponderance into more equitable relations of power between male and female unionists. Their large-scale acquiescence to male dominance in trade unions stemmed in part from the fact that, though denied positions of power in the union hierarchy, their job-related grievances were taken seriously and dealt with efficiently. While acknowledged and welcomed as workers on whose support unions crucially depended, they were denigrated as women. This alliance on the basis of class was thus fractured by gender.

Furthermore, in trying to challenge male domination in their unions, the few women energetic and courageous enough to do so, *vide* Alice Foley, took on not only local officialdom, but virtually the entire turn-of-the-century labour movement, in which the female presence was negligible outside the cotton unions. Isolated within the ranks of union officialdom, the pressure to gain acceptance, which was impossible to achieve on the basis of gender, acted upon the lone female official to adjust her views to those of the men around her, in a process of adapting to the masculine that was presumably imperceptible to herself.

The specific kinds of friction between equality in the labour process and male dominance in virtually all other social spheres were the result of the way in which mechanized cotton weaving in Lancashire had evolved historically. Closure, a potent means adopted elsewhere to prohibit women from entering specific trades, had not been a viable option. Weaving had to remain open and accessible in order to safeguard the employment of men in the industry. Owing to the long tradition of female employment, women weavers regarded their jobs as theirs by right rather than by concession, a right they were determined to defend whenever it came under attack. In these struggles their power revolved around the fact that weaving, regardless of how it was portrayed by outsiders, was a skilled trade. Consequently, employers were loath to lose tried and tested operatives, irrespective of gender.

Furthermore, since the large-scale implementation of the powerloom, no dramatic advance in production technology had occurred which would have offered the opportunity of transforming weaving into an exclusively male domain. When such advance did occur, in the shape of the automatic loom brought to Britain in the early 1900s, the opportunity to do so was seized by weaving unions with the backing of employers. Yet the specific intermingling of the dictates of economic rationality and the gender interests of men in the context of the conditions peculiar to the industry in Lancashire, coupled with women's militant defence of their right to work as part of a community struggle to preserve its members' accustomed way of life and standard of living ensured that this attempt came to nothing.

Though such conditions of female employment make the Lancashire cotton weaving industry fairly unique, it must be stressed again that this is not the reason why it has been selected for this study. The selection has been based rather on the fact that these conditions allow the construction of gender to be observed. This process, far from being confined to the cotton weaving industry, goes on everywhere all the time. Usually, it is far more difficult to discern, because gender difference has been cloaked in so many guises of objectivity and so convincingly as to appear natural. For this reason generalizations from this case study can be made. These concern, not the specific organization of the labour process, but the construction of gender.

Gender equality in the labour process had been a feature of cotton weaving in Lancashire since the collapse of handloom weaving and men's large-scale entry into factories. Yet, for women to be able to translate this experience into political action, specific conditions had to be present. Towards the close of the nineteenth century, female cotton weavers were able to draw upon two kinds of discourse to make sense of their experience in terms of equality and inequality. The labour movement argued for the right of, even the need for, members of their own class to press for recognition of working-class concerns in Parliament. Regardless of their sympathy for these demands, women of the working class had no guarantee that their specific grievances would be included in the political agenda pursued by working-class MPs.

The suffrage movement, by contrast, protested against gender being upheld as a bar to citizenship. Women weavers responded to this message of gender solidarity, inserting specific concerns to do with their class position into the movement's agenda. It bespeaks the strength of the suffrage movement in the early 1900s that it was able to build and sustain solidarity on the basis of gender across the class divide. The fusion of labour and suffrage activism effected through the intervention of the Manchester and Salford Women's Trades and Labour Council, made up of trade unionists and suffragists, marked the historical juncture enabling women weavers to turn to suffragism.

Though their struggle was successful in that, in 1918, women over the age of 30 were granted the right to vote, in the long run possession of the suffrage proved insufficient in establishing gender equality in society. Though helping to secure government measures intended to alleviate somewhat the effects of the protracted decline of the cotton industry, neither did women's involvement in the polity succeed in averting the industry's eventual demise. Despite these seeming failures, the struggle for gender equality waged by the women weavers of Lancashire is both instructive and inspiring in demonstrating relations of power to be socially constructed and hence changeable.

Notes

1 See Rose (1993, p.157).
2 Emphasizing women's agency is important because, as contrasting examples demonstrate, a more equitable gender division of domestic labour was not merely a function of the size of women's contribution to family income; see, for example, Parr (1990, p.235).
3 See Rose (1993, p.147).
4 See, for example, Gordon (1991), Canning (1996, esp. ch.7); see also Cameron (1993) for two salient examples of female textile workers at Lawrence, MA, initiating and sustaining strike action.
5 Lown (1990, p.172).
6 For the Scottish textile industry, see Gordon (1991); for the textile industry in Saxony, in particular, see Zachmann (1993) and in various parts of Germany, see Canning (1996).
7 This point is consistently emphasized by Glucksmann (2000).

8   See Clark (1997).
9   For a survey of recent research into the family wage on an international scale, see *International Review of Social History*, supplement, 1997.
10 See, for example, Canning (1996).
11 See, for example, Koven and Michel (1990).
12 See Pedersen (1993).

Glossary of Technical Terms

beam	flanged roller on which the warp is wound
bobbin	flanged wooden cylinder on which the yarn is wound
carding	disentangling and laying parallel the fibres of cotton and the removal of waste matter preparatory to spinning; operation performed in the cardroom
cardroom	see carding
cloth	technical name for woven cotton fabrics
cop	conical ball of cotton wound on the spinning frame; paper tube fitting onto a spindle to collect the yarn
count	measure of yarn by length and weight, stating how many hanks of a given length will weigh a pound; the higher the count the finer the yarn
cut	length of warp required to weave a piece of cloth; also the piece when woven
dhooties	shirtings ornamented by stripes of grey or coloured yarn and in suitable lengths for Hindu loin cloths
dobby loom	loom designed to produce more elaborate weaves by having a greater control of the raising of the warp threads
drills	very durable cotton cloth
ends	warp threads of a cloth
float	weaving fault; instead of ends being intertwined, one of the threads breaks and gets fast between cloth and healds, warp threads and intersections break; can be narrow or wide
gaiting up	setting up the loom for a particular weave
grey cloth	fabrics in an undyed or unbleached state
grey goods	see grey cloth
grinder	cardroom operative who gives new points to the teeth of the carding wires by grinding with an emery band or wheel
hank	measurement of yarn; in cotton, 840 yards

healds	looped cords furnished with an eye in the centre and used in the loom for controlling the up-and-down movement of the warp threads
manufacture	sometimes used synonymously with weaving
manufacturer	owner of a weaving mill
overlooker	supervisory worker in charge of one section of a weaving shed; keeps looms supplied with warps, sets them up for particular weaves, repairs them
pick	single throw of the shuttle in the loom, inserting a weft thread in the cloth; thread of weft placed between the warp threads in one passage of the shuttle through the shed
picking	projecting the shuttle from one side of the loom to the other
piece goods	cloth sold by the yard
piecer	mule spinner's assistant who mends the broken ends of a thread in the spinning process
piecing	joining up the threads which have broken by means of twisting
reed	metal comb fixed in a frame to keep the warp threads evenly spaced, to form a guide for the shuttle and to beat up the weft
selvedge	(or selvage) edges of a piece of cloth
shed	opening formed for the passage of the shuttle by raising some warp threads and lowering others; weaving mill
sheeting	cotton cloth used for making sheets
shirting	heavily sized common grey cloth
shuttle	bullet-shaped device for carrying the weft back and forth through the warp in the loom; made from wood, pointed at both ends and tipped with steel; hollowed out in the centre and provided with a hinged metal tongue
size	substance used for stiffening and binding fabrics
sizing	coating warp with a thin layer of starch to strengthen the yarn so that it breaks less in weaving; recipe of starch the highly paid tapesizer's secret
smash	damage that occurs in weaving when the timing of the pick is off and the shuttle tears the warp threads
stripper	male cardroom worker clearing cards from matted fibres
tackler	see overlooker
tapesizer	see sizing

tenter	juvenile assistant to fully-fledged weaver; learner in weaving
tenting	assisting an experienced weaver; common way of learning the trade
warp	threads lying lengthwise in a cloth
weft	threads lying widthwise in a cloth
yarn	spun thread

Bibliography

Primary Sources

1 Collections

Webb Collection, Collection E, Section A, vol. XLVII, Women's Labour, London School of Economics.
Women, Industry and Trade Unionism, The Gertrude Tuckwell Collection, 1890–1920, TUC Library, University of North London.
Women's Trade Union League Papers, TUC Library, University of North London.

2 Trade Association Records

Amalgamated Weavers' Association, Accrington, Northrop Weaving, Replies to Questions, 1911, Lancashire Record Office, Preston, *DDX* 1274/14/4.
Bolton & District Weavers' and Winders' Association, Minute Book, 1903–6, Bolton Archives and Local Studies, Central Library, *FT/6*.
Burnley & District Textile Workers' Union, Correspondence and Memoranda, Letter Book, 9.1.1885–5.9.1899, 4.1.1907–7.1.1913, Lancashire Record Office, Preston, *DDX* 1274/10.
Burnley Master Cotton Spinners' and Manufacturers' Association, Minute Book, 1894–1911, Lancashire Record Office, Preston, *DDX* 1145.
General Union of Associations of Loom Overlookers, Almanack and Guide, 1906–14, Manchester Central Library.
Hyde & District Power Loom Overlookers, Minute Book, 1903–4, 1908, Tameside Local Studies Library, Stalybridge, *TU8*.
Manchester, Salford and District Women's Trades Union Council, Annual Reports, 1895–1919, Local Studies Unit, Manchester Central Library, *331.88 M27*.
Manchester and Salford Women's Trades and Labour Council, Annual Reports, 1907, 1908, Working-Class Movement Library, Salford.
Preston and District Power-Loom Weavers', Winders' and Warpers' Association, Cases and Complaints, Lancashire Record Office, Preston, *DDX* 1089.
Records of the Joint Committee of the Cotton Spinners' and Manufacturers' Association and the Amalgamated Weavers' Association, 21 August 1901–end of 1914, Lancashire Record Office, Preston, *DDX* 1274/13.
Records of the Northern Counties' Amalgamated Association of Weavers, Reports

of Council Meetings, 13 July 1895–1914, Lancashire Record Office, Preston, *DDX* 1274/14.

South-East Lancashire and Cheshire Weavers' and Winders' Association, Ashton District, Minute Book, 1903–4, 1908; Manchester & Salford Branch, Minute Book; Stockport & District, Minute Book, Tameside Local Studies Library, Stalybridge, *TU6*.

Trades Union General Council Organization of Women. Summarized Report of Conference of Representatives of Unions Catering for Women Workers. Held in Transport House, Smith Square, S.W.1, on Friday January 30th, 1931, at 10.30 a.m., TUC Library, University of North London.

3 Government Publications

Board of Trade, Labour Department, Report by Miss Collet on the Statistics of Employment of Women and Girls, *PP*, 1894, LXXXI.

The Board of Trade Labour Gazette, prepared and edited at the offices of the Board of Trade, London, S.W., vol. XVI, 1908.

Departmental Committee on Humidity and Ventilation in Cotton Weaving Sheds, Minutes of Evidence and Appendices, *PP*, 1909, XV.

The Employment of Women, Report by Miss May E. Abraham on the Conditions of Work in the Cotton Industry of Lancashire and Cheshire, *PP*, 1893–94, XXXVII, Pt. I.

Report of a Committee appointed to inquire into the Working of the Cotton Cloth Factories Act, 1889, *PP*, 1897, XVII.

Report of the Departmental Committee on the Truck Acts, vol. II, Evidence (Days 1–37), *PP*, 1908, Cd.4443, lix.

Report of an Enquiry by the Board of Trade into the Earnings and Hours of Labour of Workpeople of the United Kingdom, I. Textile Trades in 1906, *PP*, 1909, LXXX; 1910, LXXXIV.

Report to the Home Office and the Local Government Board upon an Inquiry into the Alleged Danger of the Transmission of Certain Diseases from Person to Person in Weaving Sheds by means of the practice known as 'Shuttle-Kissing', by Gerald Bellhouse (one of H.M. Superintending Inspectors of Factories), Dr W.W.E. Fletcher (a Medical Inspector of the Local Government Board) and Mr D.J. Shackleton (late Senior Labour Adviser, Home Office), *PP*, 1912–13, XXVI.

Reports from the Royal Commission on the Depression of Trade and Industry, *PP*, 1886, XXI; XXII; XXIII.

Report on Strikes and Lock-Outs by the Labour Correspondent of the Board of Trade, *PP*, 1889, LXX; 1890, LXVIII; 1890–91, LXXVIII; 1893–4, LXXXIII, Pt.1; 1894, LXXXI, Pt.1; 1895, XCII; 1896, LXXX, Pt.1; 1897, LXXXIV; 1898, LXXXVIII; 1899, XCII; 1900, LXXXIII; 1901, LXXIII; 1902, XCVII; 1903, LXVI; 1904, LXXXIX; 1905, LXXVI; 1906, CXII; 1907, LXXX; 1908, XCVIII; 1909, XLIX.

Return of Rates of Wages in the Principal Textile Trades of the United Kingdom, *PP*, 1889, LXX.
Royal Commission on Labour, Minutes of Evidence (Group C), *PP*, 1892, XXXV; XXXVI, Pt. II.
Summary of Returns under s.130 of the Factory and Workshop Act, 1901, of Persons Employed in 1907 in Textile Factories, *PP*, 1909, LXXIX.

4 Memoirs

Printed

Brooks, J. Barlow (1926), *Lancashire Bred: An Autobiography*, 2 vols, Stalybridge: privately printed.
Chew, Doris Nield (ed.) (1982), *Ada Nield Chew: The Life and Writings of a Working Woman*, London: Virago.
Foley, Alice (1973), *A Bolton Childhood*, Manchester: University of Manchester Extra-Mural Department.
Hesketh, Phoebe (1992), *My Aunt Edith: The Story of a Preston Suffragette*, Preston: Lancashire County Books (1st edn London: Peter Davies, 1966).
Holt, William (1939), *I Haven't Unpacked: An Autobiography*, London: G.G. Harrap and Co.
Kenney, Annie (1924), *Memories of a Militant*, London: Edward Arnold.
Kunz, Otto (1942), *Barbara, die Feinweberin*, Lucerne: Verlag der Unionsdruckerei.
McCarthy, Margaret (1953), *Generation in Revolt*, London: William Heinemann.
Mitchell, Geoffrey (ed.) (1968), *The Hard Way Up: The Autobiography of Hannah Mitchell, Suffragette and Rebel*, London: Faber and Faber.
Smith, Deborah (1933), *My Revelation: An Autobiography*, London: Houghton Publishing Co.

Unprinted

Bolton Oral History Project, Bolton Archives and Local Studies, Central Library, *B025.178B/PRO*.
Cookson, Doris, Autumn Leaves, manuscript, Burnley Central Library, *G3*.
Early Recollections, Essay Contest Entries, Lancashire Record Office, Preston, *DDX 978*.
Grimshaw, M., Memories of Burnley, manuscript, Burnley Central Library, *G3*.
Kenny, Christine (1994), Talking to Mill Workers. Transcripts from Interviews Conducted with Bolton Textile Workers, 1991–2, 2 vols, Bolton Archives and Local Studies, Central Library, *B025.178 KEN*.
Lancashire Textile Project, Technology, Work and Leisure in a Factory Community, Bancroft Tapes, Lancaster University Library.
Manchester Studies Unit, Oral History Tapes, Manchester Metropolitan University, Tameside Local Studies Library, Stalybridge.

Middlebrook, Wilfred (1983), Trumpet Voluntary, manuscript, Brunel University Library.
North-West Sound Archive, Clitheroe, Collection of Tapes.
Roberts, Elizabeth (1981), North-West Oral History Project, Social and Family Life in Preston, 1890–1940, University of Lancaster.

5 Newspapers and Periodicals

The dates given below indicate the issues read for this study.
Blackburn Times, 15.2.1908.
Blackburn Weekly Telegraph, September 1911.
Cotton Factory Times, 1885, 1886, 1888–91; September–December 1895, 1897; June–July 1899; January 1900; June–August 1901; May, July, November 1903, 1904; November–December 1905; January–September, December 1906; September–December 1907; March, August, November 1908; March 1909; January, December 1911; August, December 1912, 1913; May–July 1927.
Daily Chronicle, 29.5.1891.
Hyde Reporter, September–December 1904; March–July 1908.
Journal of the British Association of Managers of Textile Works (Lancashire Section), 1909–14.
Lancashire Daily Post, 1.11.1893; 30.10.1906.
Liverpool Weekly Post, 30.7.1927.
New Weekly, 2.2.1895.
North Cheshire Herald, Denton and Haughton Herald, Marple Herald and Hyde and Glossop News, September–November 1904; May–July 1908.
Preston Guardian, 6.10.1906; 27.7.1907; 10.10.1908.
Textile Manufacturer, 1901–8.
Textile Mercury, 1902–8.
Textile Recorder, 1901–8.

6 Other Primary Sources

A.B.C. Magazine, vol. 1, no. 4, April 1921; no. 5, September 1921; no. 6, December 1921; vol., 2, no. 9, Christmas 1922, Tameside Local Studies Library, Stalybridge, *L677.2*.
Ashton Bros. & Co. Ltd. (1946), Introduction to the Mills, Hyde, Tameside Local Studies Library, Stalybridge, *L677.2*.
Chew, Ada Nield (1900–1902), 'Victims of Our Industrial System: The Cotton Workers of Lancashire', *Young Oxford*, **2–3**.
Chew, Ada Nield (1912), 'All in the Day's Work', *The Englishwoman*, July, 35–45.
Fletcher, A.M., An Account of the Introduction of the Northrop Loom into the Mills of Ashton Brothers & Company Limited at Hyde, Cheshire, in 1902, Tameside Local Studies Library, Stalybridge, *L677.2*.

Ford, Isabella (1900), 'Industrial Women, And How to Help Them', *Friends' Quarterly Examiner*, **34**.
Gore-Booth, Eva, 'Women Workers and Parliamentary Representation', Textile Tracts no. 1, publ. by Lancashire and Cheshire Women Textile and other Workers' Representation Committee, Manchester, Fawcett Library.
Harvey, E.C. (1909), *Labour Laws for Women and Children in the United Kingdom*, London, Fawcett Library, *344.014*.
Lancashire and Cheshire Women Textile and Other Workers' Representation Committee, Women's Suffrage Collection, Local Studies Section, Manchester Central Library, *M50*.
Making for a New Age at Ashtons, Ashton Brothers, 1961, Tameside Local Studies Library, Stalybridge, *L677.2*.
Report of a Conference between the Directors of Ashton Bros. &. Co., Ltd. and Operative Weavers' Officials, held at Bagley Field Mill, 23 March 1908, on the question of wages on the Northrop Loom, Tameside Local Studies Library, Stalybridge, *DD236*.

Secondary Sources

1 Published Books and Articles

Aitken, J.B. (1964), *Automatic Weaving*, London and Manchester: Columbine Press.
Aldcroft, D.H. (ed.) (1968), *The Development of British Industry and Foreign Competition, 1875–1914*, London: Allen and Unwin.
Alexander, Sally (1984), 'Women, Class and Sexual Difference in the 1830s and 1840s: Some Reflections on the Writing of a Feminist History', *History Workshop Journal*, **17**, 125–49.
Anderson, Adelaide (1922), *Women in the Factory*, London: John Murray.
Anderson, Gregory (ed.) (1988), *The White-Blouse Revolution: Female Office Workers Since 1870*, Manchester: Manchester University Press.
Anderson, Michael (1971), *Family Structure in Nineteenth-Century Lancashire*, Cambridge: Cambridge University Press.
Anderson, Olive (1987), *Suicide in Victorian and Edwardian England*, Oxford: Clarendon Press.
Andrew, Samuel (1887), 'Fifty Years' Cotton Trade', paper read before the Economic Section of the British Association for the Advancement of Science, Oldham.
Ashton, Owen, Fyson, Robert and Roberts, Stephen (eds) (1995), *The Duty of Discontent*, New York: Mansell.
Askwith, G.R. (1920), *Industrial Problems and Disputes*, London: John Murray.

Ayers, Pat and Lambertz, Jan (1987), 'Marriage Relations, Money and Domestic Violence in Working-Class Liverpool, 1919–1939', in Jane Lewis (ed.), *Labour and Love: Women's Experience of Home and Family, 1850–1940*, Oxford: Basil Blackwell (1st edn 1986), pp.195–219.

Bailey, Victor (1998), *'This Rash Act': Suicide Across the Life Cycle in the Victorian City*, Stanford, CA: Stanford University Press.

Banks, Olive (1986), *Becoming a Feminist: The Social Origins of 'First Wave' Feminism*, Brighton: Wheatsheaf Books.

Barker, Theo and Drake, Michael (eds) (1982), *Population and Society in Britain, 1850–1980*, London: Batsford Academic and Educational Ltd., New York: New York University Press.

Baron, Ava (ed.) (1991a), *Work Engendered: Toward a New History of American Labor*, Ithaca: Cornell University Press.

Baron, Ava (1991b), 'Gender and Labor History: Learning from the Past, Looking to the Future', in Ava Baron (ed.), *Work Engendered: Toward a New History of American Labor*, Ithaca: Cornell University Press, pp.1–46.

Barrett, Michele and McIntosh, Mary (1980), 'The "Family Wage": Some Problems for Socialists and Feminists', *Capital and Class*, **11**, 51–72.

Barton, Dorothea M. (1921–2), 'Women's Wages in the Cotton Trade', *Transactions of Manchester Statistical Society*.

Beattie, Derek (1992), *Blackburn: The Development of a Lancashire Cotton Town*, Halifax: Ryburn Publishing Ltd.

Beechey, Veronica (1987), *Unequal Work*, London: Verso.

Beer, Ursula (1990), *Geschlecht, Struktur, Geschichte*, Frankfurt am Main: Campus.

Behagg, Clive (1995), 'Narratives of Control: Informalism and the Workplace in Britain, 1800–1900', in Owen Ashton, Robert Fyson and Stephen Roberts (eds), *The Duty of Discontent*, New York: Mansell, pp.122–41.

Benenson, Harold (1991), 'The "Family Wage" and Working Women's Consciousness in Britain, 1880–1914', *Politics and Society*, **19** (1), 71–108.

Benenson, Harold (1993), 'Patriarchal Constraints on Women Workers' Mobilization: The Lancashire Female Cotton Operatives, 1842–1919', *British Journal of Sociology*, **44** (4), 613–33.

Bennett, G.A. (1948), *An Introduction to Automatic Weaving*, Manchester and London: Harlequin Press.

Bennett, W. (1951), *The History of Burnley from 1850*, Burnley: Burnley Corporation.

Berg, Maxine (1985), *The Age of Manufactures: Industry, Innovation and Work in Britain, 1700–1820*, Oxford: Oxford University Press.

Biernacki, Richard (1995), *The Fabrication of Labor: Germany and Britain, 1640–1914*, Berkeley: University of California Press.

Black, Clementina (ed.) (1984), *Married Women's Work*, London: Virago (1st edn London: G. Bell and Sons, 1915).

Blackburn, Elizabeth. K. (1980), *In and Out the Windows: A Story of the Changes in Working Class Life, 1902–77, in a Small East Lancashire Community*, Burnley: privately printed.

Blackburn, Fred (1954), *George Tomlinson*, London: William Heinemann.

Blewett, Mary H. (1990), 'Masculinity and Mobility: The Dilemma of Lancashire Weavers and Spinners in Late-Nineteenth-Century Fall River, Massachusetts', in Mark C. Carnes and Clyde Griffen (eds), *Meanings for Manhood: Constructions of Masculinity in Victorian America*, Chicago: University of Chicago Press, pp.164–77.

Blewett, Mary H. (1993), 'Deference and Defiance: Labor Politics and the Meanings of Masculinity in the Mid-Nineteenth Century New England Textile Industry', *Gender and History*, **5** (3), 398–415.

Blewett, Neil (1965), 'The Franchise in the United Kingdom, 1885–1918', *Past and Present*, **32**, 27–56.

Bolin-Hort, Per (1989), *Work, Family and the State: Child Labour and the Organization of Production in the British Cotton Industry, 1780–1920*, Lund: Lund University Press.

Bolton and District Weavers' and Winders' Association (1965), *Centenary History*, Bolton.

Boone, Gladys (1942), *The Women's Trade Union Leagues in Great Britain and the United States of America*, New York: Columbia University Press.

Boot, H.M. (1995), 'How Skilled were Lancashire Cotton Factory Workers in 1833?', *Economic History Review*, **48** (2), 283–303.

Bornat, Joanna (1977), 'Home and Work: A New Context for Trade Union History', *Oral History*, **5** (2), 101–23.

Bornat, Joanna (1988), 'Lost Leaders: Women, Trade Unionism and the Case of the General Union of Textile Workers, 1875–1914', in Angela John (ed.), *Unequal Opportunities: Women's Employment in England, 1800–1918*, Oxford: Basil Blackwell (1st edn 1986), pp.207–33.

Bowden, Sue and Higgins, David M. (1999), '"Productivity on the cheap"? The "More Looms" Experiment and the Lancashire Weaving Industry during the Inter-War Years', *Business History*, **41** (3), 21–41.

Bradley, Harriet (1987), *Men's Work, Women's Work: A History of the Sex-Typing of Jobs in Britain*, Cambridge: Polity Press, Minneapolis: University of Minnesota Press.

British Association for the Advancement of Science (1887), *On the Regulation of Wages by Means of Lists in the Cotton Industry*, Manchester.

Bruley, Sue (1993), 'Gender, Class and Party: The Communist Party and the Crisis in the Cotton Industry in England Between the Two World Wars', *Women's History Review*, **2** (1), 81–106.

Burgess, Keith (1975), *The Origins of British Industrial Relations*, London: Croom Helm.

Busfield, D.F. (1988), 'Job Definitions and Inequality: The "Unskilled"

Women Workers of the West Riding Textile Industry', *Textile History*, **19** (1), 61–82.
Cameron, Ardis (1993), *Radicals of the Worst Sort: Laboring Women in Lawrence, Massachusetts, 1860–1912*, Urbana: University of Illinois Press.
Canning, Kathleen (1994), 'Feminist History after the Linguistic Turn: Historicizing Discourse and Experience', *Signs*, **19** (2), 368–404.
Canning, Kathleen (1996), *Languages of Labor and Gender: Female Factory Work in Germany, 1850–1914*, Ithaca: Cornell University Press.
Canning, Kathleen (2002), 'Problematische Dichotomien. Erfahrung zwischen Narrativität und Materialität', *Historische Anthropoloige*, **10** (2), 163–82.
Carnes, Mark C. and Griffen, Clyde (eds) (1990), *Meanings for Manhood: Constructions of Masculinity in Victorian America*, Chicago: University of Chicago Press.
Carus-Wilson, E.M. (ed.) (1962), *Essays in Economic History*, vol. 3, London: Arnold.
Cass, Eddie (1994), 'Factory Fiction in the Cotton Factory Times', *Manchester Region History Review*, **8**, 32–43.
Cass, Eddie, Fowler, Alan and Wyke, Terry (1998), 'The Remarkable Rise and Long Decline of the *Cotton Factory Times*', *Media History*, **4** (2), 141–59.
Challand, Hilary and Walker, Michael, (1995), '"No School, No Mill; No Mill, No Money": The Half-Time Textile Worker', in Michael Winstanley (ed.), *Working Children in Nineteenth-Century Lancashire*, Preston: Lancashire County Books.
Chapman, Sydney John (1900–1901), 'A Historical Sketch of the Masters' Associations in the Cotton Industry', *Transactions of the Manchester Statistical Society*.
Chapman, Sydney John (1904), *The Lancashire Cotton Industry: A Study in Economic Development*, Manchester: University of Manchester Press.
Chenut, Helen Harden (1996), 'The Gendering of Skill as Historical Process: The Case of French Knitters in Industrial Troyes, 1880–1939', in Laura L. Frader and Sonya O. Rose (eds), *Gender and Class in Modern Europe*, Ithaca: Cornell University Press, pp.77–107.
Chesser, Elizabeth Sloan (1909–10), 'The Lancashire Operative: Women's Work in the Factory and the Home', *National Review*, **54**, 684–92.
Clapham, J.H. (1932), *An Economic History of Modern Britain: Free Trade and Steel, 1850–1886*, Cambridge: Cambridge University Press.
Clapham, J.H. (1938), *An Economic History of Modern Britain: Machines and National Rivalries (1887–1914) With an Epilogue (1914–1929)*, Cambridge: Cambridge University Press.
Clark, Anna (1997), *The Struggle for the Breeches: Gender and the Making of the British Working Class*, Berkeley: University of California Press (1st edn 1995).
Clarke, Charles Allen (1899), *The Effects of the Factory System*, London: Grant Richards.

Clegg, H.A., Fox, Alan and Thompson, A.F. (1964), *A History of British Trade Unions Since 1889*, vol. 1, 1889–1910, Oxford: Oxford University Press.

Cockburn, Cynthia (1981), 'The Material of Male Power', *Feminist Review*, **9**, 41–58, reprinted in Donald MacKenzie and Judith Wajcman (eds) (1985), *The Social Shaping of Technology*, Milton Keynes: Open University Press.

Cockburn, Cynthia (1985), *Machinery of Dominance: Women, Men and Technical Know-How*, London: Pluto Press.

Cockburn, Cynthia (1986), 'The Relations of Technology: What Implications for Theories of Sex and Class?', in Rosemary Crompton and Michael Mann (eds), *Gender and Stratification*, Cambridge: Polity Press, pp.74–85.

Cockburn, Cynthia (1991), *Brothers: Male Dominance and Technological Change*, London: Pluto Press.

Cohen, Isaac (1985), 'Workers' Control in the Cotton Industry: A Comparative Study of British and American Mule Spinning', *Labor History*, **26**, 53–85.

Cole, G.D.H. (1962), 'British Trade Unions in the Third Quarter of the Nineteenth Century', in E.M. Carus-Wilson (ed.), *Essays in Economic History*, vol. 3, London: Arnold, pp.202–21.

Coleman, D.C. and MacLeod, Christine (1986), 'Attitudes to New Techniques: British Businessmen, 1800–1950', *Economic History Review*, **39** (4), 588–611.

Collinson, David and Knights, David (1986), '"Men Only": Theories and Practices of Job Segregation in Insurance', in David Knights and Hugh Willmott (eds), *Gender and the Labour Process*, Aldershot: Gower, pp.140–78.

Copeland, Melvin T. (1909), 'Technical Developments in Cotton Manufacturing Since 1860', *Quarterly Journal of Economics*, **24**, 109–59.

Creigh, S.W. (1982), 'The Origins of British Strike Statistics', *Business History*, **24** (1), 95–106.

Creighton, Colin (1996), 'The Rise of the Male Breadwinner Family: A Reappraisal', *Comparative Studies in Society and History*, **38**, 310–37.

Crick, Martin (1994), *The History of the Social Democratic Federation*, Keele: Ryburn Publ., Keele University Press.

Crompton, Rosemary and Mann, Michael (eds) (1986), *Gender and Stratification*, Cambridge: Polity Press.

D'Cruze, Shani (1993), 'Approaches to the History of Rape and Sexual Violence: Notes Towards Research', *Women's History Review*, **1** (3), 377–96.

D'Cruze, Shani (1998), *Crimes of Outrage: Sex, Violence and Victorian Working Women*, London: UCL Press.

Davidoff, Leonore and Westover, Belinda (eds) (1986a), *Our Work, Our Lives, Our Words: Women's History and Women's Work*, Basingstoke: Macmillan and Totowa, N.J.: Barnes and Noble Books.

Davidoff, Leonore and Westover, Belinda (1986b), '"From Queen Victoria to the Jazz Age": Women's World in England, 1880–1939', in: Leonore Davidoff and Belinda Westover (eds), *Our Work, Our Lives, Our Words: Women's History and Women's Work*, Basingstoke: Macmillan and Totowa, N.J.: Barnes and Noble Books.

Davidson, Roger (1978), 'The Board of Trade and Industrial Relations, 1896–1914', *The Historical Journal*, **21** (3), 571–91.

Davies, Margaret Llewelyn (ed.) (1978), *Maternity: Letters from Working Women Collected by the Women's Co-Operative Guild*, London: Virago (1st edn London: G. Bell and Sons, 1915).

Davies, Russell (1991), '"Do Not Go Gentle into that Good Night"? Women and Suicide in Carmarthenshire, c.1860–1920', in Angela John (ed.), *Our Mothers' Land: Chapters in Welsh Women's History, 1830–1939*, Cardiff: University of Wales Press, pp.93–108.

Davin, Anna (1978), 'Imperialism and Motherhood', *History Workshop Journal*, **5**, 9–65.

Derry, T.K. (1931–2), 'The Repeal of the Apprenticeship Clauses of the Statute of Apprentices', *Economic History Review*, **3**, 67–87.

Dictionary of Labour Biography (1974), vol. 2, eds Joyce M. Bellamy and John Saville, London: Macmillan.

Downs, Laura Lee (1993a), 'If "Woman" is Just an Empty Category, Then Why Am I Afraid to Walk Alone at Night? Identity Politics Meets the Postmodern Subject', *Comparative Study of Society and History*, **35** (2), 414–37.

Downs, Laura Lee (1993b), 'Reply to Joan Scott', *Comparative Study of Society and History*, **35** (2), 444–51.

Drake, Barbara (1984), *Women in Trade Unions*, London: Virago (1st edn Labour Research Department, 1920).

DuBois, Ellen (1991), 'Woman Suffrage and the Left: An International Socialist–Feminist Perspective', *New Left Review*, **186**, 20–45.

Dupree, Marguerite (1996), 'Foreign Competition and the Interwar Period', in Mary B. Rose (ed.), *The Lancashire Cotton Industry: A History Since 1700*, Preston: Lancashire County Books, pp.265–95.

Dwork, Deborah (1987), *War is Good for Babies and Other Young Children: A History of the Infant and Child Welfare Movement in England, 1898–1918*, London: Tavistock Publications.

Dyhouse, Carol (1979), 'Working-Class Mothers and Infant Mortality in England, 1895–1914', *Journal of Social History*, **12**, 248–67.

Edgerton, David (1996), *Science, Technology and the British Industrial 'Decline', 1870–1970*, Cambridge: Cambridge University Press.

Elbaum, B. and Lazonick, William (eds) (1986), *The Decline of the British Economy: An Institutional Approach*, Oxford: Clarendon Press.

Elderton, Ethel (1914), *Report on the English Birthrate*, Eugenics Laboratory Memoirs, vols XIX and XX.

Ellison, Thomas (1968), *The Cotton Trade of Great Britain*, New York: Kelly.

Evans, Clare (1990), 'Unemployment and the Making of the Feminine During the Lancashire Cotton Famine', in Pat Hudson and W.R. Lee (eds), *Women's Work and the Family Economy in Historical Perspective*, Manchester: Manchester University Press, pp.248–70.

Farnie, D.A. (1978), 'Three Historians of the Cotton Industry: Thomas Ellison, Gerhart von Schulze-Gaevernitz, and Sydney Chapman', *Textile History*, **9**, 75–89.

Farnie, D.A. (1979), *The English Cotton Industry and the World Market, 1815–1896*, Oxford: Clarendon Press.

Feurer, Rosemary (1988), 'The Meaning of "Sisterhood": The British Women's Movement and Protective Labor Legislation, 1870–1900', *Victorian Studies*, **31**, 233–60.

Fletcher, Sheila (1980), *Feminists and Bureaucrats: A Study in the Development of Girls' Education in the Nineteenth Century*, Cambridge: Cambridge University Press.

Foster, John (1974), *Class Struggle and the Industrial Revolution: Early Industrial Capitalism in Three English Towns*, London: Weidenfeld and Nicolson.

Foulger, Wendy (1992–3), 'A Woman's Place was in Her Union', *North West Labour History Society Bulletin*, **17**, 113–19.

Fowler, Alan (1979–80), 'Trade Unions and Technical Change: The Automatic Loom Strike, 1908', *North West Labour History Society Bulletin*, **6**, 43–55.

Fowler, Alan (1988), 'Lancashire Cotton Trade Unionism in the Inter-War Years', in A.J. Jowitt and A.J. McIvor (eds), *Employers and Labour in the English Textile Industries, 1850–1939*, London: Routledge, pp.107–26.

Fowler, Alan (1999), 'Lancashire to Westminster: a study of cotton trade union officials and British labour, 1910–39', *Labour History Review*, **64** (1), 1–22.

Fowler, Alan and Fowler, Lesley (1984), 'The History of the Nelson Weavers' Association', Nelson, Burnley, Rossendale & District Textile Workers' Union.

Fowler, Alan and Wyke, Terry (eds) (1987), *The Barefoot Aristocrats: A History of the Amalgamated Association of Operative Cotton Spinners*, Littleborough: George Kelsall.

Fowler, Alan and Wyke, Terry (1993), 'Tickling Lancashire's Funny Bone: The Gradely Cartoons of Sam Fitton', *Transactions of the Lancashire and Cheshire Antiquarian Society*, **89**.

Fowler, Alan and Wyke, Terry (1995), *Mirth at the Mill: The Gradely World of Sam Fitton*, Oldham: Oldham Leisure Services.

Frader, Laura L. and Rose, Sonya O. (eds) (1996a), *Gender and Class in Modern Europe*, Ithaca: Cornell University Press.

Frader, Laura L. and Rose, Sonya O. (1996b), 'Introduction: Gender and the Reconstruction of European Working-Class History', in Laura L. Frader and Sonya O. Rose (eds), *Gender and Class in Modern Europe*, Ithaca: Cornell University Press, pp.1–36.

Frankel, M. (1955), 'Obsolescence and Technological Change in a Maturing Economy', *American Economic Review*, **45** (3), 296–315.

Freifeld, Mary (1986), 'Technological Change and the "Self-Acting" Mule: A Study of Skill and the Sexual Division of Labour', *Social History*, **11** (3), 319–43.

Frey, M. and Schleth, A. (1994), 'Examples of Data Acquisition for Fibres and the Application in the Spinning Mill', paper presented at the 22nd International Cotton Conference, Bremen, 2–5 March.

Frow, Ruth and Frow, Edmund (1976), *To Make That Future – Now! A History of the Manchester and Salford Trades Council*, Manchester: E.J. Morten.

Geertz, Clifford (1973), *The Interpretation of Cultures*, New York: Basic Books.

'Gendering Work: Historical Approaches' (1998), *Labour History Review*, **63**, special issue, eds Pamela Sharpe and Harriet Bradley.

Gibson, Roland (1948), *Cotton Textile Wages in the United States and Great Britain*, New York: King's Crown Press.

Gildemeister, Regine and Wetterer, Angelika (1992), 'Wie Geschlechter gemacht werden. Die soziale Konstruktion der Zweigeschlechtlichkeit und ihre Reifizierung in der Frauenforschung', in Gudrun-Axeli Knapp and Angelika Wetterer (eds), *Traditionen – Brüche. Entwicklungen feministischer Theorie*, Freiburg: Kore, pp.201–54.

Gittins, Diana (1982), *Fair Sex: Family Size and Structure, 1900–1939*, London: Hutchinson.

Glucksmann, Miriam (1990), *Women Assemble: Women Workers and the New Industries in Inter-War Britain*, London: Routledge.

Glucksmann, Miriam (1995), 'Some Do, Some Don't (But in Fact They All Do Really); Some Will, Some Won't; Some Have, Some Haven't: Women, Men, Work, and Washing Machines in Inter-War Britain', *Gender and History*, **7** (2), 275–94.

Glucksmann, Miriam (2000), *Cottons and Casuals: The gendered organisation of labour in time and space*, Durham: Sociologypress.

Gordon, Eleanor (1987–8), 'Women, Work and Collective Action: Dundee Jute Workers, 1870–1906', *Journal of Social History*, **21**, 27–47.

Gordon, Eleanor (1991), *Women and the Labour Movement in Scotland, 1850–1914*, Oxford: Clarendon Press.

Gordon, Eleanor and Breitenbach, Esther (eds) (1990), *The World is Ill Divided: Women's Work in Scotland in the Nineteenth and Early Twentieth Centuries*, Edinburgh: Edinburgh University Press.

Gore-Booth, Eva (1907), 'The Women's Suffrage Movement Among Trade Unionists', in Brougham Villiers (ed.), *The Case for Women's Suffrage*, London: T. Fisher Unwin, pp.50–65.

Graham, Stanley (1980), 'The Lancashire Textile Project: A Description of the Work and Some of the Techniques Involved', *Oral History*, **8** (2), 48–52.

Gray, E.M. (1937), *The Weaver's Wage: Earnings and Collective Bargaining in the Lancashire Cotton Weaving Industry*, Manchester: Victoria University, Department of Economics and Commerce.

Gray, Robert (1993), 'Factory Legislation and the Gendering of Jobs in Britain, 1830–1860', *Gender and History*, **5** (1), 56–80.

Gray, Robert (1996), *The Factory Question and Industrial England, 1830–1860*, Cambridge: Cambridge University Press.

Green, Jonathan (1986), *The Slang Thesaurus*, London: Penguin Books.
Green, Jonathan (1998), *The Cassell Dictionary of Slang*, London: Cassell.
Greenlees, Janet (1999), 'Equal Pay for Equal Work? A New Look at Gender and Wages in the Lancashire Cotton Industry, 1790–1855', in Margaret Walsh (ed.), *Working Out Gender: Perspectives from Labour History*, Aldershot: Ashgate, pp.167–90.
Groenewegen, Peter (ed.) (1994a), *Feminism and Political Economy in Victorian England*, Aldershot: Ashgate Publishing.
Groenewegen, Peter (1994b), 'A Neglected Daughter of Adam Smith: Clara Elizabeth Collet (1860–1948)', in Peter Groenewegen (ed.), *Feminism and Political Economy in Victorian England*, Aldershot: Ashgate, pp.147–73.
Groot, Gertjan de and Schrover, Marlou (eds) (1995), *Women Workers and Technological Change in Europe in the Nineteenth and Twentieth Centuries*, London: Francis and Taylor.
Hagemann-White, Carol (1993), 'Die Konstrukteure des Geschlechts auf frischer Tat ertappen? Methodische Konsequenzen einer theoretischen Einsicht', *Feministische Studien*, **2**, 68–78.
Hall, Catherine (1982), 'The Home Turned Upside Down? The Working-Class Family in Cotton Textiles, 1780–1850', in Elizabeth Whitelegg (ed.), *The Changing Experience of Women*, Oxford: Basil Blackwell, pp.17–29.
Hannam, June (1992), 'Women and the ILP, 1890–1914', in David James, Tony Jowitt and Keith Laybourn (eds), *The Centennial History of the Independent Labour Party*, Krumlin: Ryburn Academic, pp.205–28.
Hareven, Tamara K. (1977a), 'Family Time and Industrial Time: Family and Work in a Planned Corporation Town, 1900–1924', in Tamara K. Hareven (ed.), *Family and Kin in Urban Communities, 1700–1930*, New York: New Viewpoints, pp.187–207.
Hareven, Tamara K. (ed.) (1977b), *Family and Kin in Urban Communities, 1700–1930*, New York: New Viewpoints.
Hareven, Tamara K. and Langenbach, R. (1979), *Amoskeag: Life and Work in an American Factory-City in New England*, New York: Pantheon Books.
Harig, H., Bäumer, R. and Gerardi, H. (1994), 'The Reproducibility of Strength Measurements on Raw Cotton', paper presented at the 22nd International Cotton Conference, Bremen, 2–5 March.
Harley, C.K. (1974), 'Skilled Labour and the Choice of Technique in Edwardian Industry', *Explorations in Economic History*, **11**, 391–414.
Harrison, Barbara (1993), 'Are Accidents Gender Neutral? The Case of Women's Industrial Work in Britain, 1880–1914', *Women's History Review*, **2** (2), 253–75.
Harrison, Royden (1985), 'Introduction', in Royden Harrison and Jonathan Zeitlin (eds), *Divisions of Labour: Skilled Workers and Technological Change in Nineteenth Century England*, Brighton: Harvester Press, pp.1–18.
Harrison, Royden and Zeitlin, Jonathan (eds) (1985), *Divisions of Labour: Skilled*

Workers and Technological Change in Nineteenth Century England, Brighton: Harvester Press.

Hausen, Karin (ed.) (1993), *Geschlechterhierarchie und Arbeitsteilung. Zur Geschichte ungleicher Erwerbschancen von Männern und Frauen*, Göttingen: Vandenhoeck & Ruprecht.

Hill, Jeffrey (1997), *Nelson: Politics, Economy, Community*, Edinburgh: Keele University Press.

Hoff, Ernst-H. (ed.) (1990), *Die doppelte Sozialisation Erwachsener*, Munich: DJI-Verlag.

Holcombe, Lee (1983), *Wives and Property: Reform of the Married Women's Property Law in Nineteenth-Century England*, Toronto: University of Toronto Press.

Holton, Sandra Stanley (1988), *Feminism and Democracy: Women's Suffrage and Reform Politics in Britain, 1900–1918*, Cambridge: Cambridge University Press (1st edn 1986).

Hopwood, Edwin (1969), *The Lancashire Weavers' Story*, Manchester: Amalgamated Weavers' Association.

Horrell, Sara and Humphries, Jane (1997), 'The Origins and Expansion of the Male Breadwinner Family: The Case of Nineteenth-Century Britain', *International Review of Social History*, **42**, supplement: The Rise and Decline of the Male Breadwinner Family?, ed. Angélique Janssens, pp.25–64.

Howell, David (1983), *British Workers and the Independent Labour Party, 1888–1906*, Manchester: Manchester University Press.

Huck, Gerhard (ed.) (1980), *Sozialgeschichte der Freizeit*, Wuppertal: Hammer.

Hudson, Pat and Lee, W.R. (eds) (1990), *Women's Work and the Family Economy in Historical Perspective*, Manchester: Manchester University Press.

Hunt, E.H. (1981), *British Labour History, 1815–1914*, London: Weidenfeld and Nicolson, Atlantic Highlands, NJ: Humanities Press.

Hunt, Karen (1996), *Equivocal Feminists: The Social Democratic Federation and the Woman Question, 1884–1911*, Cambridge: Cambridge University Press.

Innes, John W. (1938), *Class Fertility Trends in England and Wales, 1876–1934*, Princeton, NJ: Princeton University Press.

James, David, Jowitt, Tony and Laybourn, Keith (eds) (1992), *The Centennial History of the Independent Labour Party*, Krumlin: Ryburn Academic.

Jenkins, D.T. (1979), 'The Cotton Industry in Yorkshire', *Textile History*, **10**, 75–95.

Jewkes, John (1930), 'The Localisation of the Cotton Industry', *Economic History*, **2** (5), 91–106.

Jewkes, John and Gray, E.M. (1935), *Wages and Labour in the Lancashire Cotton Spinning Industry*, Manchester: Victoria University, Department of Economics and Commerce.

Jewkes, John and Jewkes, Sylvia (1966), 'A Hundred Years of Change in the Structure of the Cotton Industry', *Journal of Law and Economics*, **9**, 115–34.

Joannou, Maroula and Purvis, June (eds) (1998), *The Women's Suffrage Movement: New Feminist Perspectives*, Manchester: Manchester University Press.

John, Angela (1980), *By the Sweat of Their Brow: Women Workers at Victorian Coal-Mines*, London: Routledge.

John, Angela (ed.) (1988), *Unequal Opportunities: Women's Employment in England, 1800–1918*, Oxford: Basil Blackwell (1st edn 1986).

John, Angela (ed.) (1991), *Our Mothers' Land: Chapters in Welsh Women's History, 1830–1939*, Cardiff: University of Wales Press.

Jones, G.F. (1933), *Increasing Return*, Cambridge: Cambridge University Press.

Jordan, Ellen (1989), 'The Exclusion of Women from Industry in Nineteenth-Century Britain', *Comparative Studies in Society and History*, **31**, (2), 273–96.

Jowitt, J.A. and McIvor, A.J. (eds) (1988), *Employers and Labour in the English Textile Industries, 1850–1939*, London: Routledge.

Joyce, Patrick (1980), *Work, Society and Politics: The Culture of the Factory in Later Victorian England*, Brighton: Harvester Press.

Kenny, Stephen (1982), 'Sub-regional Specialization in the Lancashire Cotton Industry, 1884–1914: A Study in Organizational and Locational Change', *Journal of Historical Geography*, **8** (1), 41–63.

Kent, Susan Kingsley (1987), *Sex and Suffrage in Britain, 1860–1914*, Princeton, NJ: Princeton University Press.

Kessler, Suzanne and McKenna, Wendy (1978), *Gender: An Ethnomethodological Approach*, New York: Wiley.

Kessler-Harris, Alice (1990), *A Woman's Wage: Historic Meanings and Social Consequences*, Lexington, KY: University of Kentucky Press.

Kirk, Neville (1985), *The Growth of Working-Class Reformism in Mid-Victorian England*, London: Croom Helm.

Knapp, Gudrun-Axeli (1990), 'Zur widersprüchlichen Vergesellschaftung von Frauen', in Ernst-H. Hoff (ed.), *Die doppelte Sozialisation Erwachsener*, Munich, DJI-Verlag, pp.17–52.

Knapp, Gudrun-Axeli and Wetterer, Angelika (eds) (1992), *Traditionen – Brüche. Entwicklungen feministischer Theorie*, Freiburg: Kore.

Knight, Patricia (1977), 'Women and Abortion in Victorian and Edwardian England', *History Workshop Journal*, **4**, 57–81.

Knights, David and Willmott, Hugh (eds) (1986), *Gender and the Labour Process*, Aldershot: Gower.

Koven, Seth and Michel, Sonya (1990), 'Womanly Duties: Maternalist Politics and the Origins of Welfare States in France, Germany, Great Britain and the United States, 1880–1920', *American Historical Review*, **95**, 1076–1108.

Lambertz, Jan (1985), 'Sexual Harassment in the Nineteenth Century English Cotton Industry', *History Workshop Journal*, **19**, 29–61.

Lamphere, Louise (1985), 'Bringing the Family to Work: Women's Culture on the Shop Floor', *Feminist Studies*, **11** (3), 519–40.

Lancaster Regionalism Group (eds) (1985), *Localities, Class and Gender*, London: Pion.
Laqueur, Thomas (1990), *Making Sex: Body and Gender from the Greeks to Freud*, Cambridge, MA: Harvard University Press.
Larrabeiti, Michelle de (1998), 'Conspicuous Before the World: The Political Rhetoric of Chartist Women', in Eileen Janes Yeo (ed.), *Radical Femininity: Women's Self-Representation in the Public Sphere*, Manchester: Manchester University Press, pp.106–26.
Lazonick, William (1979), 'Industrial Relations and Technical Changes: The Case of the Self-Acting Mule', *Cambridge Journal of Economics*, **3**, 231–62.
Lazonick, William (1981a), 'Competition, Specialization and Industrial Decline', *Journal of Economic History*, **41** (1), 31–8.
Lazonick, William (1981b), 'Factor Costs and the Diffusion of Ring Spinning in Britain Prior to World War I', *Quarterly Journal of Economics*, **96**, 89–109.
Lazonick, William (1981c), 'Production Relations, Labor Productivity and Choice of Technique: British and U.S. Cotton Spinning', *Journal of Economic History*, **41** (3), 491–516.
Lazonick, William (1983), 'Industrial Organisation and Technological Change: The Decline of the British Cotton Industry', *Business History Review*, **57** (2), 195–236.
Lazonick, William (1986), 'The Cotton Industry', in B. Elbaum and William Lazonick (eds), *The Decline of the British Economy: An Institutional Approach*, Oxford: Clarendon Press, pp. 18–50.
Lazonick, William and Mass, William (1984), 'The Performance of the British Cotton Industry, 1870–1913', *Research in Economic History*, **9**, 1–44.
Leidner, Robin (1991), 'Serving Hamburgers and Selling Insurance: Gender, Work and Identity in Interactive Service Jobs', *Gender and Society*, **5** (2), 154–77.
Leneman, Leah (1998), 'A truly national movement: the view from outside London', in Maroula Joannou and June Purvis (eds), *The Women's Suffrage Movement: New Feminist Perspectives*, Manchester: Manchester University Press, pp.37–50.
Leunig, Timothy (2001), 'New Answers to Old Questions: Explaining the Slow Adoption of Ring Spinning in Lancashire, 1880–1913', *Journal of Economic History*, **61** (2) 439–66.
Lewenhak, Sheila (1977), *Women and Trade Unions: An Outline History of Women in the British Trade Union Movement*, London: Ernest Benn Ltd.
Lewis, Gifford (1988), *Eva Gore-Booth and Esther Roper: A Biography*, London: Pandora.
Lewis, Jane (1984), *Women in England, 1870–1950: Sexual Divisions and Social Change*, Brighton: Wheatsheaf Books.
Lewis, Jane (ed.) (1987), *Labour and Love: Women's Experience of Home and Family, 1850–1940*, Oxford: Basil Blackwell (1st edn 1986).
Lewis, Jane and Rose, Sonya O. (1995), '"Let England Blush": Protective Labor

Legislation, 1820–1914', in Ulla Wikander, Alice Kessler-Harris and Jane Lewis (eds), *Protecting Women: Labor Legislation in Europe, the United States and Australia, 1880–1920*, Urbana: University of Illinois Press, pp.91–124.

Lichfield, R. Burr (1978), 'The Family and the Mill: Cotton Mill Work, Family Work Patterns and Fertility in Mid-Victorian Stockport', in Anthony Stephen Wohl (ed.), *The Victorian Family: Structure and Stresses*, London: Croom Helm, pp.180–95.

Liddington, Jill (1977), 'Working-Class Women in the North West', *Oral History*, **5** (2), 31–45.

Liddington, Jill (1984), *The Life and Times of a Respectable Radical: Selina Cooper, 1864–1946*, London: Virago.

Liddington, Jill and Norris, Jill (1985), *One Hand Tied Behind Us: The Rise of the Women's Suffrage Movement*, London: Virago (1st edn 1978).

Longworth, James H. (1987), *The Cotton Mills of Bolton, 1780–1985: A Historical Directory*, Bolton: Bolton Museum and Art Gallery.

Lorber, Judith (1994), *Paradoxes of Gender*, New Haven: Yale University Press.

Lown, Judy (1990), *Women and Industrialization: Gender at Work in Nineteenth-Century England*, Minneapolis: University of Minnesota Press.

Lüdtke, Alf (1980), 'Arbeitsbeginn, Arbeitspausen, Arbeitsende', in Gerhard Huck (ed.), *Sozialgeschichte der Freizeit*, Wuppertal: Hammer, pp.95–122, reprinted Alf in Lüdtke (1993), *Eigen-Sinn: Fabrikalltag, Arbeitererfahrungen und Politik vom Kaiserreich bis in den Faschismus*, Hamburg: Ergebnisse Verlag.

Machtan, Lothar (1981), 'Zum Innenleben deutscher Fabriken im 19. Jahrhundert: Die formelle und die informelle Verfassung von Industriebetrieben anhand von Beispielen aus dem Bereich der Textil- und Maschinenproduktion', *Archiv für Sozialgeschichte*, **21**, 179–236.

MacLeod, Christine (1992), 'Strategies for Innovation: The Diffusion of New Technology in Nineteenth-Century British Industry', *Economic History Review*, **45** (2), 285–307.

Mark-Lawson, Jane (1988), 'Occupational Segregation and Women's Politics', in Sylvia Walby (ed.), *Gender Segregation at Work*, Milton Keynes: Open University Press, pp.157–73

Mappen, Ellen (1984), 'Introduction', in Clementina Black (ed.), *Married Women's Work*, London: Virago (1st edn London: G. Bell and Sons, 1915), pp.i–xxi.

Mappen, Ellen (ed.) (1985), *Helping Women at Work: The Women's Industrial Council, 1889–1914*, London: Hutchinson.

Mappen, Ellen (1988), 'Strategists for Change: Social Feminist Approaches to the Problems of Women's Work', in Angela John (ed.), *Unequal Opportunities: Women's Employment in England, 1800–1918*, Oxford: Basil Blackwell (1st edn 1986), pp.235–59.

Marrison, Andrew (1996), 'Indian Summer, 1870–1914', in Mary B. Rose (ed.), *The Lancashire Cotton Industry: A History Since 1700*, Preston: Lancashire County Books, pp.238–64.

Marsden, Richard (1884), *Cotton Spinning: Its Development, Principles and Practice*, London: G. Bell and Sons.

Marsden, Richard (1895), *Cotton Weaving: Its Development, Principles, and Practice*, London: G. Bell and Sons

Martin, Ross M. (2000), *The Lancashire Giant: David Shackleton, Labour Leader and Civil Servant*, Liverpool: Liverpool University Press.

Mass, William (1989), 'Mechanical and Organisational Innovation: The Drapers and the Automatic Loom', *Business History Review*, **63** (4), 876–929.

Mass, William and Lazonick, William (1990), 'The British Cotton Industry and International Competitive Advantage: The State of the Debates', *Business History*, **32** (4), 9–65.

McClelland, Keith (1989), 'Some Thoughts on Masculinity and the "Representative Artisan" in Britain, 1850–1880', *Gender and History*, **1** (2), 164–77.

McClelland, Keith (1996), 'Rational and Respectable Men: Gender, the Working Class and Citizenship in Britain, 1850–1867', in Laura L. Frader and Sonya O. Rose (eds), *Gender and Class in Modern Europe*, Ithaca: Cornell University Press, pp.280–93.

McFeely, Mary Drake (1988), *Lady Inspectors: The Campaign for a Better Workplace, 1893–1921*, Oxford: Basil Blackwell.

McIvor, Arthur J. (1988), 'Cotton Employers' Organisations and Labour Relations, 1890–1939', in J.A. Jowitt and A.J. McIvor (eds), *Employers and Labour in the English Textile Industries, 1850–1939*, London: Routledge, pp.1–26.

McIvor, Arthur J. (1996), *Organised Capital: Employers' Associations and Industrial Relations in Northern England, 1880–1939*, Cambridge: Cambridge University Press.

McLaren, Angus (1977), 'Women's Work and Regulation of Family Size', *History Workshop Journal*, **4**, 70–81.

McLaren, Angus (1978), *Birth Control in Nineteenth-Century England*, London: Croom Helm.

Melling, Joseph (1980), '"Non-Commissioned Officers": British Employers and Their Supervisory Workers, 1880–1920', *Social History*, **5** (2), 183–221.

Messenger, Betty (1988), *Picking Up the Linen Threads*, Belfast: Blackstaff Press.

Milkman, Ruth (1987), *Gender at Work: The Dynamics of Job Segregation During World War II*, Urbana: University of Illinois Press.

More, Charles (1980), *Skill and the English Working Class, 1870–1914*, London: Croom Helm.

Morgan, Carol E. (1992), 'Women, Work and Consciousness in the Mid-Nineteenth-Century English Cotton Industry', *Social History*, **17**, 23–41.

Morgan, Carol E. (1996), 'The Domestic Image and Factory Culture: The Cotton District in Mid-Nineteenth-Century England', *International Labor and Working-Class History*, **49**, 26–46.

Morgan, Carol E. (2001), *Women Workers and Gender Identities, 1835–1913: The cotton and metal industries in England*, London: Routledge.
Norris, Jill (1988), '"Well Fitted for Females": Women in the Macclesfield Silk Industry', in J.A. Jowitt and A.J. McIvor (eds), *Employers and Labour in the English Textile Industries, 1850–1939*, London: Routledge, pp.187–202.
Pankhurst, Sylvia (1988), *The Suffragette Movement: An Intimate Account of Persons and Ideals*, London: Virago (1st edn London: Longman, 1931).
Park, Jihang (1988), 'The British Suffrage Activists of 1913: An Analysis', *Past & Present*, **120**, 147–62.
Parr, Joy (1990), *The Gender of Breadwinners: Women, Men, and Change in Two Industrial Towns, 1880–1950*, Toronto: University of Toronto Press.
Partridge, Eric (1984), *A Dictionary of Slang and Unconventional English*, ed. Paul Beale, London: Routledge & Kegan Paul.
Pedersen, Susan (1993), *Family, Dependence, and the Origins of the Welfare State: Britain and France, 1914–1945*, Cambridge: Cambridge University Press.
Phillips, Andrew (1994), 'Women on the Shop Floor: The Colchester Rag Trade, 1918–1950', *Oral History*, **22**, 56–65.
Phillips, Anne and Taylor, Barbara (1980), 'Sex and Skill: Notes Towards a Feminist Economics', *Feminist Review*, **6**, 79–88.
Pope, Rex (2000), 'Unemployed Women in Inter-war Britain: the case of the Lancashire weaving district', *Women's History Review*, **9** (4), 743–59.
Porter, J.H. (1967), 'Industrial Peace in the Cotton Trade, 1875–1913', *Yorkshire Bulletin of Economic and Social Research*, **19** (1), 49–61.
Reiter, Rayna Rapp (ed.) (1975), *Toward an Anthropology of Women*, New York: Monthly Review Press.
Roberts, Elizabeth (1982a), 'Working-Class Standards of Living in Three Lancashire Towns, 1890–1914', *International Review of Social History*, **27**, 43–65.
Roberts, Elizabeth (1982b), 'Working Wives and Their Families', in Theo Barker and Michael Drake (eds), *Population and Society in Britain, 1850–1980*, London: Batsford Academic and Educational Ltd. and New York: New York University Press, pp.140–71.
Roberts, Elizabeth (1986), *A Woman's Place: An Oral History of Working-Class Women, 1890–1940*, Oxford: Basil Blackwell (1st edn 1984).
Roberts, Robert (1977), *The Classic Slum: Salford Life in the First Quarter of the Century*, Harmondsworth: Penguin Books Ltd (1st edn Manchester: Manchester University Press, 1971).
Robson, R. (1957), *The Cotton Industry in Britain*, London: Macmillan.
Rose, Mary B. (1986), *The Gregs of Quarry Bank Mill*, Cambridge: Cambridge University Press.
Rose, Mary B. (1996), 'Introduction: The Rise of the Cotton Industry in Lancashire to 1830', in Mary B. Rose (ed.), *The Lancashire Cotton Industry: A History Since 1700*, Preston: Lancashire County Books, pp.1–28.

Rose, Mary B. (ed.) (1996), *The Lancashire Cotton Industry: A History Since 1700*, Preston: Lancashire County Books.
Rose, Mary B. (2000), *Firms, Networks and Business Values: The British and American Cotton Industries since 1750*, Cambridge: Cambridge University Press.
Rose, Sonya O. (1986), '"Gender at Work": Sex, Class and Industrial Capitalism', *History Workshop Journal*, **21**, 113–31.
Rose, Sonya O. (1988), 'Gender Antagonism and Class Conflict: Exclusionary Strategies of Male Trade Unionists in Nineteenth-Century Britain', *Social History*, **13** (2), 191–208.
Rose, Sonya O. (1992), *Limited Livelihoods*, London: Routledge and Berkeley: University of California Press.
Rose, Sonya O. (1993), 'Gender and Labor History: The Nineteenth-Century Legacy', *International Review of Social History*, **38**, supplement, 145–62.
Rose, Sonya O. (1996),'Protective Labor Legislation in Nineteenth-Century Britain: Gender, Class, and the Liberal State', in Laura L. Frader and Sonya O. Rose (eds), *Gender and Class in Modern Europe*, Ithaca: Cornell University Press, pp.193–210.
Rosen, Andrew (1974), *Rise Up, Women! The Militant Campaign of the Women's Social and Political Union, 1903–1914*, London: Routledge.
Ross, Ellen (1993), *Love and Toil: Motherhood in Outcast London, 1870–1918*, Oxford: Oxford University Press.
Rothwell, Roy (1975),'The British Northrop: A Case Study of Decline and Renaissance', *Textile Institute and Industry*, **13**.
Rubin, Gayle (1975), 'The Traffic in Women: Notes on the Political Economy of Sex', in Rayna Rapp Reiter (ed.), *Toward an Anthropology of Women*, New York: Monthly Review Press, pp.157–210.
Sadler, M.E. (ed.) (1907), *Continuation Schools in England and Elsewhere*, Manchester: Victoria University.
Sandberg, Lars G. (1969), 'American Rings and English Mules: The Role of Economic Rationality', *Quarterly Journal of Economics*, **73**, 25–43.
Sandberg, Lars G. (1974), *Lancashire in Decline*, Columbus: Ohio State University Press.
Sandiford, Peter (1907), 'The Half-Time System in the Textile Trade', in M.E. Sadler (ed.), *Continuation Schools in England and Elsewhere*, Manchester: Victoria University.
Savage, Michael (1982), 'Control at Work: North Lancashire Cotton Weaving, 1890–1940', Lancaster Regionalism Group, working paper 7.
Savage, Michael (1985), 'Capitalist and Patriarchal Relations at Work: Preston Cotton Weaving, 1890–1940', in Lancaster Regionalism Group (eds) (1985), *Localities, Class and Gender*, London: Pion, pp.177–94.
Savage, Michael (1987), *The Dynamics of Working-Class Politics: The Labour Movement in Preston, 1880–1940*, Cambridge: Cambridge University Press.

Savage, Michael (1988), 'Women and Work in the Lancashire Cotton Industry, 1890–1939', in J.A. Jowitt and A.J. McIvor (eds), *Employers and Labour in the English Textile Industries, 1850–1939*, London: Routledge, pp.203–23.

Saxonhouse, Gary R. and Wright, Gavin (1984), 'New Evidence on the Stubborn English Mule and the Cotton Industry, 1878–1920', *Economic History Review*, **37** (4), 507–19.

Scholliers, Peter (1995), 'Grown-Ups, Boys and Girls in the Ghent Cotton Industry: The Voortman Mills, 1835–1914', *Social History*, **20** (2), 201–18.

Scholliers, Peter (1996), *Wages, Manufacturers and Workers in the Nineteenth Century Factory: The Voortman Cotton Mill in Ghent*, Oxford: Berg.

Schulze-Gävernitz, Gerhart von (1892), *Der Großbetrieb: ein wirtschaftlicher und sozialer Fortschritt. Eine Studie auf dem Gebiete der Baumwollindustrie*, Leipzig: Duncker und Humblot.

Schwarzkopf, Jutta (1991), *Women in the Chartist Movement*, Basingstoke: Macmillan.

Scott, Gillian (1997), 'Working-Class Feminism? The Women's Co-operative Guild, 1880s–1914', in Eileen Janes Yeo (ed.), *Mary Wollstonecraft and 200 Years of Feminisms*, London: Rivers Oram Press.

Scott, Gillian (1998a), '"As a War-Horse to the Beat of Drums": Representations of Working-Class Femininity in the Women's Co-operative Guild, 1880s to the Second World War', in Eileen Janes Yeo (ed.), *Radical Femininity: Women's Self-Representation in the Public Sphere*, Manchester: Manchester University Press, pp.196–219.

Scott, Gillian (1998b), *Feminism and the Politics of Working Women: The Women's Co-operative Guild, 1880s to the Second World War*, London: UCL Press.

Scott, Joan Wallach (1986), 'Gender: A Useful Category of Historical Analysis', *American Historical Review*, **91**, 1053–75.

Scott, Joan Wallach (1988), *Gender and the Politics of History*, New York: Columbia University Press.

Scott, Joan Wallach (1991), 'The Evidence of Experience', *Critical Inquiry*, **17**, 772–97.

Scott, Joan Wallach (1993), 'The Tip of the Volcano', *Comparative Study of Society and History*, **35** (2), 438–43.

Scott, Joan Wallach (ed.) (1996), *Feminism and History*, Oxford: Oxford University Press.

Seccombe, Wally (1986), 'Patriarchy Stabilized: The Construction of the Male Breadwinner Norm in Nineteenth-Century Britain', *Social History*, **11** (1), 53–76.

Seccombe, Wally (1990), 'Starting to Stop: Working-Class Fertility Decline in Britain', *Past & Present*, **126**, 151–88.

Shanley, Mary Lyndon (1989), *Feminism, Marriage, and the Law in Victorian England, 1850–1895*, Princeton, NJ: Princeton University Press.

Shortland, Ann (n.d.), 'The Effect of the Cotton Industry and Changing Industrial Structure on the Development of Hyde'.

Singleton John (1991), *Lancashire on the Scrapheap: The Cotton Industry, 1945–1970*, Oxford: Oxford University Press.

Singleton, John (1996), 'The Decline of the British Cotton Industry Since 1940', in Mary B. Rose (ed.), *The Lancashire Cotton Industry: A History Since 1700*, Preston: Lancashire County Books, pp.296–324.

Smith, Roland (1961), 'An Oldham Limited Liability Company, 1875–1896', *Business History*, **4** (11), 34–53.

Soldon, Norbert C. (1978), *Women in British Trade Unions, 1874–1976*, Dublin: Gill and Macmillan.

Stephenson, Jayne D. and Brown, Callum G. (1990),'The View from the Workplace: Women's Memories of Work in Sterling, c.1910–c.1950', in Eleanor Gordon and Esther Breitenbach (eds), *The World is Ill Divided: Women's Work in Scotland in the Nineteenth and Early Twentieth Centuries*, Edinburgh: Edinburgh University Press.

Summerfield, Penny (1998), *Reconstructing Women's Wartime Lives: Discourse and subjectivity in oral histories of the Second World War*, Manchester: Manchester University Press.

Szreter, Simon (1996), *Fertility, Class and Gender in Britain, 1860–1940*, Cambridge: Cambridge University Press.

Taylor, Barbara (1983), *Eve and the New Jerusalem: Socialism and Feminism in the Nineteenth Century*, London: Virago.

Thompson, Paul (1975), *The Edwardians: The Remaking of British Society*, London: Weidenfeld and Nicolson.

Thompson, Paul (1988), 'Playing at Being Skilled Men: Factory Culture and Pride in Work Skills Among Coventry Car Workers', *Social History*, **13** (1), 45–69.

Tickner, Lisa (1987), *The Spectacle of Women: Imagery of the Suffrage Campaign, 1907–14*, London: Chatto & Windus.

Timmins, Geoffrey (1993), *The Last Shift: The Decline of Handloom Weaving in Nineteenth-Century Lancashire*, Manchester: Manchester University Press.

Timmins, Geoffrey (1996), 'Technological Change', in Mary B. Rose (ed.), *The Lancashire Cotton Industry: A History Since 1700*, Preston: Lancashire County Books, pp.29–62.

Tippett, L.H.C. (1969), *A Portrait of the Lancashire Textile Industry*, London: Oxford University Press.

Toews, John (1987), 'Intellectual History after the Linguistic Turn: The Autonomy of Meaning and the Irreducibility of Experience', *American Historical Review*, **92**, 879–907.

Toms, J.S. (1996), 'Integration, Innovation, and the Progress of a Family Cotton Enterprise: Fielden Bros. Ltd., 1889–1914', *Textile History*, **27** (1), 77–100.

Toms, Steven (1998), 'Windows of Opportunity in the Textile Industry: The

Business Strategies of Lancashire Entrepreneurs, 1880–1914', *Business History*, **40** (1), 1–25.
Townsend, Irving U. (1902), 'The Northrop Loom', *Scientific American*, **4** (1393), supplement, 22, 324–5.
Tuckwell, Gertrude and Smith, Constance (1908), *The Worker's Handbook*, London: Duckworth and Co.
Tuckwell, Gertrude, Smith, Constance, Macarthur, Mary, Tennant, May, Adler, Nettie, Anderson, Adelaide and Black, Clementina (1908), *Woman in Industry from Seven Points of View*, London: Duckworth and Co.
Turner, H.A. (1962), *Trade Union Growth, Structure and Policy: A Comparative Study of the Cotton Unions*, London: George Allen and Unwin Ltd.
Tyson, R.E. (1968), 'The Cotton Industry', in D.H. Aldcroft (ed.), *The Development of British Industry and Foreign Competition, 1875–1914*, London: Allen and Unwin, pp.100–127.
Valenze, Deborah (1991), 'The Art of Women and the Business of Men: Women's Work and the Dairy Industry, c.1740–1840', *Past & Present*, **130**, 142–69.
Valverde, Mariana (1987), '"Giving the Female a Domestic Turn": The Social, Legal and Moral Regulation of Women's Work in British Cotton Mills, 1820–1850', *Journal of Social History*, **21**, 619–34.
Villiers, Broughton (ed.) (1907), *The Case for Women's Suffrage*, London: T. Fisher Unwin.
Vincent, David (1982), *Bread, Knowledge and Freedom: A Study of Nineteenth-Century Working Class Autobiography*, London: Methuen.
Walby, Sylvia (ed.) (1988), *Gender Segregation at Work*, Milton Keynes: Open University Press.
Walsh, Margaret (ed.) (1999), *Working Out Gender: Perspectives from Labour History*, Aldershot: Ashgate Publishing.
Walton, John (1992), *Fish and Chips and the British Working Class, 1870–1940*, Leicester: Leicester University Press.
Webb, Sidney (1891), 'The Alleged Differences in the Wages Paid to Men and Women for Similar Work', *Economic Journal*, **1**, 634–62.
Webb, Sidney and Webb, Beatrice (1897), *Industrial Democracy*, London: Longman.
Westwood, Sallie (1984), *All Day Every Day: Factory and Family in the Making of Women's Lives*, Urbana: University of Illinois Press.
Wetterer, Angelika (ed.) (1995), *Die soziale Konstruktion von Geschlecht in Professionalisierungsprozessen*, Frankfurt am Main: Campus.
Whipp, Richard (1985), 'Labour Markets and Communities: An Historical View', *Sociological Review*, **33** (3–4), 768–91.
White, Joseph L. (1978), *The Limits of Trade Union Militancy: The Lancashire Textile Workers, 1910–14*, Westport, CT: Greenwood Press.
White, Joseph L. (1982), 'Lancashire Cotton Textiles', in Chris Wrigley (ed.), *A History of British Industrial Relations, 1875–1914*, Brighton: Harvester Press, pp. 209–29.

Whitehead, Joyce (n.d.), 'How the Unions Tried to Keep Women Out of Office: A Case Study: Alice Foley', Bolton Archives and Local Studies, Central Library.

Whitehead, Joyce (1987), 'No Place for a Lady: How the Unions Tried to Keep Women Out of Office', *North West Labour History Society Bulletin*, **12**, 17–23.

Whitelegg, Elizabeth (ed.) (1982), *The Changing Experience of Women*, Oxford: Basil Blackwell.

Wikander, Ulla, Kessler-Harris, Alice and Lewis, Jane (eds) (1995), *Protecting Women: Labor Legislation in Europe, the United States, and Australia, 1880–1920*, Urbana: University of Illinois Press.

Williams, Christine (1989), *Gender Differences at Work: Women and Men in Nontraditional Occupations*, Berkeley: University of California Press.

Williams, Raymond (1976), *Keywords: A Vocabulary of Culture and Society*, London: Fontana.

Winstanley, Michael (ed.) (1995), *Working Children in Nineteenth-Century Lancashire*, Preston: Lancashire County Books.

Winstanley, Michael (1996), 'The Factory Workforce', in Mary B. Rose (ed.), *The Lancashire Cotton Industry: A History Since 1700*, Preston: Lancashire County Books, pp.121–53.

Wohl, Anthony Stephen (ed.) (1978), *The Victorian Family: Structure and Stresses*, London: Croom Helm.

Wood, G.H. (1910), *The History of Wages in the Cotton Trade During the Past Hundred Years*, London: Sherratt and Hughes.

Wrigley, Chris (ed.) (1982), *A History of British Industrial Relations, 1875–1914*, Brighton: Harvester Press.

Yeo, Eileen Janes (ed.) (1997), *Mary Wollstonecraft and 200 Years of Feminisms*, London: Rivers Oram Press.

Yeo, Eileen Janes (ed.) (1998), *Radical Femininity: Women's Self-Representation in the Public Sphere*, Manchester: Manchester University Press.

Zachmann, Karin (1993), 'Männer arbeiten, Frauen helfen. Geschlechtsspezifische Arbeitsteilung und Maschinisierung in der Textilindustrie des 19. Jahrhunderts', in Karin Hausen (ed.), *Geschlechterhierarchie und Arbeitsteilung. Zur Geschichte ungleicher Erwerbschancen von Männern und Frauen*, Göttingen: Vandenhoeck & Ruprecht, pp.71–96.

2 Unpublished Works

Adams, Janice (1996), 'A Study of Infant Mortality in St. Helens, Burnley and Nelson in the Years 1899–1914', unpublished MA dissertation, University of Lancaster.

Bann, J.E. (1976), 'The Changing Distribution of the Cotton Industry in Hyde', unpublished BA dissertation, University of Newcastle.

Bather, Leslie (1956), 'A History of Manchester and Salford Trades Council', unpublished PhD thesis, University of Manchester.

Bowker, David (1983), 'Ashton Weavers in the Age of Labour Unrest, 1910–20', unpublished BA dissertation, Manchester Polytechnic.
Bryan, Susan M. (1977), 'The Women's Suffrage Question in the Manchester Area, 1890–1906', unpublished MA dissertation, University of Manchester.
Busfield, Deirdre F. (1986), 'Sex and Skill in the West Riding: Women's Employment in Yorkshire, 1850–1914', unpublished DPhil dissertation, University of York.
Cass, E.F. (1996), 'The Cotton Factory Times, 1885–1937: A family newspaper and the Lancashire cotton community', unpublished PhD thesis, Lancaster University.
Firth, P.A. (1986), 'Skilled Work and Workers in North East Lancashire: A Consideration of Cotton Trades and Textile Engineering, 1890–1914', unpublished PhD thesis, University of Salford.
Frost, Diane (1988), 'Women's Suffrage in Bolton, 1900–1914', unpublished MA dissertation, University of Lancaster.
Hall, Alan Anthony (1975), 'Social Control and the Working-Class Challenge in Ashton-under-Lyne, 1886–1914', unpublished MA dissertation, University of Lancaster.
Healey, Dermot, 'Overlookers', unpublished typescript.
Hewitt, Margaret (1953), 'The Effect of Married Women's Employment in the Cotton Textile Districts on the Organization and the Structure of the Home in Lancashire, 1840–1880', unpublished PhD thesis, University of London.
Mark-Lawson, Jane (1987), 'Women, Welfare and Urban Politics: A Comparative Analysis of Luton and Nelson, 1917–1934', unpublished PhD thesis, University of Lancaster.
Mass, William N. (1984), 'Technological Change and Industrial Relations: The Diffusion of Automatic Weaving in the United States and Britain', unpublished PhD thesis, Boston College.
McIvor, Arthur J. (1983), 'Employers' Associations and Industrial Relations in Lancashire, 1890–1939', unpublished PhD thesis, University of Manchester.
Paul, D.P. (1988), 'The Women's Labour League of Great Britain, 1906–18', unpublished PhD thesis, University of North Carolina at Chapel Hill.
Riley, J.H. (1981), 'The More Looms System', unpublished MA dissertation, University of Manchester.
Ross, Priscilla (1991), 'A Town Like Nelson: The Social Implications of Technical Change in a Lancashire Mill Town', unpublished DPhil dissertation, University of Sussex.
Savage, Michael (1981), 'Unions and Workers in the Cotton Industry of Preston, c.1890–1895', unpublished MA dissertation, University of Lancaster.
Scott, Gillian (1988), '"The Working Class Women's Most Active and Democratic Movement": The Women's Co-operative Guild from 1883 to 1950', unpublished PhD thesis, University of Sussex.
Trodd, Geoffrey N. (1978), 'Political Change and the Working Class in Blackburn and Burnley, 1880–1914', unpublished PhD thesis, University of Lancaster.

Index

abortion 143
    advertisements for abortifacients 143
abstinence, culture of 143
Accrington 19
    suicide 91–3, 97
    Weavers' Friendly Society 88
    workforce composition 30–31
acquisition of skill *see* apprenticeships;
    skill, acquisition; training
agency 2–3, 27
anti-driving campaign *see* driving system
apprenticeships
    tacklers 67
    weavers 60
    see also skill, acquisition; training
Ashton 19, 21
Ashton Bros., Hyde 110–14, 115, 117,
    118–19, 120–22, 124, 125–6
automatic (Northrop) loom
    at Ashton Bros., Hyde 111–14, 121–2,
        125–6
    averting opposition 104–5
    gender division of labour 105–10, 125–9
    strikes
        1904 114–17
        1908 117–21
    vs. Lancashire (mechanical) loom 110,
        122, 123–4

Banks, Thomas (president of the Preston
    weavers' union) 106
Birtwistle, Thomas (secretary of Weavers'
    Amalgamation) 153
Blackburn 19, 20, 21, 24
    driving system 86
    workforce composition 31, 33
Blackburn List 22, 23
Blackburn Weavers' Association 88, 152
bobbin looms 115–16
Bolton 19, 21, 31, 152, 154
bread-winner wage 108–10
British Association of Managers of Textile
    Works 116

British Northrop Loom Company 124
Brooklands Agreement (1893) 24
bullying 91
Burnley 19, 20, 21, 23, 24, 33
    driving system 86
    infant mortality rate 107
    New Textile Operatives' Society
        (Weavers' Department) 156
    weavers' union 153, 155, 164–5
    weavers' wages 35, 40–41

Chew, Ada Nield (trade union organizer
    and suffragist) 41, 89–90, 96,
    114–15, 146, 156
child labour
    age of entry 26, 29
    half-timers 29
    skill acquisition 59–61, 87
    working hours 26–7
childbearing
    fertility control 143–6
    infant mortality rate 105–6, 107, 116
Chorley 20, 21, 30–31
cleaning machinery 28
cloth quality 56–7, 62, 70
    fining 26, 70, 94–6
cloth-lookers 91, 94, 95
Cockburn, Cynthia 5
Collet, Clara (labour correspondent of the
    Board of Trade) 34, 38, 44, 141
Colne 19, 20, 30–31
Commission on Humidity and Ventilation
    63–4
Commission on Trade and Depression of
    Industry 149
competition, gendered 63–6, 67–9
composition of workforce 29–34
Cooper, Selina (trade unionist and
    suffragist) 145–6, 162, 164, 165, 168
cooperative weaving mills 20
Cotton Cloth Committee 63
Cotton Cloth Factories Acts 26
Cotton Factory Times 8–9, 36

cotton famine 111
'culture of abstinence' 143

Darwen 19, 20
  suicide 85–7, 88, 89–90, 91, 93, 97
  weavers' union 88
Devine, Nellie (committee member of Oldham weavers' union) 91, 151
Dickenson, Sarah (trade union organizer and suffragist) 157, 158, 161, 164, 166
discipline *see* tacklers (overlookers)
dismissal 87, 88, 92
division of labour, gendered 4–5
  automatic (Northrop) loom 105–10, 125–9
  in paid and unpaid work 5, 139–42
  spinning sector 4, 29
domestic service 58, 126, 167
Drake, Barbara 42, 44
Draper (George) & Sons 104, 123–4
driving system 83–5
  Accrington suicide 91–3
  Darwen suicide 85–7, 88, 89–90, 91, 93, 97
  fining 26, 70, 94–5
  gendered exploitation 88–90, 96–8
  industrial manners 90–91
  slate system 85, 86, 87, 90

economic development (1873–1914) 15–18
employers/mill owners 24
  automatic (Northrop) loom 110
  driving system 90–91, 92
  industrial manners 90–91
  industrial relations 21–5
  paternalism 25, 41
Evans, Clare 167
experience 2, 10
exploitation, gendered 88–90, 96–8

Factories and Workshops Act 25–6
Factory Acts 25–7, 28, 29
factory legislation 25–9
Fairhurst, Helen (president of Wigan weavers' union) 164
family pressures 87
family as unit of production 72–3
family wage 61, 87, 107, 108–10, 141–2, 187–8
female work culture 69–72
fertility control 143–6
fining 26, 70, 94–6

Fletcher, A.M. (Managing Director, Ashton Bros., Hyde) 116–17
Foley, Alice (trade unionist) 42, 70, 154
Freifeld, Mary 55

Gender
  competition 63–6, 67–9
  concept 1–3
    history of 1, 2, 3–4
  and cotton industry 4–5
  division of labour on automatic (Northrop) loom 105–10, 125–9
  and labour history 3
  relations of couples 142, 144
  relations at the workplace and in the home 5, 70–71, 139–42
  social construction of 1–2, 3
Gibson, Roland 37–8, 40
Gittins, Diana 139, 140, 142, 144
Glucksmann, Miriam 139, 140–41, 142
Gore-Booth, Eva (trade union organizer and suffragist) 157, 161, 164, 166, 168
Greenlees, Janet 44–5
Greg, Henry Philips ((vice-)chairman Ashton Bros., Hyde) 112–13, 124

half-time system 29, 38–9
handloom weaving 22
Haslam, Mary (Bolton suffragist) 45
health and safety issues
  shuttles 27–8
  steam 26, 63–4
housework
  delegation 139
  husbands' participation in 139–40, 141
  'Mary Anne nights' 140
humour/jokes 68, 70, 71
Hyde, Ashton Bros. 110–14, 115, 117, 118–19, 120–22, 124, 125–6
Hyde and Hadfield Weavers' Association 118, 119, 147

illness 70, 93, 154
imprisonment 95
Independent Labour Party 162
industrial manners 90–91
industrial relations 21–5
  see also unions
infant mortality rate 105–6, 107, 116
informal parties 71–2
innovation of technology 122–6

job satisfaction, women weavers 57–9
joint decision making 144
joint role relationships 142
Joint Standing Committee of Employers and Operatives 24–5, 86, 87, 92
jokes/humour 68, 70, 71
Joyce, Patrick 41, 83

Keenan, Nellie (Salford and District Powerloom Weavers' Union official) 158, 159, 164, 166
Kessler-Harris, Alice 5, 26–7
Kilburn, Martha Ann (Rochdale weaver resisting fining) 95, 96, 97, 98

labour history, gendered 3
Labour Party 163, 164, 165
Lancashire and Cheshire Women Textile and Other Workers' Representation Committee 163
Lancashire (mechanical) loom 103–4
  vs. automatic (Northrop) loom 110, 122, 123–4
language of tacklers 69, 90, 91
Lazonick, William 122, 123, 125
Lewis, Jane and Rose, Sonya 27
Liddington, Jill 41–2, 162
limited liability companies 20, 21
local specialization 18–21
local variation in wages 37–40
looms
  bobbin 115–16
  handlooms 22
  Lancashire (mechanical) 103–4, 122, 123–4
  machine complement size 35–7, 62–3, 92, 104, 115–16
  mechanical knowledge/maintenance 64–8
  and weavers' skill 57
  see also automatic (Northrop) loom

machine complement size 35–7, 62–3, 92, 104, 115–16
machinery and masculinity 4–5
McIvor, Arthur J. 24, 25
male domination of unions 151–4, 186–9
male union officials 147, 148–9, 151
male weavers
  fining 94
  retirement 58
  suicide 93
  –tacklers relationship 67–9

managers 87, 91, 95
Manchester 20, 21, 32
Manchester and Salford Women's Trades Council 157–60, 161
Manchester and Salford Women's Trades and Labour Council 161
manufacturers see employers/mill owners
Marland-Brodie, Annie (trade union organizer) 92, 96, 156–7, 158
married women 32–4, 105–8, 125–6
  see also family wage; gender, division of labour; housework
Marsden see Nelson
'Mary Anne nights' 140
masculinity
  and housework 139–40, 141
  and machinery 4–5
  power relations 91, 94
  tacklers 65, 66–9, 90, 91
  weavers 141–2, 145, 170
Mass, William 104, 123, 125
mechanical knowledge/maintenance of looms 64–8
mechanization 122–6
  spinning 29, 54–5
  see also automatic (Northrop) loom; Lancashire (mechanical) loom
mill owners see employers/mill owners
mule spinners
  'labour aristocracy' 53
  self-actor 54, 55, 56
  vs. ring spinners 123–4
mutual support 70–71, 73

National Association of Powerloom Overlookers 93
Nelson 19, 20–21
  socialist weavers 58, 145–6
  union membership 154
  workforce composition 30–31
North Lancashire Power Loom Weavers' Association 23
North and North East Lancashire Cotton Spinners' and Manufacturers' Association 110–11
Northern Counties' Amalgamated Association of Weavers (Weavers' Amalgamation) 23, 25, 26, 29, 45
  anti-driving campaign 86, 95, 96
  automatic (Northrop) loom 105, 108–9, 111–12, 113, 116, 117, 120, 121–2
  Shackleton, David (president) 108–9, 120, 151, 153, 164

unionization of women 151, 153–4, 157, 158–9, 160
Northern Counties' Federation of Textile Trades 112
Northrop loom *see* automatic loom

old age 58–9
Oldham 19, 20, 21
   unions 147, 148, 151, 152
   workforce composition 31, 32
oral history 9-10
overlookers *see* tacklers (over lookers)

paternalism of employers 25, 41
pay
   bread-winner wage 108–10
   family wage 61, 87, 107, 108–10, 141–2, 187–8
   and fining 26, 70, 94–5
   local variation 37–40
   machine complement size 35–7
   married couples 33–4
   negotiated 23, 25
   rates 5, 24, 35–7
   standard price lists 22–3, 38
   tacklers (poundage) 64, 86, 87, 93
   weaver–tenter/spinner–piecer relationships 61
   women weavers 34–45
   see also driving system
pensions 59
Phillips, Anne and Taylor, Barbara 55–6
physical strength 63
piecer–spinner relationship 61, 84
political activism *see* socialist weavers; suffrage movement; unions
Pope, William (secretary of Hyde weavers' association) 118, 119
poundage 64, 86, 87, 93
power relations 91, 94
   see also masculinity
powerloom *see* Lancashire (mechanical) loom
Preston 20, 21, 23, 24
   fertility rate 144
   married women's employment 106–7
   suffrage 162
   weavers' union 73, 88, 106, 152–3
   workforce composition 30–32
private enterprises 20
productivity *see* driving system

Reddish, Sarah (cooperator, trade union organizer, suffragist) 164, 166, 168
regional concentration 18–21
Report on Earnings 36–7
resilience 63–4
resistance
   fining 95–6
   mechanization 122–6
   women weavers 69–70
   see also suffrage movement; unions
retirement 58, 59
Return of Rates of Wages (1889) 37
ring spinners 29, 167
   vs. mule spinners 123–4
Roberts, Elizabeth 107, 138, 139, 141, 142, 144
Rochdale 19, 21, 31, 33, 95–6
Roper, Esther (suffragist) 166
Rose, Mary 124
Rose, Sonya 27, 119, 150
Rossendale 20, 21

safety *see* health and safety issues
Salford 32
Salford and District Powerloom Weavers' Union 158–9
Sandberg, Lars 122, 125
sanitary conditions 28–9
Savage, Michael 30, 33, 38, 57, 62, 73, 107–8, 144
Scott, Joan 1
SDF *see* Social Democratic Federation
self-actor spinners 54, 55, 56
sexual harassment 65, 66, 69
Shackleton, David (president of Weavers' Amalgamation) 88, 108–9, 120, 151, 153, 164
shopfloor mores 70
shopfloor tensions 67–9
shuttle(s)
   changing 104
   health and safety issues 27–8
skill 57, 73–4
   acquisition 59–63, 87
   see also apprenticeships; training
   competition 63–6, 67–9
   consciousness, women weavers 57–9
   content of weaving 56–7
   definitions of 53–6
   tacklers 66–7
slate system 85, 86, 87, 90
social construction
   of gender 1–2, 3

of skill 54
Social Democratic Federation (SDF) 145, 155–6, 166
socialist weavers
  Burnley 155–6
  Nelson 58, 145–6
solidarity 69–70, 73
  women-only unions 159–60
spinner–piecer relationship 61, 84
spinning sector 19, 20, 21
  division of labour 4, 29
  mechanization 29, 54–5
  strikes 24
  unions 21–2, 148
  see also mule spinners; ring spinners
standard price lists 22–3, 38
standard working day 26
steaming 26, 63–4
strike breakers ('knobsticks') 120, 150
strikes 24, 25, 114–21, 148–9, 150
suffrage movement 137, 145, 146, 165–8, 190
  and unions 160–65
suicides
  female weavers 85–7, 88, 89–90, 91–3, 96, 97
  male weavers 93
Szreter, Simon 143, 144

tacklers (overlookers) 64–6, 68, 69, 73, 83–4, 85–6, 92, 93, 155
  apprenticeships 67
  language 69, 90, 91
  –male weavers relationship 67–9
  masculinity 65, 66–9, 90, 91
  pay (poundage) 64, 86, 87, 93
  unions 67, 93
Technical Instruction Act (1889) 66
technology, innovation 122–6
Ten Hours Movement 27
tenters 61–2
Textile Mercury 90, 105–6, 113, 123
Textile Recorder 104–5, 113
Textile Workers' Representation Committee 164
Throstle Bank Mill 114, 118
Todmorden 21
trade unionism *see* unions
training 55, 62
  see also apprenticeships; skill, acquisition
Truck Acts 26, 94–5
Truck Committee 91, 151

Turner, H.A. 54–5

Uniform Standard List (1892) 23, 38
union officials
  female 151–4, 156–7
  male 147, 148–9, 151
unions 21–2, 23–5, 146–54
  anti-driving campaign 86, 87, 88–90, 92–3, 94, 95–7
  benefits of membership 155–7
  control of labour supply 54–5, 67
  female officials 151–4, 156–7
  male domination 151–4, 186–9
  male officials 147, 148–9, 151
  spinning sector 21–2, 148
  strikes 24, 25, 114–21, 148–9, 150
  and suffrage movement 160–65
  support of equal pay 45
  support of female autonomy 157–60
  support of training 55
  tacklers (overlookers) 67, 93
  women's membership 148–9, 151, 159–60, 163–4, 166
  women-only (Manchester and Salford) 158–60, 161
  see also Northern Counties' Amalgamated Association of Weavers (Weavers' Amalgamation)

Varley, Julia (trade unionist and suffragist) 164–5
voting rights *see* suffrage movement

wages *see* driving system; pay
Weavers' Amalgamation *see* Northern Counties' Amalgamated Association of Weavers
weaving sector 19, 20, 21
  workforce composition 29–31
weaving unions *see* unions
Webb, S. and Webb, B. 42–4
weddings 71
White, Joseph L. 25, 30, 38
Wigan 32, 151
Wilkinson, William H. (secretary of Weavers' Amalgamation) 45
winders 167–8
women weavers 183–90
  married 32–4, 105–8, 125–6
  skill consciousness 57–9
  wages 34–45
  work culture 69–72

see also specific subjects
Women's Cooperative Guild 146, 163, 166
Women's Trade Union League (WTUL) 89, 96, 114–15, 156, 157
Women's Trade Union Review 89, 92
work ethic 138

workforce composition 29–34
working conditions 25–9
working hours 26–7

yarn quality 56–7, 84
Yorkshire Factory Times 89